One of the more troubling aspects of the ferment in macroeconomics that followed the demise of the Keynesian dominance in the late 1960s has been the inability of many of the new ideas to account for unemployment and, in particular, its cyclical variation. This involuntary unemployment remains unexplained because equilibrium in most economic models occurs with supply equal to demand: If this equality holds in the labor market, there is no involuntary unemployment. *Efficiency Wage Models of the Labor Market* explores the reasons why there are labor market equilibria with employers preferring to pay wages in excess of the market-clearing wage and thereby explains involuntary unemployment.

This volume brings together a number of the important articles on efficiency wage theory. The collection is preceded by a strong, integrative introduction, written by the editors, in which the hypothesis is set out and the variations, as described in subsequent chapters, are discussed.

George Akerlof is Professor of Economics at the University of California, Berkeley; Janet Yellen is Professor of Economics at the School of Business Administration, University of California, Berkeley.

D0631140

Efficiency Wage Models of the Labor Market

Efficiency Wage Models of the Labor Market

Edited by

GEORGE A. AKERLOF AND JANET L. YELLEN
University of California, Berkeley

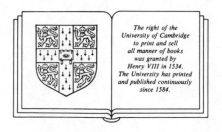

The right of the
University of Cambridge
to print and sell
all manner of books
was granted by
Henry VIII in 1534.
The University has printed
and published continuously
since 1584.

CAMBRIDGE UNIVERSITY PRESS

Cambridge
London   New York   New Rochelle
Melbourne   Sydney

Published by the Press Syndicate of the Unversity of Cambridge
The Pitt Building, Trumpington Street, Cambridge CB2 1RP
32 East 57th Street, New York, NY 10022, USA
10 Stamford Road, Oakleigh, Melbourne 3166, Australia

First published 1986

Printed in the United States of America

Library of Congress Cataloging-in-Publication Data
Main entry under title:
Efficiency wage models of the labor market.
Includes bibliographies
1. Wages – Econometric models.   I. Akerlof,
George A., 1940– .   II. Yellen, Janet L.
(Janet Louise), 1946– .
HD4909.E35   1986   331.2'1'0724   85-31373

British Library Cataloguing in Publication Data
Efficiency wage models of the labor market.
1. Wages – Econometric models
I. Akerlof, George A.   II. Yellen, Janet L.
331.2'1'0724   HD4915

ISBN 0 521 32156 5 hard covers
ISBN 0 521 31284 1 paperback

To our mothers,
ROSALIE C. AKERLOF
and
ANNA RUTH YELLEN

Contents

Acknowledgments for Reprinted Articles

George A. Akerlof, "Labor Contracts as Partial Gift Exchange," *Quarterly Journal of Economics*, volume 97, pp. 543–69, November 1982. Copyright President and Fellows of Harvard College, 1982. Reprinted by permission of John Wiley & Sons, Inc.

Guillermo A. Calvo and Stanislaw Wellisz, "Hierarchy, Ability, and Income Distribution," *Journal of Political Economy*, volume 87, pp. 991–1010, October 1979. Copyright 1979 by the Unversity of Chicago Press. Reprinted by permission.

James E. Foster and Henry Y. Wan, Jr., "Involuntary Unemployment as a Principal-Agent Equilibrium," *American Economic Review*, volume 74, pp. 476–84, June 1984. Copyright 1984 by the American Economic Association. Reprinted by permission.

Edward P. Lazear and Robert L. Moore, "Incentives, Productivity, and Labor Contracts," *Quarterly Journal of Economics*, volume 99, pp. 275–95, May 1984. Copyright President and Fellows of Harvard College, 1984. Reprinted by permission of John Wiley & Sons, Inc.

Harvey Leibenstein, "The Theory of Underemployment in Densely Populated Back ward Areas," *Economic Backwardness and Economic Growth*, Chapter 6, 1963. John Wiley & Sons, Inc. Reprinted by permission of the author.

James M. Malcomson, "Work Incentives, Hierarchy, and Internal Labor Markets," *Journal of Political Economy*, volume 92, pp. 486–507, June 1984. Copyright 1984 by the University of Chicago Press. Reprinted by permission.

Steven C. Salop, "A Model of the Natural Rate of Unemployment," *American Economic Review*, volume 69, pp. 117–25, March 1979. Copyright 1979 by the American Economic Association. Reprinted by permission.

Carl Shapiro and Joseph E. Stiglitz, "Equilibrium Unemployment as a Worker Discipline Device," *American Economic Review*, volume 74, pp. 433–44, June 1984. Copyright 1984 by the American Economic Association. Reprinted by permission.

Robert M. Solow, "Another Possible Source of Wage Stickiness," *Journal of Macroeconomics*, volume 1, pp. 79–82, Winter 1979. Copyright 1979 by The Wayne State University Press. Reprinted by permission.

Andrew Weiss, "Job Queues and Layoffs in Labor Markets with Flexible Wages," *Journal of Political Economy*, volume 88, pp. 526–38, June 1980. Copyright 1980 by the University of Chicago Press. Reprinted by permission.

Janet L. Yellen, "Efficiency Wage Models of Unemployment," *American Economic Review*, volume 74, pp. 200–5, March 1984. Copyright 1984 by the American Economic Association. Reprinted by permission. [Refers to sections of the Introduction in this book that are based on the Yellen article.]

Introduction

George A. Akerlof and Janet L. Yellen
University of California, Berkeley

For more than 60 years, since the long depression of the 1920s in Great Britain, the key problem in macroeconomics has been the explanation of unemployment, which is seemingly involuntary and varies with aggregate demand. Most markets seem to clear, but not the labor market. Why? Even in the absence of major real shocks, such as materials shortages, there are large fluctuations in output that seem to be correlated with aggregate demand. Why?

An answer to these questions was given by Pigou and Keynes in the 1930s: With sticky money wages, labor markets will not clear if demand is low, and decreases in demand will usually cause decreases in output and increases in unemployment. But, in economics as in child-rearing, answers usually beget further questions. This challenge, which did not arise until almost 35 years after the publication of *The General Theory* (Keynes, 1936), resulted in the inevitable questions: Why should money wages be sticky? Do sticky wages correspond to rational economic behavior? And, if sticky wages are not rational, is there another way to explain business cycles in the absence of sticky money wages?

Attempts to answer these questions have led to a sequence of important developments: search theory, the new classical macroeconomics, implicit contract theory, and staggered contract theory, all of which have been interesting and some of whose results have been surprising indeed. But, for a variety of both empirical and theoretical reasons, these approaches have failed to explain cyclically fluctuating levels of involuntary unemployment.

Recently there has been developed a new class of models – efficiency wage models – which, appropriately adapted, can explain cyclically varying involuntary unemployment. All these models have in common that in equilibrium an individual firm's production costs are reduced if it pays a wage in excess of market-clearing, and, thus, there is equilibrium involuntary unemployment.

Without equivocation or qualification, we view efficiency wage models as

We would especially like to thank Joseph Stiglitz for valuable conversations that aided our thinking in writing this introduction. We are also indebted to David Estenson, Lawrence Katz, Michael Reich, and James Wilcox for valuable comments. Financial support for this research was provided by the National Science Foundation under grant number SES84-01130.

providing the framework for a sensible macroeconomic model, capable of explaining the stylized facts characterizing business cycles. Such a macroeconomic model must have at least five features: It must have involuntary unemployment; shifts in aggregate demand must change equilibrium output and employment, at least in the short run; over the course of the business cycle, productivity must behave procyclically; more skilled workers must have lower unemployment rates; and the quit rates should decrease with higher unemployment. Later in this introduction, we shall indicate how each of these features naturally arises from an efficiency wage framework, although as yet no model has been constructed with all of these features simultaneously. But let us not get ahead of our story. First, let us review the efficiency wage literature and explain the selection of articles in this book.

Review of Efficiency Wage Models

This book is a primer on efficiency wage models. The ten articles that have been chosen for this volume fall roughly into three groups. The first group offers various rationales for efficiency-wage-generated unemployment; it includes the chapters by Solow (1979), Shapiro and Stiglitz (1984), Foster and Wan (1984), Akerlof (1982), Salop (1979), and Weiss (1980). The second category gives alternative implications, in terms of contract forms and internal labor markets, for the type of assumptions made in some of the efficiency wage models of unemployment; it includes the chapters by Calvo and Wellisz (1979), Lazear and Moore (1984), and Malcomson (1984). The third category, the Leibenstein (1957) chapter, describes the original use of efficiency wage models in development economics.[1]

Efficiency wage models are all based on a convincing and coherent explanation as to why firms may find it unprofitable to cut wages in the presence of involuntary unemployment. The models surveyed are variants of the efficiency wage hypothesis, according to which labor productivity depends on the real wage paid by the firm. If wage cuts harm productivity, then cutting wages may end up raising labor costs. We shall first describe some of the general implications of the efficiency wage hypothesis in its simplest form and then describe four distinct microeconomic approaches that justify the relation between wages and productivity. These approaches identify four benefits of higher wage payments: reduced shirking of work by employees due to a higher cost of job loss, lower turnover, improvement in the average quality of job applicants, and improved morale.

The potential relevance of the efficiency wage hypothesis in explaining

---

[1] The next section describing efficiency wage models is taken from Yellen (1984) with slight modifications.

involuntary unemployment and other stylized labor market facts can be seen in a rudimentary model. Consider an economy with identical, perfectly competitive firms, each firm having a production function of the form $q = f(e(\omega)n)$, where n is the number of employees, e is effort per worker, and ω is the real wage. A profit-maximizing firm that can hire all the labor it wants at the wage it chooses to offer (see **Solow,** 1979; Stiglitz, 1976a)[2] will offer a real wage, ω^*, satisfying the "Solow condition": The elasticity of effort with respect to the wage is unity. The wage ω^* is known as the efficiency wage, and this wage choice minimizes labor cost per efficiency unit. Each firm should then optimally hire labor up to the point where its marginal product, $e(\omega^*)f'(e(\omega^*)n^*)$, is equal to the real wage ω^*. As long as the aggregate demand for labor falls short of aggregate labor supply and ω^* exceeds labor's reservation wage, the firm will be unconstrained by labor market conditions in pursuing its optimal policy, so that equilibrium will be characterized by involuntary unemployment. Unemployed workers would strictly prefer to work at the real wage ω^* rather than to be unemployed, but firms will not hire them at that wage or at a lower wage. Why? For the simple reason that any reduction in the wage paid would lower the productivity of all employees already on the job. Thus the efficiency wage hypothesis explains involuntary unemployment.

Extended in simple ways this hypothesis also explains four other labor market phenomena: real wage rigidity, the dual labor market, the existence of wage distributions for workers of identical characteristics, and discrimination among observationally distinct groups. Real wage rigidity at the firm or industry level is a straightforward implication of the model. Suppose that there is a decline in the relative price of the product sold by a particular firm. There will be no change in the efficiency wage for the firm. The firm's optimal response to a reduction in the value of the marginal product of labor is to lay off workers.

Dual labor markets can be explained by the assumption that the wage–productivity nexus is important in some sectors of the economy but not in others. For sectors where the efficiency wage hypothesis is relevant – the primary sector – we find job rationing and voluntary payment by firms of wages in excess of market-clearing; in the secondary sector, where the wage–productivity relationship is weak or nonexistent, we should observe fully neoclassical behavior. The market for secondary sector jobs clears, and anyone can obtain a job in this sector, although it might be at lower pay.

Theorists who emphasize the importance of unemployment due to the frictions of the search process have frequently found it difficult to explain the reasons for a distribution of wage offers in the market. The efficiency wage

---

[2] Boldface names in reference citations indicate chapters in this book.

hypothesis also offers a simple explanation for the existence of wage differentials that might motivate the search process emphasized by Phelps and others. If the relationship between wages and effort differs among firms, each firm's efficiency wage will differ and, in equilibrium, there will emerge a distribution of wage offers for workers of identical characteristics.

The efficiency wage hypothesis also explains discrimination among workers with different observable characteristics. Employers may know that the functions relating effort to wages differ across groups. Then each group has its own efficiency wage and corresponding "efficiency labor cost." If these labor costs differ, it will pay firms to hire first only employees from the lowest cost group. Any unemployment that exists will be confined to labor force groups with higher costs per efficiency unit. With fluctuations in demand, these groups will bear a disproportionate burden of layoffs.

Microfoundations of the Efficiency Wage Model

Why should labor productivity depend on the real wage paid by firms? In the context of less developed countries, for which the hypothesis was first advanced, the links between wages, nutrition, and illness were emphasized (**Leibenstein,** 1957). Recent theoretical work has advanced a convincing case for the relevance of this hypothesis to developed economies. In this section, four different microeconomic foundations for the efficiency wage model are described and evaluated.

The Shirking Model

In most jobs, workers have some discretion concerning their performance. Rarely can employment contracts rigidly specify all aspects of a worker's performance. Piece rates are often impracticable because monitoring is too costly or too inaccurate. Piece rates may also be nonviable because the measurements on which they are based are unverifiable by workers, creating a moral hazard problem. Under these circumstances, the payment of a wage in excess of market-clearing may be an effective way for firms to provide workers with the incentive to work rather than shirk. (See Bowles, 1981, 1985; Calvo, 1979; Eaton and White, 1982; **Foster** and **Wan,** 1984; Gintis and Ishikawa, 1983; Miyazaki, 1984; **Shapiro** and **Stiglitz,** 1984; and Stoft, 1982.) The details of the models differ somewhat, depending on what is assumed measurable, at what cost, and the feasible payment schedules.

Bowles, Calvo, Eaton–White, Foster–Wan, Shapiro–Stiglitz, and Stoft assume that it is possible to monitor individual performance on the job, even though imperfectly. In the simplest model, due to Shapiro–Stiglitz, workers can decide whether to work or to shirk. Workers who shirk have some chance of getting caught, with the penalty of being fired. This has been termed "cheat–threat" theory by Stoft because, if there is a cost to being fired, then the threat of being sacked if caught cheating creates an incentive not to shirk. Equilibrium then entails unemployment. If all firms pay an identical wage and if there is full employment, there would be no cost to shirking and it would pay all workers, assuming that they get pleasure from loafing on the job, to shirk. Under these circumstances, it pays each firm to raise its wage to eliminate shirking. When all firms do this, average wages rise and employment falls. In equilibrium all firms pay the same wage above market-clearing, and unemployment, which makes job loss costly, serves as a worker discipline device. Unemployed workers cannot bid for jobs by offering to work at lower wages. If the firm were to hire a worker at a lower wage, it would be in the worker's interest to shirk on the job. The firms know this and the worker has no credible way of promising to work if he is hired.

The shirking model does *not* predict, counterfactually, that the bulk of those unemployed at any time are those who were fired for shirking. If the threat associated with being fired is effective, little or no shirking and sacking will actually occur. Instead, the unemployed are a rotating pool of individuals who have quit jobs for personal reasons, who are new entrants to the labor market, or who have been laid off by firms with declines in demand. Pareto optimality, with costly monitoring, will entail some unemployment, since unemployment plays a socially valuable role in creating work incentives. But the equilibrium unemployment rate will not be Pareto optimal (see **Shapiro** and **Stiglitz,** 1984).

In contrast to the simple efficiency wage model, the shirking model adds new arguments to the firm's effort function – the average wage, aggregate unemployment, and the unemployment benefit. The presence of the unemployment rate in the effort function yields a mechanism whereby changes in labor supply affect equilibrium wages and employment. New workers increase unemployment, raising the penalty associated with being fired and inducing higher effort at any given wage. Firms, accordingly, lower wages and, as a result, hire more labor. In a provocative recent Brookings paper, Weisskopf, Bowles, and Gordon (1983) have used the presence of the unemployment benefit in the effort function to explain the secular decline in productivity in the United States. They argue that a major part of the productivity slowdown is attributable to loss of employer control due to a reduction in the cost of job loss. The shirking model also offers an interpretation of hierarchical wage differentials, in excess of productivity differences (**Calvo** and **Wellisz,** 1979).

All these models suffer from a similar theoretical difficulty: Employment contracts that are more ingenious than the simple wage schemes considered can reduce or eliminate involuntary unemployment. In the cheat-threat model, the introduction of employment fees allows the market to clear efficiently as long as workers have sufficient capital to pay them (see Eaton and White, 1982). Unemployed workers would be willing to pay a fee to gain employment. Fees lower labor cost, giving firms an incentive to hire more workers. If all firms charge fees, any worker who shirks and is caught knows that he will have to pay another fee to regain employment. This possibility substitutes for the threat of unemployment in creating work incentives. Devices that function similarly are bonds posted by workers when initially hired and forfeited if found cheating as well as fines levied on workers caught shirking. The threat of forfeiting the bond or paying the fine substitutes for the threat of being fired. Lazear (1979, 1981) has demonstrated the use of seniority wages to solve the incentive problem. Workers can be paid a wage less than their marginal productivity when they are first hired with a promise that their earnings will later exceed their marginal productivity. The upward tilt in the age–earnings profile provides a penalty for shirking: The present value of the wages paid can fall to the market-clearing level, eliminating involuntary unemployment. **Lazear** and **Moore** (1984) give a good summary of the theoretical model described in Lazear's earlier papers; in addition, by comparing the steepness of age–earnings profiles and lifetime discounted earnings of employed and self-employed workers, they discriminate between that part of the earnings profile due to incentive effects and that part due to on-the-job training. They find support for the hypothesis that the slope of earnings profiles are significantly affected by incentives.

As a theoretical objection to these schemes, employers would be subject to moral hazard in evaluating workers' effort. Firms would have an obvious incentive to declare workers shirking and appropriate their bonds, collect fines, or replace them with new fee-paying workers. In Lazear's model, in which the firm pays a wage in excess of marginal product to senior workers, there is an incentive for the firm to fire such workers, replacing them with young workers who are paid less than their productivity. The seriousness of this moral hazard problem depends on the ability of workers to enforce honesty on the firm's part. If effort is observable both by the firm and by the worker and if it can be verified by outside auditors, the firm will be unable to cheat workers. Even without outside verification, Lazear (1981) has shown how a firm's concern for its reputation can overcome the moral hazard problem. Bhattacharya (1983), Green and Stokey (1983), Lazear and Rosen (1981), **Malcomson** (1984), and Nalebuff and Stiglitz (1983) have suggested tournament contracts, which also can overcome the moral hazard problem. The firm commits itself to a fixed-wage plan in which a high wage is paid to a fraction of workers and a low wage to the remaining fraction according to an ex post, possibly random ranking of their effort levels. By precommitting itself to such a plan with a fixed wage bill, the firm's moral hazard problem disappears.

The Labor Turnover Model

Firms may also offer wages in excess of market-clearing to reduce costly labor turnover (see **Salop,** 1979; Schlicht, 1978; and Stiglitz 1974.) The formal structure of the labor turnover model is identical to that of the shirking model. Workers will be more reluctant to quit the higher the relative wage paid by the current firm and the higher the aggregate unemployment rate. If all firms are identical, then one possible equilibrium has all firms paying a common wage above market-clearing with involuntary unemployment serving to diminish turnover.

The theoretical objection to the prediction of involuntary unemployment in this model again concerns the potential for more sophisticated employment contracts to provide Pareto-superior solutions. As Salop explains, the market for new hires fails to clear because an identical wage is paid to both trained and untrained workers. Instead, new workers could be paid a wage equal to the difference between their marginal product and their training cost. A seniority wage scheme might accomplish this, although, if training costs are large and occur quickly, it might prove necessary to charge a fee to new workers. In contrast to the shirking model, an employment or training fee scheme could be used without the problem of moral hazard. It is no longer in any firm's interest to dismiss trained workers; explicit contracts could probably be written to insure that training is actually provided to fee-paying workers. Although moral hazard thus appears to be a less formidable barrier to achieving neoclassical outcomes via fees or bonds than in the shirking model, capital market imperfections or institutional or sociological constraints may, in fact, make them impractical.

Adverse Selection

Adverse selection yields further reason for a relation between productivity and wages. Suppose that performance on the job depends on "ability" and that workers are heterogeneous in ability. If ability and workers' reservation wages are positively correlated, firms with higher wages will attract more able job candidates. (See Malcomson, 1981; Stiglitz, 1976b; **Weiss,** 1980.) In such a model, each firm pays an efficiency wage and optimally turns away applicants offering to work for less than that wage. The willingness of an individual to work for less than the going wage places an upper bound on his ability, raising the firm's estimate that he is a lemon. The model provides an explanation of wage differentials and different layoff probabilities for observationally distinct groups due to statistical discrimination if it is known that different groups have even slight differences in the joint distributions of ability and acceptance wages. However, for the adverse selection model to provide a convincing account of involuntary unemployment, firms must be unable either to measure effort and pay piece rates after workers are hired or to fire workers whose output is too low. Clever firms may also be able to mitigate adverse selection in hiring by designing self-selection or screening devices that induce workers to reveal their true characteristics.

Sociological Models

The theories reviewed up to this point are neoclassical in their assumption of individualistic maximization by all agents. Solow (1981) has argued, however, that wage rigidity may more plausibly be due to social conventions and principles of appropriate behavior, which are not entirely individualistic in origin. **Akerlof** (1982) has provided the first explicitly sociological model leading to the efficiency wage hypothesis. He uses a variety of interesting evidence from sociological studies to argue that each worker's effort depends on the work norms of his group. In Akerlof's partial gift exchange model, the firm can succeed in raising group work norms and average effort by paying workers a gift of wages in excess of the minimum required in return for their gift of effort above the minimum required. The sociological model can explain phenomena that seem inexplicable in neoclassical terms: Why firms don't fire workers who turn out to be less productive; why piece rates are avoided even when feasible; and why firms set work standards that are exceeded by most workers. In a later paper, Akerlof (1984) explores alternative sociological foundations for the efficiency wage hypothesis. Sociological considerations governing the effort decisions of workers are also emphasized in Marxian discussions of the extraction of labor from labor power (see, for example, Bowles, 1981, 1985).

Summary

In the preceding review of the literature, the bonding issue was emphasized as the most serious theoretical difficulty regarding efficiency wage models. Because of the theoretical importance of this issue, this collection has included two articles (**Lazear** and **Moore,** 1984; and **Malcomson,** 1984) that implicitly carry this "bonding" criticism. More complicated contracts can be more efficient and therefore obviate the need for unemployment as a "worker discipline device." In practice, we do not know how seriously to take this criticism. There are, quite possibly, many easy and practical reasons why complicated contracts are difficult to use: For example, invidious comparisons are likely to be made more frequently when the contracts are more complicated, and the possibilities for disagreement or misunderstanding between the contracting parties will increase with the complexity of the contract. If such

practical difficulties are in fact significant, it should be easy, although probably also inelegant, to model them and thereby weaken the bonding argument.

Seven Questions Regarding Efficiency Wage Models of Unemployment and Their Answers

Aside from bonding there are seven other major questions that naturally arise
regarding the ability of efficiency wage models to explain involuntary unemployment. In fact, we believe there are natural answers to each of these questions. These questions will be posed and answered.

Question 1

The fundamental idea underlying efficiency wage models is the willingness
of employers to pay higher wages than necessary to hire their current labor
force. Is not such an idea implausible, since it is contrary to the fundamental
tenet of supply and demand theory that buyers pay the lowest price they can
to purchase goods while sellers charge the highest price at which they can sell
goods? Is it not counterintuitive that any market could be otherwise, even
granted the serious considerations of quality (in terms of effort and morale)
that make the labor market different from the market for standardized commodities, such as wheat?

For most markets for goods and assets the supply–demand description seems
to be a good one: Most buyers in such markets fairly actively seek the lowest
available price for goods of given quality. But casual observation suggests
that in labor markets this cannot be the case. Persons of equal ability often
seem to have jobs with very different returns or, alternatively stated, similar
jobs have very different working conditions and pay. The classic evidence of
pay dispersion for similar jobs is given by Dunlop's (Dunlop, 1957) dramatic
table of average wages of *unionized* truck drivers by industry in the Boston
area in July, 1951 (see Table 1). Similar evidence for nonunion workers, as
we believe exists, would indicate that many employers are paying more than
necessary to attract their employees.

Efficiency wage theorists, it turns out, are not alone in subscribing to a
view of labor markets in which some employers pay more than necessary to
attract labor. Dual labor market theory would divide the labor force into two
groups: There are, on the one hand, some unlucky persons who are in the
"secondary labor market," where wages and other conditions are determined
by supply and demand; on the other hand, most workers are in the primary
labor market, where wages are not uniform and workers' treatment in all
respects is better than in the market-clearing secondary market. For some
reason or other, then, in such markets those institutions that are part of the

Table 1. *Union scale for motortruck drivers*
(Boston, July, 1951)[a]

Magazine	$2.25
Newspaper, day	2.16
Oil	1.985
Building construction	1.85
Paper handlers, newspaper	1.832
Beer, bottle and keg	1.775
Grocery, chain store	1.679
Meat-packing house, 3–5 tons	1.64
Bakery	1.595
Wholesale	1.57
Rendering	1.55
Coal	1.518
Garbage disposal	1.50
General hauling	1.50
Food service, retail	1.475
Ice	1.45
Armored car	1.405
Carbonated beverage	1.38
Wastepaper	1.38
Linen supply	1.342
Movers, piano and household	1.30
Scrap, iron and metal	1.20
Laundry, wholesale	1.20

[a]Bureau of Labor Statistics, *Union Wages and Hours: Motortruck Drivers and Helpers* (July 1, 1951), Bulletin 1052, pp. 9–10. (From Dunlop, 1957, p. 21.)

primary sector pay more than necessary to obtain their labor; if the wages in excess of market-clearing are not counterintuitive for the theory of dual labor markets, neither should they be for efficiency wage models.

Question 2

The second potential problem for efficiency wage models as an explanation for *involuntary* unemployment arises because of the existence of a secondary sector. With a secondary sector all workers can get a job. Does that not imply that all unemployment is *voluntary?* In some sense that is true. But Robert Hall has pointed out that in dual labor markets, there will be positive unemployment, with the marginal unemployed worker just indifferent between unemployment (which presumably enhances his probability of finding a primary sector job) and employment in the secondary labor market. A dual labor market economy of this sort, with primary sector and secondary sector employment and with equilibrium unemployment, can be constructed to behave just like a Keynesian model. Changes in aggregate demand will affect output and employment. And, although it is true that every unemployed worker might be able to get a secondary sector job (so that in *one sense* there is no *involuntary* unemployment), it is also true that unemployed workers would be more than willing to work in primary sector jobs at prevailing wage rates. In *that sense* such workers are *involuntarily* unemployed.

Question 3

The third question regarding simple efficiency wage models concerns their predictions about cyclical variation in productivity. According to Okun's Law, higher unemployment rates correspond to lower labor productivity. In addition, real wages tend not to decline in economic downturns. These stylized facts appear inconsistent with the predictions of simple efficiency wage models. In the simplest efficiency wage model (e.g., Shapiro–Stiglitz), a downturn caused by a decline in the marginal productivity of labor due to a decline in the real price of output should lower real wages and leave productivity (effort) unchanged. Should real wages fail to fall, higher unemployment rates would cause workers to be more fearful of losing their jobs (or less ungrateful for having them, in the "gift exchange" version), and, therefore, at higher unemployment rates, workers will put in added effort to increase productivity. Thus productivity would be expected to rise in economic downturns.

There is at least some microeconomic evidence that workers sometimes do behave that way. The famed Hawthorne experiment is often cited as showing how workers' productivity increased in response to random changes in the environment. A recent statistical analysis of the data, however, reveals that the increases in productivity could also be explained by the worsening economic conditions of the times: The Hawthorne experiment was made just as the economy was moving into the Great Depression, and the increases in productivity, which seemed so random at the time, could have been caused by workers' increasing fears of job loss. (See Franke and Kaul, 1978.)

But, this microeconomic evidence from the Hawthorne experiment notwithstanding, the macroeconomic evidence remains: It must still be explained why productivity increases as unemployment rates fall. We believe that long-term (implicit) contracts offer a straightforward reason for these productivity changes, as a simple model will demonstrate. The existence of these contracts could easily be incorporated into an efficiency wage model.

Consider then the following rudimentary model that attempts to explain procyclical behavior of productivity *independently* of efficiency wages. Let there be an initial period in which all contracts are made between firms and workers. Each contract is contingent upon the true state of the world that is subsequently revealed in the next period. States of the world differ according to the real price $p(\theta)$ paid for firms' outputs. In the initial period a firm hires n workers. An implicit contract is then signed with these workers specifying their effort, income, and probability of employment in each state of the world θ (with the effort and income also dependent on whether workers are employed or unemployed). There is no *ex post* mobility. By assumption – corresponding to the convention in most implicit contract models and also corresponding to the reality of the forty-hour week for most workers – workers are either fully employed or not at all. If fully employed, a worker has income $\omega_1(\theta)$ and effort $e_1(\theta)$. If unemployed, the worker has income $\omega_2(\theta)$ and effort $e_2(\theta)$. The utility of an employed worker is

$$u[e_1(\theta)] + v[\omega_1(\theta)].\tag{1}$$

The utility of an unemployed worker is

$$u[e_2(\theta)] + v[\omega_2(\theta)] + w.\tag{2}$$

The worker is employed with probability $q(\theta)$. The firm's output Q is produced according to the production function

$$Q = f(e_1 qn),\tag{3}$$

where qn is the number of workers employed.

In equilibrium, a worker attracted to a firm must be paid "market utility" $\bar{u}$, so that a maximizing firm sets the contract $\{e_1(\theta), e_2(\theta), \omega_1(\theta), \omega_2(\theta), q(\theta), n\}$ that maximizes expected profits,

$$\underset{\theta}{E}\{p(\theta)f(e_1(\theta)q(\theta)n) - q(\theta)\omega_1(\theta)n - (1 - q(\theta))\omega_2(\theta)n\},\tag{4}$$

subject to the condition of paying the worker his expected "market utility" $\bar{u}$,

$$\bar{u} = \underset{\theta}{E}\{q(\theta)(u(e_1(\theta)) + v(\omega_1(\theta))) + (1 - q(\theta))(u(e_2(\theta)) + v(\omega_2(\theta) + w))\}.\tag{5}$$

Three questions naturally arise about the nature of these contracts: about income, about employment, and about effort. *How does income vary with* $p(\theta)$? Straightforward calculations from maximizing the profit function (4) subject to the utility constraint (5) show that income is independent of θ and it is also independent of whether the worker is employed or unemployed. (Of course this result depends on the separability of the utility function.) *How*

does employment vary with $p(\theta)$? In each state of the world θ all workers will
be fully employed with probability one if the marginal revenue product of the
nth worker (working at the optimal effort) exceeds the value of additional
leisure plus the value of the difference between the effort of employed workers and unemployed workers. *How does effort vary with $p(\theta)$?* The key marginal condition with respect to effort obtained from differentiating the Lagrangian [of (4) subject to (5)] with respect to $e_1(\theta)$ is

$$\frac{p(\theta)f'(e_1(\theta)q(\theta)n)n}{u'(e_1(\theta))} = -\lambda, \tag{6}$$

where λ is the Lagrange multiplier associated with $\bar{u}$. Inspection of (6) shows
that states of the world with higher $p(\theta)$ will be associated with higher levels
of effort $e_1(\theta)$ provided that $q(\theta)$ is on its upper boundary of 1. The marginal
condition obtained by differentiating the Lagrangian with respect to $q(\theta)$ shows

$$p(\theta)f'[e_1(\theta)q(\theta)n]e_1(\theta)n = \lambda[u(0) + w - u(e_1(\theta))]. \tag{7}$$

Taking (6) and (7) together (for $q<1$) yields the condition for optimal effort
for states where there is some unemployment:

$$e_1u'(e_1) = u(e_1) - u(0) - w. \tag{8}$$

As can be seen, effort is independent of p in such states. In sum, effort increases, although not strictly, with p.

What relationship will exist between productivity and employment in this
model? Although the relationship could go either way, it is likely to be the
case that productivity is typically higher in times of full employment than it
is, on average, in times with unemployment. In this model, labor productivity
initially declines as $p(\theta)$ and $q(\theta)$ increase as a consequence of diminishing
returns to labor. Once $q(\theta) = 1$, however, productivity and output both increase with $p(\theta)$ because of increased effort.

The preceding results, we believe, conform to everyday reality: Workers
generally work faster when there is more work to be done. In terms of a
testable hypothesis, all things being equal, the queues at checkout counters at
supermarkets move more quickly the longer they are, while pay and the willingness of workers to accept these jobs are determined by long-run average
conditions.

We claim then that the addition of effort to the production function with
long-term contracts yields a natural explanation for procyclic productivity,
even though in single period (or single state-of-the world) contracts it would
appear as if productivity varied negatively rather than positively with the level
of employment. Implicit contracts over wages would also explain the apparent
constancy of real wages in the face of employment fluctuations. [An alterna-

tive explanation is based on near-rational wage-setting (see answer to Question 7).] Implicit contracts together with efficiency wage models *jointly* explain Okun's Law and involuntary unemployment.

Question 4

A fourth problem with efficiency wage theory concerns the Solow equilibrium condition: In equilibrium the elasticity of effort with respect to the real wage is unity. With the production function $q = f(en)$ and with $e = e(\omega)$, the effort–wage elasticity of unity minimizes the cost per labor efficiency unit. However, it may be objected that an effort–wage elasticity of unity is quite high, and, if this elasticity never is that high, then there cannot be an equilibrium with unemployment in an efficiency wage model.

Yet a further difficulty makes this problem with efficiency wages seem worse. Suppose the labor supply function has the property that there are some workers willing to work at a *zero* wage. If workers at a zero wage put in any work at all, there cannot be an equilibrium with unemployment since, at a zero wage, labor cost per labor efficiency unit is minimized. Both of these objections can be answered.

One answer to the first objection regarding high effort–wage elasticities concerns the endogeneity of the unemployment rate. Let us suppose, as might be realistic, that, if the unemployment rate is zero and with a market-clearing wage, a very large fraction of the population would shirk. At such low unemployment rates, it could also be true that only modest wage payments by individual firms in excess of market-clearing would induce workers to quit shirking. If that is the case, then at low unemployment rates there are, quite plausibly, high effort–wage elasticities.

A second answer involves a realistic alteration to most of the efficiency wage models that relaxes the Solow condition. This condition is based on a production function of the sort $q = f(en)$, with output a function of labor efficiency units, which are the product of effort and labor, *en*. Other plausible production functions, as shall be demonstrated, will have a lower equilibrium effort–wage elasticity. The labor efficiency unit representation of the production function suggests that the harm done by shirking labor is limited to a reduction in the shirking labor's own labor input. But that is unrealistic. Poor labor not only produces less in its own right, but it also misuses other inputs. Therefore the downside risk from shirking labor is usually not limited by the smaller amount of its own labor input: It may include the wastage of scarce opportunities inherent in the job itself, poor use of other current inputs, or, in some cases, the destruction, theft, or wastage of capital assets. Representation of the downside risk of low-effort labor as resulting in additional *costs* to the firm other than those of hiring more labor to replace the lost effort will result in an equilibrium effort–wage elasticity lower than unity. We offer a simple illustrative example.

Suppose that a *single worker* controls the water flow from a large dam. The output from the dam is proportional to the worker's effort:

$$q = ke. \tag{9}$$

The value of a unit of output is 1. In this example the worker who shirks not only wastes his own effort, he also wastes the potential rents from the dam.

Let us look at the equilibrium effort–wage elasticity for this dam. The dam's profits, if privately owned, will be

$$ke(\omega) - \omega, \tag{10}$$

where we have assumed effort depends on ω. If the managers of the dam wish to maximize $ke(\omega)$, they will choose a wage rate ω^* so that

$$ke'(\omega^*) - 1 = 0, \tag{11}$$

or

$$e'(\omega^*) = 1/k. \tag{12}$$

When the dam has positive rents,

$$ke(\omega^*) > \omega^*, \tag{13}$$

and substitution of (13) in (12) shows

$$\frac{e'(\omega^*)}{e(\omega^*)} \cdot \frac{1}{\omega^*} < 1. \tag{14}$$

The opposite case of zero rents is of negligible interest here, since in that case the dam cannot be profitably operated.

Why is the equilibrium elasticity of effort lower here than in Solow's model? In Solow's model a laborer who does not work hard will not waste the firm's potential since additional workers can be hired. But in this example *only one worker can work on the dam*. The failure of that one worker to work hard not only results in the loss due to his low labor power, but it also wastes another resource: the potential positive returns from the dam itself. In this example of the dam, a high level of effort is more important than in Solow's model, and, therefore, the equilibrium effort–wage elasticity is lower. We are convinced that examples of this sort are more realistic than $q = f(en)$ and, as a result, our confidence in equilibrial profit-maximizing supra-market-clearing wages is enhanced.

Let us now turn to the second objection regarding the Solow equilibrium condition of unit elasticity of the effort–wage function: If $e(0)$ is positive while labor supply is vertical, so that there is positive labor supply at a zero wage, then the firm's effective labor costs (i.e., costs per labor efficiency unit) are minimized at a *zero* wage.

In a dual labor economy, such as Hall's, this problem disappears. The argument is due to Annable (1984). In such a model, primary sector firms choose a wage to maximize $e(\omega)/\omega$ on the condition that the wage paid exceeds *that in the secondary sector*. Effort at wages below those paid by the secondary sector are irrelevant to this maximization problem, and, thus, the issue of positive effort and labor supply at near zero wages is irrelevant.

Question 5

The fifth potential problem with efficiency wage models concerns the *distribution* of unemployment: Do not such models predict that high-education, high-skill workers, whose performance is most likely to be difficult to observe and evaluate, have higher unemployment rates than low-education, low-skill workers? In models of the Shapiro–Stiglitz type with "unemployment as a worker discipline device" this will be the case if high- and low-skill workers have the same utility functions for work and leisure. But, in fact, it is usually thought that workers' commitment to work varies positively with the skill requirements of their jobs. Consider an extension of the Shapiro–Stiglitz model with two types of workers: one type, skilled workers, who get no utility from shirking; the other type, unskilled workers, who do get utility from shirking as in the earlier model. The skilled will have no unemployment while the unskilled will have unemployment as a worker discipline device. Thus, if workers who are more skilled, or jobs requiring more skill, also are associated with less desire for shirking, efficiency wage models might well predict the observed negative correlation between skill (or education) and unemployment.

Question 6

In search theoretic models, there are more quits when unemployment rises. Does this occur in efficiency wage models?

In the efficiency wage models of involuntary unemployment, as unemployment rises it takes unemployed workers longer to get a job. As a result the loss to an individual quitter rises with unemployment in an efficiency wage model that has been adapted to yield cyclically varying unemployment due to aggregate demand shocks. (See question 7 for a description for such a model.)

Question 7

A final question of efficiency wage models concerns the existence of a business cycle. Any efficiency wage model based on pure maximization must, of necessity, be a *real* model. The equilibrium of such a model will be *neutral:* If all exogenous nominal variables change proportionately, the equilibrium set of endogenous nominal variables will change in the same proportion with the equilibrium set of real variables unchanged. Equilibrium unemployment will, therefore, be unaffected by money supply changes in simple efficiency wage models. Furthermore, in most simple efficiency wage models the aggregate supply function will be vertical at the level of output corresponding to the natural rate of unemployment. With such a vertical supply curve, shifts in aggregate demand, by either fiscal or monetary policy, will have no effect on equilibrium output or employment. In consequence, are efficiency wage models a dead end in explaining demand-generated business cycles or in explaining the efficacy of Keynesian or monetarist demand-oriented policies of controlling macroeconomic fluctuations?

Efficiency wage models, as it turns out, have the property that, with minor modifications, aggregate demand does affect equilibrium income and employment (see Akerlof and Yellen, 1985). In efficiency wage models, wages are *chosen* by the firm to maximize profits as the interior solution to a maximization problem. Failure to choose wages in precisely optimal fashion results in little loss to the firm, so that sticky wages in response to shocks result in only small losses to a firm that does not *exactly* maximize. Such behavior is *near-rational*. A similar property is true for an individual firm that *chooses* a price that trades the advantages of additional sales at lower prices against the advantage of greater revenue per item sold at higher prices: This firm will also lose relatively little by maintaining a sticky price in the presence of shocks caused by demand shifts.

The preceding two results can be neatly used in a model of response to a demand shock. Suppose that an economy is composed of monopolistically competitive firms whose labor supplies effort according to a simple efficiency wage model, $e = e(\omega)$. Suppose, further, that this economy is initially in a long-run equilibrium in which all agents are precisely maximizing. This equilibrium has an efficiency wage which is above market-clearing, and a natural rate of unemployment u^*. Then a money supply shock occurs that increases the money supply by a fraction ϵ.

In the short run following this shock, a fraction β of the firms do *not* maximize. Instead, they keep their money wages and prices constant, taking the demand that comes at their sticky prices and employing labor to supply this demand. (The remaining firms choose profit-maximizing prices and wages.) The firms with inertial, rather than maximizing, profits and wages lose something small as a result of their failure to maximize; their profits could be larger, but only by an amount approximately proportional to the square of ϵ. But, due to this nonmaximizing behavior, employment and output will respond significantly to this shock: The change in output and employment will be approximately proportional to ϵ.

A model of this sort can easily be constructed. There are monopolistically competitive firms with demand functions

$$X = (p/\bar{p})^{-\eta}(M/\bar{p}), \tag{15}$$

where X is output demanded, p is the individual firm's price, $\bar{p}$ is the average price of all firms, and M is the money supply.

Output is produced by individual firms according to the production function

$$q = (en)^{\alpha}. \tag{16}$$

And effort depends on wages according to the function

$$e = -a + b\omega^{\gamma}. \tag{17}$$

Finally, the supply of labor, which is an endogenous variable, is chosen greater than the demand for labor at the cost-minimizing efficiency wage.

The response of this system, initially in a long-run fully maximizing equilibrium, can be examined when the money supply changes by a fraction ϵ, on the assumption that a fraction of firms keep sticky prices and pay sticky wages. The loss to nonmaximizing firms due to their behavior can be calculated as a function of ϵ, namely $L(\epsilon)$. This loss is second order in ϵ, since $L(0) = 0$ and $L'(0) = 0$. But the elasticity of employment with respect to ϵ is nonzero. With examples of finite changes in the money supply, this translates into small percentage losses in profits to the nonmaximizing firms, while at the same time this failure to maximize can cause demand shocks to have significant impacts on output and employment.

Since this behavior of the macrosystem may seem mysterious, we offer the general logic as to why this system behaves in this way: Why small departures from maximization can cause significant deviations from the maximizing equilibrium. This generalized logic will show why all efficiency wage models will have the basic property that profits, but not employment, will be insensitive to money (and/or real) wage stickiness.

Consider a shock that perturbs an equilibrium in which all agents are maximizing. Sticky wage and price behavior will be near-rational for any agent whose objective function is differentiable as a function of *his own wages and prices*. The error in wages or prices caused by inertial behavior will result in losses to the agent that are second order in terms of the policy shock, since at the equilibrium prior to the shock, the agent chose prices and/or wages so that the marginal benefits of higher prices and/or wages were just offset by the marginal costs. An error in wages and prices, therefore, has a second-order effect on the value of the objective function. This is just an application of the envelope theorem. But the sticky wage and price behavior, while it has a second-order effect (in terms of the money shock parameter ϵ) on the profits

Is the assertion of an absolute labor surplus true? There are two general bases for the belief in the existence of agricultural underemployment in backward economies:[1] (1) casual observation and (2) statistical comparisons of output between what are sometimes assumed to be roughly comparable areas. Although it is impossible to check the casual observer, it is a fact that this type of observation is made time and time again by different people. What can be observed, and what is indisputable, is the existence of exceedingly small holdings and the belief that in other areas a man can cultivate much larger holdings. The statistical observations are of a similar nature. First, an attempt is made to reduce all land to something like units of land of equal or equivalent quality. Then a comparison is made of the number of workers per similar acre of land. Such calculations must, of necessity, be of a rough and ready kind both because of the poorness of the initial statistics and because of the practical difficulties of converting land in various areas possessing quite different characteristics into some sort of comparable units. Nevertheless, despite the rough and ready nature of the methods, the results are not without persuasive power. For it often appears that in some areas the land is cultivated by less than 50 per cent of the labor force used in less developed areas, and yet higher yields are achieved.[2] It is usually difficult to take into account the differences in capital available in different areas. But can this alone account for the vast differences that are observed?

Especially persuasive is the observation that one very often finds in the same area, with precisely the same climatic and soil conditions, both large holdings and small holdings, and yet the large holdings do not use proportionately more manpower although they do have at least as high a yield per acre. Of course, here too, it may be very difficult to account for the differences in capital that may exist.

One possible explanation, for at least part of the picture, is that we have to distinguish between two types of disguised unemployment. The first type is one in which it would be possible to delete a portion of the labor force, reorganize the labor force in some manner or other, make no additions whatsoever to any of the other factors of production, and obtain no smaller yield with the smaller labor force than with the larger

---

[1] See Wilbert Moore, *Economic Demography of Eastern and Southern Europe*, League of Nations, 1945, Chapters 3 and 4; Also Ragnar Nurkse, *Problems of Capital Formation in Underdeveloped Countries*, New York, Oxford University Press, 1953; Doreen Warriner, *Economics of Peasant Farming*, London, Oxford University Press, 1939; W. Arthur Lewis, "Reflections on South East Asia," *District Bank Review* (December 1952), p. 11.

[2] See, for example, the tables in Moore, *op. cit.*, Chapter 3.

one. In this case, the marginal productivity of labor on the land may be said to be zero. Additional manpower would not increase output at all.

A second type of disguised unemployment is involved in the case where a subtraction of a portion of the labor force will yield a smaller output no matter what sort of reorganization of the smaller labor force takes place. Similarly, an addition to the labor force would result in a higher total yield. The sense in which we can have disguised unemployment in this case is that with additional resources or means of creating additional employment opportunities *of the right kind, more effort* could be obtained from the existing labor force. This type of unemployment is due to the seasonal nature of the production process in agriculture, coupled with the fact that there is a lack of alternative employment outlets.

In the second case, the agricultural labor force may be said to suffer from disguised unemployment in the same sense that taxi-drivers may be said to suffer from disguised unemployment. During the daily peak periods, all taxis find riders and if there were additional taxis, they would find additional riders. But during other times of the day a great many of the taxis are idle. The hours of idleness may outweigh the hours during which they are delivering passengers. In this sense, they may be said to be partially unemployed or to suffer from disguised unemployment. Also, any reduction in the labor force of taxi-drivers would raise the average number of riders per taxi.

This second type of disguised unemployment is much easier to understand since it fits in with usual economic ideas. In this case, the marginal productivity of labor is positive and the wage rate is positive. It is directly related to the seasonal type of production process that is fairly well understood. The entire agricultural labor force can be used effectively during the sowing and harvesting seasons but not during the in-between periods. While the marginal productivity of labor is probably exceedingly low in this case, its marginal return may still be sufficient to maintain it at a subsistence level. It is also probable, in view of the fact that the marginal productivity of labor is so low, that the ability to substitute capital for labor is very high. Hence, the introduction of a small amount of capital would permit the elimination of a large portion of the labor force and yet permit the maintenance of the same level of output. Perhaps this second type of disguised unemployment accounts for some of the presumed underemployment that is allegedly observed.

But the first type of disguised unemployment is much more difficult to explain and its existence cannot be dismissed. We shall therefore consider this type of underemployment in the rest of this chapter.

enthusiasm, in a more lethargic fashion, and probably with a greater degree of absenteeism.[10]

The direct connection between calorie intake and productivity is shown very clearly in a number of studies by Kraut and Muller made in Germany between 1942 and 1945.[11] Twenty men building earth embankments shifted 1.5 tons of earth per hour per man when they consumed 2400 calories, but when the calorie intake was raised to 2900 the output rose to 2.2 tons per man (and at the same time body weight increased by about 9 pounds per man). Allowing 1600 to 1800 calories for metabolism and relaxation, we see that (approximately) a 60 per cent increase in "working" calories leads to an almost 50 per cent increase in output. But of greater interest for our purposes is that a 21 per cent increase in total calorie intake results in an almost 50 per cent rise in output. In another study of 31 miners an increase of 1200 to 1600 work calories led to an increase in output from 7 to 9.6 tons per day. The experience of miners in the Ruhr district also reported by Kraut and Muller confirmed these general results. On the average, the mining of a ton of coal required about 1200 calories, and when, during the war period, the calorie intake of the miners was reduced, output fell proportionately, and when at a later stage the diet was increased, production rose proportionately. Even more spectacular results are reported in a study of construction workers in Central America where it was found that the efficiency of workers increased threefold when they were provided with an adequate calorie allowance. Since the original calorie intake of the workers is not reported, it is not possible to compare the relative change in calorie intake with the relative increase in output, but the report is, nevertheless, suggestive of the sort of results that can be obtained by increasing the calorie intake of workers.[12]

It would be easy to continue to pile up additional experimental and empirical evidence relating not only calorie intake to output, but also relating other nutritive elements to output either directly or indirectly

---

[10] See R. K. Mukerjee, "Food and Food Requirements of the Indian Labourers," *Indian Journal of Economics,* Vol. XII, 1932, p. 263. The inverse relation between quality of diet and absenteeism seems to be fairly well established. On this point see also C. E. A. Winslow, *The Cost of Sickness and the Price of Health,* World Health Organization, Geneva, 1951, pp. 35 ff.

[11] "Calorie Intake and Industrial Output," *Science,* Vol. 104 (1946), pp. 495–497. In this connection see also the more recent studies by G. Lehman, E. A. Muller, and H. Spitzer, "Der Caloriebedarf bei gewerblicher Arbeit," *Arbeitsphysiologie,* Vol. 14 (1949–1950), pp. 166 ff. Here they determine the extent of the deterioration in work output resulting from different levels of calorie feeding, and develop prediction tables for various workers for various occupations.

[12] Winslow, *op. cit.,* p. 33.

through their effect on debilitating diseases, absenteeism, lethargy, etc. But enough has been said to suggest our main point. There is an obvious and clear cut relationship between income and output, and furthermore, it is clear that up to some point, the effective work units are increased as wages are increased.

It follows from the above discussion that we must distinguish between the supply of labor-time (that is, man-hours or man-years) and the supply of work (or effort), and between the average and marginal

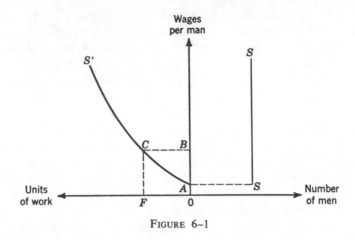

FIGURE 6–1

product per man and the average and marginal product per unit of work. We must keep these distinctions in mind throughout the rest of this discussion. The significance and implications of these distinctions can probably best be seen with the aid of figures 6–1, 6–2, and 6–3 that follow.

In figure 6–1 we illustrate the distinction between the supply of labor-time and the supply of units of work. In the short period the supply of labor-time may be said to be approximately fixed, and hence the supply curve of labor-time is the vertical line SS, as shown in the right quadrant of the figure. Below some minimum wage the work force would starve and there would be no work forthcoming. Therefore, the supply of labor-time starts only above that minimum wage OA necessary to sustain life in the labor force. However, the number of units of work supplied will increase gradually as wage rates and consumption rises. Hence, the curve AS' in the left quadrant of figure 6–1 slopes upward gradually to the left. Each point on the curve indicates the number of units of work that would be forthcoming in response to a given wage rate. Of course, above a certain wage the supply of work curve becomes absolutely vertical. In other words, beyond some point, increases in consumption are unlikely to add appreciably to the health, vigor, and vitality of the average worker so that the work performed per unit of time is no greater than at a lower wage.

Now, what this means is that the average productivity (and the marginal productivity) of a group of men will depend on their wage. Up to some point, the higher the wage the higher the per capita productivity for the group, because the higher the wage the greater the units of work per man. The nature of this relationship is illustrated by the

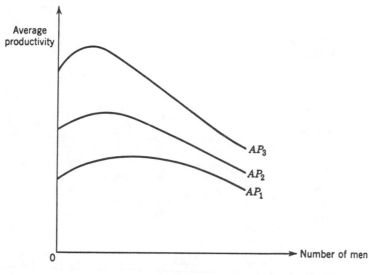

FIGURE 6–2

family of average productivity curves in figure 6–2. Each curve in figure 6–2 illustrates what happens to average productivity as the number of men in the work force increases. As usual we assume that beyond some point, diminishing returns are in effect, and, therefore, beyond some point the average productivity curves are negatively inclined. AP_1 is the average productivity curve for a low wage (say w_1), AP_2 is the average productivity curve for a somewhat higher wage (say w_2), and AP_3 is the average productivity curve for a still higher wage. The curves are always above each other because for any given number of men the higher the wage, up to some point, the higher the output.

As usual for each average productivity curve there is a related (and derived) marginal productivity curve. Of course, just as there is a separate average productivity curve for each wage there is also a separate marginal productivity curve for each wage. And it is the relation between the different marginal productivity curves for different wage rates that is of special interest for our purposes.

As already indicated, we expect the average productivity curves for different wage rates to be one above the other, but it is important to observe that this need not always be the case for the related marginal productivity curves. Indeed the interesting case for our purposes, and the one that we shall concentrate on, is the case where the marginal productivity curves for different wage rates cross each other. This is the case that we illustrate in figure 6–3.

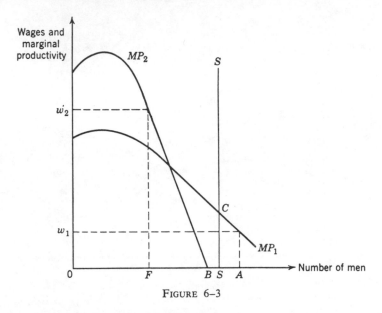

FIGURE 6–3

The curves marked MP_1 and MP_2 in figure 6–3 are the marginal productivity curves under consideration. The MP curve for a higher wage rate is likely to start at a higher level than one for a lower wage, but beyond the point where diminishing returns are in effect, the marginal curves for the higher wage rates may fall much more rapidly than the marginal curves for the lower rate.

Consider the two curves MP_1 and MP_2 in figure 6–3. The marginal productivity per man curve (MP_1) for the low wage rate w_1 falls much more slowly than does the marginal productivity curve (MP_2) for the high wage rate w_2. At some point the marginal productivity curve for the high wage rate will fall below the one for the low rate. To see the reason for this we have to observe that there are two forces in operation that work in opposite directions. (1) On one hand the higher the wage the more units of work that are put forth per man per unit of time. (2) But on the other hand, as more units of work are put forth, the marginal product per *unit of work* declines. Beyond some point the marginal product per unit of work may decline quite rapidly. The rate of decline may be so rapid that for the higher curve (representing more work units per man) the rate of decline in the marginal product per man (as men are added) is greater than it is for the lower curve (MP_1). It is, therefore, possible for the higher wage curve (MP_2) to cross the lower wage curve (MP_1) and then fall below it. In other words, beyond some point, we expect the declining marginal productivity per unit of work to become more important than the fact that each man accomplishes more units of work.

Let us look again at the possibility depicted in figure 6–3 and see what it implies in terms of the problem under consideration. We note first that the curve MP_1 is drawn in such a way that at its related wage there is actually a scarcity of labor. As drawn, the supply of labor is equal to OS but the demand is OA, assuming that demand is determined at the point at which the marginal product equals the wage. The reason for this possibility is not difficult to conceive. At this low wage (w_1) the labor force is in such a low state of health, vigor, and vitality, that it produces relatively few units of work and, as a consequence, the marginal product per final unit of work as well as the marginal product per man is considerably above the wage rate. Or, what is the same thing, the number of work units produced are so few at this low wage that the existing resources could be combined advantageously with more units of work. At the low wage w_1 more men can be hired before the marginal product is equal to the wage per man. As the curve is drawn the reverse is true with respect to the curve marked MP_2 and the related wage w_2. At the wage w_2 the supply of labor on SS is greater than the demand of OF, assuming that the demand is determined at the point where the marginal product is equal to the wage.

What all this implies is that at very low wages there may be a labor deficit because the units of work produced per man are so few. But at higher wages the units of work per man increase so rapidly that a labor surplus is created. For the underdeveloped areas this may mean that the allegedly observed manpower surpluses in agriculture do not really exist when wages are very low, but that they do indeed become a fact when wages rise sufficiently.

In addition it is worth observing (in figure 6–3) that at the low wage (w_1) the marginal product of the fully employed labor force is in fact above zero ($= SC$), but at the higher wage the marginal product per man may fall to zero (as at point B) or even below zero.

Institutional Rigidities, Wage Rates, and Marginal Productivity Theory

An interesting consequence of the wage-productivity relation discussed in the last section is that we can show that there are circumstances under which it is to the benefit of landowners to pay a wage above the competitive level. Specifically, we shall see that in circumstances where competition among the visibly unemployed depresses wage rates toward the zero level, it may be to the benefit of landlords as a group to operate under institutional arrangements (or traditions) that would not permit wages to fall to their competitive levels, but, rather, to operate under conditions which permit wage rates above competitive levels.

We shall not examine in detail the specific type of institutional arrangements that would enable landlords to employ the entire labor force at a wage in excess of their marginal product, but it is not difficult to think of some possibilities. The appropriate institutional arrangements will usually arise from the historical situation under which the backward economy operates. A system of serfdom, where landlords have to utilize all the serfs born on and tied to the land, is essentially of this nature. Another system of this nature is that which, by virtue of its mores, permits people born into certain castes to perform only a limited range of tasks. Other institutional arrangements of this type are found in various backward economies. The point of the discussion that follows is that such institutions need not be irrational, and indeed, we shall see that such institutional arrangements may lead to a greater total product than otherwise.

To see that the results mentioned above are actually possible we need to continue our analysis from the point where we left it in the previous section. Starting with the marginal productivity curves in figure 6–3, we shall build up through diagrammatical illustrations (figures 6–4, 6–5, and 6–6) a comparison of the possible outcomes to landlords as a group under two alternative situations: (1) the situation wherein landlords can ignore the effects of visible unemployment and (2) the situation wherein visible unemployment does have a depressing effect on the wage rate, and in which the effect on the wage rate also affects landlords' incomes.

In figure 6–4 we draw a family of marginal productivity curves similar to those in figure 6–3. Each curve is related to a specific wage rate. As before, the curve MP_1 indicates the alternative marginal productivities per man for alternatively greater numbers of men if the wage rate is w_1. MP_2 is the marginal productivity curve if the wage rate is w_2, and so on. Let us suppose that landlords as a group can hire any number of men they wish without regard to the possible results of a labor deficit or of a labor surplus, and also without regard to the possible consequences of such a deficit or surplus. How many men would they hire? In other words, we examine the demand side first without regard to supply conditions. (Later, of course, we shall take into account the supply aspect.) For each wage rate and its related marginal productivity curve there is

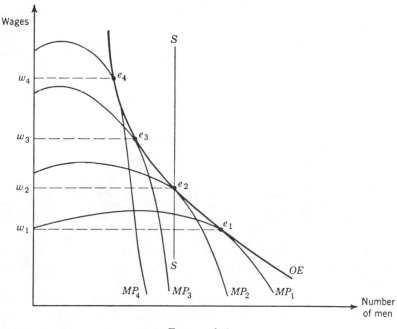

FIGURE 6–4

an optimum number of men whom landlords as a group would hire if they were to maximize their group income. The optimum number of men to be hired is determined, as usual, at the point where the wage is equal to the marginal product of the labor force. In figure 6–4, for the curve MP_1, this optimum point is e_1, where the marginal product is equal to w_1. Similarly, we obtain e_2, e_3, for the curves MP_2, MP_3, and so on. Thus for every wage we obtain the optimum number of men to be hired. The locus of such optimum employment points is indicated by the curve OE in figure 6–4. This curve is, *in a sense,* a demand curve for labor. At each wage it tells us the number of workers that landlords as a group would hire if they had a choice of hiring the number that would maximize their group income without regard to the consequences of any labor deficit or surplus that may be involved.

In figure 6–5 we combine the curve OE and the related inelastic supply curve for labor *SS*. We observe that at the higher wage rates the optimum number of men employed is less than the supply, whereas at the very low wage rates the reverse is true. A question that comes to mind is whether the *OE* curve need cross the *SS* curve at any point. Generally speaking, it is probable that there would always be some wage rate so low that the optimum employment would be greater than the supply.

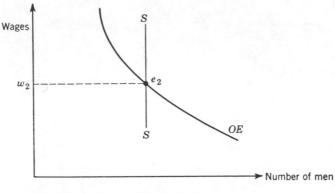

FIGURE 6–5

But we need not worry about this general point at present. For present purposes it is sufficient if we concentrate on the possibilities depicted in our graphs.

The next step in our argument is to relate the points on the optimum employment curve with the net revenues obtained by landlords at various wage rates. Associated with every wage rate and every optimum number of men employed there is a given net revenue to landlords as a group. This relationship is illustrated by the curve *OR* in figure 6–6. (For each *MP* curve the net revenue is equal to the area under the marginal productivity curve that is above the "wage line.") For every wage rate and related point on the *OE* curve there is a related net revenue shown on the left quadrant of figure 6–6. The locus of these points may be called the *optimum employment revenue curve OR*.

Next, suppose that the *entire* labor force is employed. Then, in a similar fashion, we can obtain the *full employment* revenue curve *FR*. That is, for every wage, assuming that the full labor force *SS* is employed, there is a related net revenue that will accrue to the landlords. At some wage rates the employment of the full labor force will involve employing a greater number of workers than landlords wish to employ and, at other wage rates, a smaller number than that which would maximize their group incomes.

Some remarks about the shape of the curves *OR* and *OF* and their relationship to each other are of special interest. Consider first the general shape of the optimum employment revenue curve *OR*. (As usual we assume diminishing returns per unit of work.) For exceedingly low wage rates per man, the amount of effort per man is also exceedingly low, hence the marginal product per man is very low. In this case a great many units are each doing very little work. The per capita costs

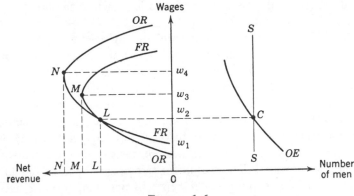

FIGURE 6–6

of coordinating the work force, and other overhead costs, are likely to be high in relation to output. It seems reasonable to believe that there is some very low wage rate at which the net revenue due to landlords would be just slightly above zero. As wages increase, as effort per man grows, and as the optimum number of men decline, overhead costs per *unit of work* decline accordingly, and, as a consequence, we would expect net revenue to rise. At least two general factors are responsible for increases in net revenue as wages rise: (1) As wages rise, work per man may increase more than the proportionate increase in wages. (2) With the greater amount of units of work produced by the work force, it may be possible to combine resources and labor so that we come closer to the optimum combination of factors and, as a result, increase the output per unit of work. Up to some wage rate, net revenue is likely to increase as wages increase. However, beyond a certain wage, we would certainly expect a reversal of this tendency, for beyond some point, an increase in wages will bring with it no increase whatsoever in units of work supplied per man, and, therefore, at some wage, as wages rise, the units of work done per man will increase less proportionately than wages. Hence, beyond some point the higher the wage rate, the less the net revenue. Of course, at some very high wage rate the net revenue will drop to zero since there is obviously a wage that is greater than the maximum productivity per man possible. For these reasons we depict the OR curve, as illustrated in figure 6–6, in the shape of a "U" on its side.

The main thing to observe about the full employment revenue curve is that at each wage rate, except one, the full employment revenue is always less than the optimum employment revenue. Of course, at the wage where the optimum employment curve OE crosses the labor supply curve SS, the optimum employment revenue and the full employment revenue are identical. In figure 6–6 this is shown at the point L where the FR curve touches the OR curve.

It should be clear that the full employment revenue curve need not be at a maximum above the wage w_2 where the labor supply and the optimum employment are equal. Although it is true that at wages above w_2 the full employment revenue must always be less than the optimum employment revenue (since there must be a reduction from the optimum employment revenue occasioned by the necessity of employing excess manpower whose wages are below their marginal product), it may nevertheless be that the full employment revenue is higher than what it was at a lower wage. The reason for this possibility is similar to those reasons given in explaining the increase in optimum revenue as wages rise. Namely, above the wage w_2, the work units per man increase by a greater proportion than the increase in wages, and this effect may, up to some point, be more significant than the depressing effect of the greater wages bill on net revenue.

Three points in our illustration (N, M, and L, on the curves OR and FR) are especially worthy of attention. If landlords could pay any wage they pleased and could hire any number of workers, they would pay a wage of w_4 and achieve the maximum net revenue possible, ON. But at this wage there would be an excess supply of labor. If there were some means of eliminating the excess labor in a costless fashion, this would be the optimum solution from the landlords' point of view.

But if there is nowhere for "surplus" labor to go, and competition among the unemployed and the employed depresses wages, the wage rate will decline below the level, w_4. The wage decline will continue as long as an excess supply exists, and wages will eventually drop to w_2, the wage at which the optimum employment curve crosses the labor supply curve. *But at this point net revenue drops to level OL.* It is clear that in our graphical illustration employers can improve their position, by employing the entire labor force (simultaneously raising wages to w_3), and consequently can enjoy a net revenue of OM, which of course is greater than OL. This is the best solution under the circumstances, because as long as they leave some of the excess labor unemployed, there is the danger of wage rates being driven down to a level at which revenue is less than OM. Hence, landlords, as a group, are in an improved position if institutional arrangements permit them to employ the entire labor force, pay a wage of w_3, and yet not utilize the entire labor force. Possibilities and institutional arrangements of this sort *can* account for the phenomenon of disguised unemployment.[13]

Let us examine some of the characteristics of the solution in our diagrammatical illustration. First, we note that this solution (a wage of w_3 and a net revenue of OM) can account for the existence of surplus labor and of disguised unemployment. At this wage the labor force could cultivate more land with the same auxiliary resources if there were more land available. Second, and this is a crucial aspect of the foregoing argument, we see that under the postulated conditions the wage can be above the marginal product of labor. Indeed, it is to the benefit of both landlords and labor that this be the case.

The essential aspect of the argument is that the position of landlords can be improved by employing excess labor, where the units of work produced are related to the wage, rather than by employing the "optimum" amount of labor which permits the unemployed surplus to drive wages down to a level where the amount of work produced is reduced to such an extent that the landlords' net revenue is lower than otherwise.

Let us now consider the extreme case where M and L coincide, that is, where the maximum full employment revenue is at the wage at which the optimum employment curve and the supply of labor curve cross. In this case, the landlords' optimum solution is to pay a wage, w_2, and to hire the entire labor supply. Labor's marginal product will be equal to the wage. It may appear that under such circumstances the situation depicted is not quite consistent with the notion of an excess labor supply and disguised unemployment. Determining such consistency depends on how we interpret the notion of excess labor. It is true that in this case (where M and L coincide) at the optimum wage w_2 there is no surplus of labor, and the marginal product is above zero. But if our criterion is that excess labor exists where the existing labor supply can cultivate more land, this criterion can be met even in this extreme case. For under these circumstances the existing labor force could cultivate more land if they received some portion of the produce of the additional land cultivated. Given a greater output, we would expect some increase in

---

[13] Indeed, we have illustrated the possibility that such institutional arrangements may lead to a greater total product than otherwise. Thus, we come to the rather curious conclusion that, far from being a vice, institutional arrangements that permit a degree of disguised unemployment may actually enable the economy to be more productive than otherwise.

wages, which in turn would lead to more units of work per man, thus enabling the fixed labor force to cultivate more land. However, it is of interest to note that should the country undergo industrialization and try to shift some of the labor force off the land without increasing wages per man, we would have a shortage of labor. This last may perhaps shed some light on situations like those experienced by some of the countries in the Soviet orbit, where a shortage of labor appeared in the agricultural sector after attempts at forced industrialization were put into effect, whereas prior to this, it was believed that there was a considerable amount of disguised unemployment.

Postscript

While the wage–productivity relation in "The Theory of Underemployment . . ." emphasized the physical aspects of an effort–wage relation, there are also significant psychological aspects to be considered. It is of interest that Ancel Keys, in *The Biology of Starvation* (University of Minnesota Press, 1950, Vol. II), shows that sustained low-calorie diets have significant psychological and motivational impacts, such as apathy, lack of desire to work, and impaired ability to concentrate. Clearly, adverse motivational consequences also result from other components of working contexts in urban areas and play a role in determining effort. If wages are positively correlated with working conditions, then wages can be used as a proxy for such conditions. This would give us a basis for an effort–wage relation for urban contexts in developing countries. For such a model, see my chapter "Efficiency Wages, X-Efficiency, and Urban Unemployment" in *Economic Development and Planning, Essays in Honour of Jan Tinbergen* (ed. Willy Sellekaerets, Macmillan, London, 1974).

H.L.
Harvard University
November 1985

ROBERT M. SOLOW

Massachusetts Institute
of Technology

Another Possible Source of Wage Stickiness

A number of hypotheses have been advanced to explain wage stickiness. This article explores another reason why wage stickiness might be in an employer's interest: the relationship between productivity and the wage rate. If the wage enters the short-run production function, a cost-minimizing firm will leave its wage offer unchanged, no matter how its output varies, if and only if the wage enters the production function in a labor-augmenting way.

One could argue—and I would argue—that the most interesting and important line of work in current macro theory is the attempt to reconstruct plausible microeconomic underpinnings for a recognizably Keynesian macroeconomics. The best developed approach to this task, which has just achieved at least a local maximum in Malinvaud (1977), starts from the presumption that the nominal wage, or some other equally important price, is sticky.[1] I say "sticky" rather than "rigid" because the wage is allowed to move; the presumption is only that it does not move quickly enough to clear the labor market in a reasonable time.

A theory that rests on sticky wages owes itself an explanation of wage stickiness. Why does the wage not move flexibly to clear the labor market? The literature has produced several answers to that question, generally not mutually exclusive. Keynes gave one answer in the *General Theory:* in a decentralized labor market, every change in a nominal wage is also a change in relative wages; workers can and do resist reductions in their relative wages in the only way the institutions allow—by resisting wage cuts even in soft labor markets.[2] The recent revival of interest in macro theory has produced alternative accounts. Hahn (1976) and Negishi (1974) suggest a sort of kinked perceived demand curve, both for labor and for produced commodities. The current favorite seems to be the implicit contract: wage stickiness is a rational market response to the fact that employers are less risk averse than workers, combined with the

---

[1]See also Barro and Grossman (1976).
[2]For a recent discussion of this idea, see Trevithick (1976).

existence of some sources of income for unemployed workers.[3] There are undoubtedly other possibilities.

One of the attractive features of the implicit contract approach is that it brings the employer into the act. Whether or not it is surprising that unemployed workers do not try to undercut the still-employed by offering to work for less than the going wage, it requires explanation that employers do not typically solicit wage-cutting behavior. In the implicit contract model, the employer has tacitly given up that ploy in return for a lower going wage than would otherwise prevail. I want to suggest yet another reason why wage stickiness might be in the employer's interest.

Part of the folklore of the labor market is that "you get what you pay for." An employer who did try to induce wage-cutting in a buyer's market might find that the short-run gain was more than offset by hidden longer-run costs. Bad morale may lead to lower productivity or even to carelessness verging on sabotage. A reputation as a lousy employer will carry over to tighter labor market conditions and lead to adverse selection in recruiting and perhaps even worse productivity performance. Suppose we try to formalize this piece of home-made sociology.

Consider an employer who is sales-constrained in the market for output, q. Labor, n, is the only variable input in the short run, and the labor market is imperfect enough so that the employer has some choice of the wage, w, to be offered. (Since I will not be considering price changes, w can do duty both as nominal and real wage.) However, the employer knows that realized productivity will depend on the wage quoted, with the two rising or falling together. This may come about either by selectivity in recruiting or behavior on the job.

Let $q = f(n,w)$ be the short-run production function, giving output as an increasing function of employment and the wage. The partial inverse $n = n(q,w)$ will exist and exhibit labor requirements as an increasing function of the rate of output and a decreasing function of the wage. Prime cost is then $w \cdot n(q,w)$. For given q, the firm naturally chooses the wage that minimizes cost. The first-order condition is

$$n(q,w) + wn_w(q,w) = 0 \ , \tag{1}$$

and I will suppose that this represents a unique interior minimum. For each rate of output given by the market there is a best wage for the firm to quote, obtained by solving (1). Thus (1) defines w as a function of q.

The sensitivity of the quoted wage to business cycle variations in output is measured by dw/dq, obtained by implicit differentiation of (1).

---

[3]For a summary and references see Gordon (1977).

For the ultimate in wage stickiness, we can ask when $dw/dq = 0$. The answer is: when and only when $n_q + wn_{wq} = 0$, for (q,w) satisfying (1). Use (1) to substitute for the explicit w, and we find a partial differential equation for wage-stickiness-at-all-levels-of-output:

$$n_w \cdot n_q - n \cdot n_{wq} = 0 . \tag{2}$$

It is easily checked that $\partial^2 \log n/\partial q \, \partial w = n^{-2}(n \cdot n_{qw} - n_q \cdot n_w)$, so (2) is equivalent to $\partial^2 \log n/\partial q \, \partial w = 0$. The general solution of (2) is therefore

$$\log n = A(q) + B(w) , \tag{3}$$

where A and B are arbitrary functions (increasing and decreasing, respectively). Now, setting $e^A = a$ and $e^{-B} = b$, we have $n = a(q)/b(w)$ or, finally,

$$q = g[b(w)n] , \tag{4}$$

where g (the inverse function of a) and b are arbitrary increasing functions.

The upshot is: if the wage enters the short-run production function, a cost minimizing firm will leave its wage offer unchanged no matter how its output varies if and only if the wage enters the production function in a labor augmenting way. And in that case, the cost minimizing wage is the one that minimizes the cost of a unit of effort or effective labor, while employment is varied to meet output needs. Now this condition may be special, but it is not implausible. It requires simply that higher morale or higher quality of personnel affect production like an increase in effort. And in any case it would be enough for macro theory if the condition were only approximately met and the wage only nearly invariant.

I find this story fairly easy to believe. It can not be the whole story of wage stickiness, however. For one thing, although wage stability may be good for morale, presumably instability of employment is not. Why is it better for firms to offer stable wages than to offer stable employment? Perhaps because, except in the worst of times, the number laid off is only a small fraction of the number of workers attached to a typical firm, and everyone knows that. Wage cutting might therefore have far more drastic effects on morale than would layoffs. In any case, the factor emphasized here does not exclude any of the other factors mentioned in the literature, nor is it excluded by them.

The underlying point of this paper must be as old as the hills. This particular formulation began life as an exam question in the graduate macro course at M.I.T. At about the same time, I came across an unpublished paper, by Negishi (1976), which states the easier sufficiency half of the theorem proved above. Negishi also gives a reference to Rees (1973, p. 226). This is especially nice, although Rees merely mentions the phenomenon, because at last we come to someone who actually knows something about real labor markets.

Received: June 10, 1977

References

Barro, R.J. and H.I. Grossman. *Money, Employment and Inflation.* Cambridge and New York: Cambridge University Press, 1976.

Gordon, R.J. "The Theory of Domestic Inflation." *American Economic Review* 67 (February 1977): 128–134.

Hahn, F.H. "On Non-Walrasian Equilibria." Institute for Mathematical Studies in the Social Sciences, Stanford University, Technical Report No. 203, 1976.

Malinvaud, Edmond. *The Theory of Unemployment Reconsidered.* Yrijo Jahnsson Lectures, Oxford: Basil Blackwell, 1977.

Negishi, Takaski. "Involuntary Unemployment and Market Imperfection." *Economic Studies Quarterly* 25 (April 1974): 32–41.

———. "Microeconomic Foundations of Keynesian Macroeconomics." Mimeographed, Summer 1976.

Rees, Albert. *The Economics of Work and Pay.* New York: Harper and Row, 1973.

Trevithick, G.A. "Money Wage Inflexibility and the Keynesian Labour Supply Function." *Economic Journal* 86 (June 1976): 327–32.

Equilibrium Unemployment as a Worker Discipline Device

By CARL SHAPIRO AND JOSEPH E. STIGLITZ*

Involuntary unemployment appears to be a persistent feature of many modern labor markets. The presence of such unemployment raises the question of why wages do not fall to clear labor markets. In this paper we show how the information structure of employer-employee relationships, in particular the inability of employers to costlessly observe workers' on-the-job effort, can explain involuntary unemployment[1] as an equilibrium phenomenon. Indeed, we show that imperfect monitoring necessitates unemployment in equilibrium.

The intuition behind our result is simple. Under the conventional competitive paradigm, in which all workers receive the market wage and there is no unemployment, the worst that can happen to a worker who shirks on the job is that he is fired. Since he can immediately be rehired, however, he pays no penalty for his misdemeanor. With imperfect monitoring and full employment, therefore, workers will choose to shirk.

To induce its workers not to shirk, the firm attempts to pay more than the "going wage"; then, if a worker is caught shirking and is fired, he will pay a penalty. If it pays one firm to raise its wage, however, it will pay all firms to raise their wages. When they all raise their wages, the incentive not to shirk again disappears. But as all firms raise their wages, their demand for labor decreases, and unemployment results. With unemployment, even if all firms pay the same wages, a worker has an incentive not to shirk. For, if he is fired,

an individual will not immediately obtain another job. The equilibrium unemployment rate must be sufficiently large that it pays workers to work rather than to take the risk of being caught shirking.

The idea that the threat of firing a worker is a method of discipline is not novel. Guillermo Calvo (1981) studied a static model which involves equilibrium unemployment.[2] No previous studies have treated general market equilibrium with dynamics, however, or studied the welfare properties of such unemployment equilibria. One key contribution of this paper is that the punishment associated with being fired is endogenous, as it depends on the equilibrium rate of unemployment. Our analysis thus goes beyond studies of information and incentives within organizations (such as Armen Alchian and Harold Demsetz, 1972, and the more recent and growing literature on worker-firm relations as a principal-agent problem) to inquire about the equilibrium conditions in markets with these informational features.

The paper closest in spirit to ours is Steven Salop (1979) in which firms reduce turnover costs when they raise wages; here the savings from higher wages are on monitoring costs (or, at the same level of monitoring, from increased output due to increased effort). As in the Salop paper, the unemployment in this paper is definitely involuntary, and not of the standard search theory type (Peter Diamond, 1981, for example). Workers have perfect information about all job opportunities in our model, and unemployed workers strictly prefer to work at wages less than the prevailing market wage (rather than to remain unemployed); there are no vacancies.

*Woodrow Wilson School of Public and International Affairs, and Department of Economics, respectively, Princeton University, Princeton, NJ 08540. We thank Peter Diamond, Gene Grossman, Ed Lazear, Steve Salop, and Mike Veall for helpful comments. Financial support from the National Science Foundation is appreciated.
[1] By involuntary unemployment we mean a situation where an unemployed worker is willing to work for less than the wage received by an equally skilled employed worker, yet no job offers are forthcoming.

[2] In his 1979 paper, Calvo surveyed a variety of models of unemployment, including his hierarchical firm model (also with Stanislaw Wellisz, 1979). There are a number of important differences between that work and this paper, including the specification of the monitoring technology.

The theory we develop has several important implications. First, we show that unemployment benefits (and other welfare benefits) increase the equilibrium unemployment rate, but for a reason quite different from that commonly put forth (i.e., that individuals will have insufficient incentives to search for jobs). In our model, the existence of unemployment benefits reduces the "penalty" associated with being fired. Therefore, to induce workers not to shirk, firms must pay higher wages. These higher wages reduce the demand for labor.

Second, the model explains why wages adjust slowly in the face of aggregate shocks. A decrease in the demand for labor will ultimately cause a lower wage and a higher level of unemployment. In the transition, however, the wage decrease will match the growth in the unemployment pool, which may be a sluggish process.

Third, we show that the market equilibrium which emerges is not, in general, Pareto optimal, where we have taken explicitly into account the costs associated with monitoring. There exist, in other words, interventions in the market that make everyone better off. In particular, we show that there are circumstances in which wage subsidies are desirable. There are also circumstances where the government should intervene in the market by supplying unemployment insurance, even if all firms (rationally) do not. A (small) turnover tax is desirable, because high turnover increases the flow of job vacancies, and hence the flow out of the unemployment pool, making the threat of firing less severe.

Additionally, our theory provides predictions about the characteristics of labor markets which cause the natural rate (i.e., equilibrium level) of unemployment to be relatively high: high rates of labor turnover, high monitoring costs, high discount rates for workers, significant possibilities for workers to vary their effort inputs, or high costs to employers (such as broken machinery) from shirking.

Finally, our theory shows how wage distributions (for identical workers) can persist in equilibrium. Firms which find shirking particularly costly will offer higher wages than other firms do. The dual role wages play by allocating labor and providing incentives for employee effort allows wage dispersion to persist.

Although we have focused our analysis on the labor market, it should be clear that a similar analysis could apply to other markets (for example, product or credit markets) as well. This paper can be viewed as an analysis of a simplified general equilibrium model of an economy in which there are important principal-agent (incentive) problems, and in which the equilibrium entails *quantity constraints* (job rationing). As in all such problems, it is important to identify what is observable, and, based on what is observable, what are the set of feasible contractual arrangements between the parties to the contract. Under certain circumstances, for instance, workers might issue performance bonds and this might alleviate the problems with which we are concerned in this paper. In Section III we discuss the role of alternative incentive devices.

In the highly simplified model upon which we focus here, all workers are identical, all firms are identical, and thus, in equilibrium, all pay the same wage. The assumption that all workers are the same is important, because it implies that being fired carries no stigma (the next potential employer knows that the worker is no more immoral than any other worker; he only infers that the firm for which the worker worked must have paid a wage sufficiently low that it paid the worker to shirk). We have made this assumption because we wished to construct the simplest possible model focussing simply on incentive effects, in which adverse selection considerations play no role. In a sequel, we hope to explore the important interactions between the two fundamental information problems of adverse selection and moral hazard.[3]

The assumption that all firms are the same is not critical for the existence of equilibrium unemployment. Firm heterogeneity will, however, lead to a wage distribution. If the

---

[3] Other studies have focused on quantity constraints (rationing) with adverse-selection problems. See Stiglitz (1976), Charles Wilson (1980), Andrew Weiss (1980), and Stiglitz and Weiss (1981).

damage that a particular firm incurs as a result of a worker not performing up to standard is larger, the firm will have an incentive to pay the worker a higher wage. Similarly, if the cost of monitoring (detecting shirking) for a firm is large, that firm will also pay a higher wage. Thus, even though workers are all identical, workers for different firms will receive different wages. There is considerable evidence that, in fact, different firms do pay different wages to workers who appear to be quite similar (for example, more capital intensive firms pay higher wages). The theory we develop here may provide part of the explanation of this phenomenon.

In Section I, we present the basic model in which workers are risk neutral. Quit rates and monitoring intensities are exogenous. A welfare analysis of the unemployment equilibrium is provided. In Section II, we comment on extensions of the analysis to situations where monitoring intensities and quit rates are endogenous, and where workers are risk averse. Section III compares the role of unemployment as an incentive device with other methods of enforcing discipline on the labor force.

I. The Basic Model

In this section we formulate a simple model which captures the incentive role of unemployment as described above. Extensions and modifications of this basic model are considered in subsequent sections.

A. Workers

There are a fixed number, N, of identical workers, all of whom dislike putting forth effort, but enjoy consuming goods. We write an individual's instantaneous utility function as $U(w, e)$, where w is the wage received and e is the level of effort on the job. For simplicity, we shall assume the utility function is separable; initially, we shall also assume that workers are risk neutral. With suitable normalizations, we can therefore rewrite utility as $U = w - e$. Again, for simplicity, we assume that workers can provide either minimal effort ($e = 0$), or some fixed positive level of

$e > 0$.[4] When a worker is unemployed, he receives unemployment benefits of $\bar{w}$ (and $e = 0$).

Each worker is in one of two states at any point in time: employed or unemployed. There is a probability b per unit time that a worker will be separated from his job due to relocation, etc., which will be taken as exogenous. Exogenous separations cause a worker to enter the unemployment pool. Workers maximize the expected present discounted value of utility with a discount rate $r > 0$.[5] The model is set in continuous time.

B. The Effort Decision of a Worker

The only choice workers make is the selection of an effort level, which is a discrete choice by assumption. If a worker performs at the customary level of effort for his job, that is, if he does not shirk, he receives a wage of w and will retain his job until exogenous factors cause a separation to occur. If he shirks, there is some probability q (discussed below), per unit time, that he will be caught.[6] If he is caught shirking he will be fired,[7] and forced to enter the unemployment pool. The probability per unit time of acquiring a job while in the unemployment pool (which we call the job acquisition rate, an endogenous variable calculated below) determines the expected length of the unemployment spell he must face. While unemployed he receives unemployment compensation of $\bar{w}$ (also discussed below).

---

[4] Including effort as a continuous variable would not change the qualitative results.

[5] That is, we assume individuals are infinitely lived, and have a pure rate of time preference of r. They maximize

$$W = E \int_0^\infty u(w(t), e(t)) \exp(-rt) \, dt,$$

where we have implicitly assumed that individuals can neither borrow nor lend. Allowing an exponential death rate would not alter the structure of the model; neither would borrowing in the risk-neutral case.

[6] For now we take q as exogenous; later it will be endogenous. The assumption of a Poisson detection technology, like a number of the other assumptions employed in the analysis, is made to ensure that the model has a simple stationary structure.

[7] This will be firm's optimal policy in equilibrium.

The worker selects an effort level to maximize his discounted utility stream. This involves comparison of the utility from shirking with the utility from not shirking, to which we now turn. We define V_E^S as the expected lifetime utility of an employed shirker, V_E^N as the expected lifetime utility of an employed nonshirker, and V_u as the expected lifetime utility of an unemployed individual. The fundamental asset equation for a shirker is given by

(1) $rV_E^S = w + (b+q)(V_u - V_E^S),$

while for a nonshirker, it is

(2) $rV_E^N = w - e + b(V_u - V_E^N).$

Each of these equations is of the form "interest rate times asset value equals flow benefits (dividends) plus expected capital gains (or losses)."[8] Equations (1) and (2) can be solved for V_E^S and V_E^N:

(3) $V_E^S = \dfrac{w + (b+q)V_u}{r+b+q};$

(4) $V_E^N = \dfrac{(w-e)+bV_u}{r+b}.$

The worker will choose not to shirk if and only if $V_E^N \geq V_E^S$. We call this the *no-shirking condition* (*NSC*), which, using (3) and (4), can be written as

(5) $w \geq rV_u + (r+b+q)e/q \equiv \hat{w}.$

Alternatively, the *NSC* also takes the form $q(V_E^S - V_u) \geq e$. This highlights the basic im-

plication of the *NSC*: unless there is a penalty associated with being unemployed, everyone will shirk. In other words, if an individual could immediately obtain employment after being fired, $V_u = V_E^S$, and the *NSC* could never be satisfied.

Equation (5) has several natural implications. If the firm pays a sufficiently high wage, then the workers will not shirk. The critical wage, $\hat{w}$, is higher

(a) the higher the required effort (e),
(b) the higher the expected utility associated with being unemployed (V_u),
(c) the lower the probability of being detected shirking (q),
(d) the higher the rate of interest (i.e., the relatively more weight is attached to the short-run gains from shirking (until one is caught) compared to the losses incurred when one is eventually caught),
(e) the higher the exogenous quit rate b (if one is going to have to leave the firm anyway, one might as well cheat on the firm).

C. *Employers*

There are M identical firms, $i=1,\ldots,M$. Each firm has a production function $Q_i = f(L_i)$, generating an aggregate production function of $Q = F(L)$.[9] Here L_i is firm i's effective labor force; we assume a worker contributes one unit of effective labor if he does not shirk. Otherwise he contributes nothing (this is merely for simplicity). Therefore firms compete in offering wage packages, subject to the constraint that their workers choose not to shirk. We assume that $F'(N) > e$, that is, full employment is efficient.

The monitoring technology (q) is exogenous. Monitoring choices by employers are analyzed in the following section. We assume

---

[8]A derivation follows: taking V_u as given and looking at a short time interval $[0,t]$ we have

$$V_E = wt + (1-rt)[btV_u + (1-bt)V_E],$$

since there is probability bt of leaving the job during the interval $[0,t]$ and since $e^{-rt} \approx 1 - rt$. Solving for V_E, we have

$$V_E = [wt + (1-rt)btV_u]/[1-(1-rt)(1-bt)].$$

Taking limits as $t \to 0$ gives (1). Equation (2) can be derived similarly.

[9]That is,

$$F(L) \equiv \max_{\{L_i\}} \sum f_i(L_i)$$

such that $\Sigma L_i = L$. This assumes that in market equilibrium, labor is efficiently allocated, as it will be in the basic model of this section. The modifications required for more general cases, when different firms face different critical no-shirking wages, $\hat{w}_i$, or have different technologies, are straightforward.

that other factors (for example, exogenous noise or the absence of employee specific output measures) prevent monitoring of effort via observing output.

A firm's wage package consists of a wage, w, and a level of unemployment benefits, $\overline{w}$.[10] Each firm finds it optimal to fire shirkers, since the only other punishment, a wage reduction, would simply induce the disciplined worker to shirk again.

It is not difficult to establish that all firms offer the smallest unemployment benefits allowed (say, by law).[11] This follows directly from the *NSC*, equation (5). An individual firm has no incentive to set $\overline{w}$ any higher than necessary. An increase in $\overline{w}$ raises V_u and hence requires a higher w to meet the *NSC*. Therefore, increases in $\overline{w}$ cost the firm both directly (higher unemployment benefits) and indirectly (higher wages). Since the firm has no difficulty attracting labor (in equilibrium), it sets $\overline{w}$ as small as possible. Hence we can interpret $\overline{w}$ in what follows as the minimum legal level, which is offered consistently by all firms.

Having offered the minimum allowable $\overline{w}$, an individual firm pays wages sufficient to induce employee effort, that is, $w = \hat{w}$ to meet the *NSC*. The firm's labor demand is given by equating the marginal product of labor to the cost of hiring an additional employee. This cost consists of wages and future unemployment benefits. For $\overline{w} = 0$,[12] the labor demand is given simply by $f'(L_i) = \hat{w}$, with aggregate labor demand of $F'(L) = \hat{w}$.

---

[10] More complex employment contracts, for example, wages rising with seniority, are discussed in Section III. With our assumptions of stationarity and identical workers, employers cannot improve on the simple employment provisions considered here.

[11] We are implicitly assuming that the firm cannot offer $\overline{w}$ only to workers who quit. This is so because the firm can always fire a worker who wishes to quit, and it would be optimal for the firm to do so.

[12] For $\overline{w} > 0$ the expected cost of a worker is the wage cost for the expected employment period of $1/b$, followed by $\overline{w}$ for the expected period of unemployment, $1/a$. This generates labor demand given by

$$f'(L_i) = w + \overline{w}b/(a+r).$$

D. *Market Equilibrium*

We now turn to the determination of the equilibrium wage and employment levels. Let us first indicate heuristically the factors which determine the equilibrium wage level.

If wages are very high, workers will value their jobs for two reasons: (a) the high wages themselves, and (b) the correspondingly low level of employment (due to low demand for labor at high wages) which implies long spells of unemployment in the event of losing one's job. In such a situation employers will find they can reduce wages without tempting workers to shirk.

Conversely, if the wage is quite low, workers will be tempted to shirk for two reasons: (a) low wages imply that working is only moderately preferred to unemployment, and (b) high employment levels (at low wages there is a large demand for labor) imply unemployment spells due to being fired will be brief. In such a situation firms will raise their wages to satisfy the *NSC*.

Equilibrium occurs when each firm, taking as given the wages and employment levels at other firms, finds it optimal to offer the going wage rather than a different wage. The key market variable which determines individual firm behavior is V_u, the expected utility of an unemployed worker. We turn now to the calculation of the equilibrium V_u.[13]

The asset equation for V_u, analogous to (1) and (2), is given by

$$(6) \qquad rV_u = \overline{w} + a(V_E - V_u),$$

where a is the job acquisition rate and V_E is the expected utility of an employed worker (which equals V_E^N in equilibrium). We can now solve (4) and (6) simultaneously for V_E and V_u to yield

$$(7) \qquad rV_E = \frac{(w-e)(a+r)+\overline{w}b}{a+b+r};$$

$$(8) \qquad rV_u = \frac{(w-e)a+\overline{w}(b+r)}{a+b+r}.$$

---

[13] We have already shown that all firms offer the same employment benefits $\overline{w}$, so V_u is indeed a single number, i.e., an unemployed person's utility is independent of his previous employer.

50   **Carl Shapiro and Joseph E. Stiglitz**

Substituting the expression for V_u (i.e., (8)) into the *NSC* (5) yields the *aggregate NSC*

(9) $w \geq \bar{w} + e + e(a + b + r)/q.$

Notice that the critical wage for nonshirking is greater: (a) the smaller the detection probability q; (b) the larger the effort e; (c) the higher the quit rate b; (d) the higher the interest rate r; (e) the higher the unemployment benefit ($\bar{w}$); and (f) the higher the flows out of unemployment a.

We commented above on the first four properties; the last two are also unsurprising. If the unemployment benefit is high, the expected utility of an unemployed individual is high, and therefore the punishment associated with being unemployed is low. To induce individuals not to shirk, a higher wage must be paid. If a is the probability of obtaining a job per unit of time, $1/a$ is the expected duration of being unemployed. The longer the duration, the greater the punishment associated with being unemployed, and hence the smaller the wage that is required to induce nonshirking.

The rate a itself can be related to more fundamental parameters of the model, in a steady-state equilibrium. In steady state the flow *into* the unemployment pool is bL where L is aggregate employment. The flow *out* is $a(N - L)$ (per unit time) where N is the total labor supply. These must be equal, so $bL = a(N - L)$, or

(10) $a = bL/(N - L).$

Substituting for a into (9), the aggregate *NSC*, we have

(11) $w \geq e + \bar{w} + \dfrac{e}{q} \left(\dfrac{bN}{(N - L)} + r \right)$

$= e + \bar{w} + (e/q)(b/u + r) \equiv \hat{w},$

where $u = (N - L)/N$, the unemployment rate. This constraint, the aggregate *NSC*, is graphed in Figure 1. It is immediately evident that *no shirking is inconsistent with full employment*. If $L = N$, $a = +\infty$, so any shirking worker would immediately be re-

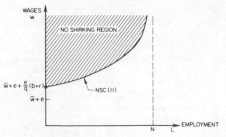

FIGURE 1. THE AGGREGATE NO-SHIRKING CONSTRAINT

hired. Knowing this, workers will choose to shirk.

The equilibrium wage and employment level are now easy to identify. Each (small) firm, taking the aggregate job acquisition rate a as given, finds that it must offer at least the wage $\hat{w}$. The firm's demand for labor then determines how many workers are hired at the wage. Equilibrium occurs where the aggregate demand for labor intersects the aggregate *NSC*. For $\bar{w} = 0$, equilibrium occurs when

$$F'(L) = e + (e/q)(bN/(N - L) + r).$$

The equilibrium is depicted in Figure 2.[14] It is important to understand the forces which cause E to be an equilibrium. From the firm's point of view, there is no point in raising wages since workers are providing effort and the firm can get all the labor it wants at w^*. Lowering wages, on the other hand, would induce shirking and be a losing idea.[15]

From the worker's point of view, *unemployment is involuntary*: those without jobs would be happy to work at w^* or lower, but cannot make a credible promise not to shirk at such wages.

---

[14]Aggregate labor demand is $F'(L)$ only when $\bar{w} = 0$ (see fn. 12).
[15]We have assumed that output is zero when an individual shirks, but we need only assume that a shirker's output is sufficiently low that hiring shirking workers is unprofitable.

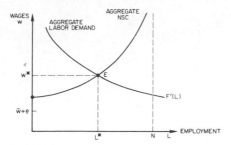

FIGURE 2. EQUILIBRIUM UNEMPLOYMENT

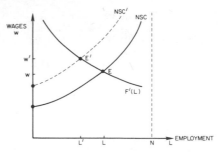

FIGURE 3. COMPARATIVE STATICS

Note: A decrease in the monitoring intensity q, or an increase in the quit rate b, leads to higher wages and more unemployment

Notice that the type of unemployment we have characterized here is very different from search unemployment. Here, all workers and all firms are identical. There is perfect information about job availability. There is a different information problem: firms are assumed (quite reasonably, in our view) not to be able to monitor the activities of their employees costlessly and perfectly.

E. *Simple Comparative Statics*

The effect of changing various parameters of the problem may easily be determined. As noted above, increasing the quit rate b, or decreasing the monitoring intensity q, decreases incentives to exert effort. Therefore, these changes require an increase in the wage necessary (at each level of employment) to induce individuals to work, that is, they shift the NSC curve upwards (see Figure 3). On the other hand, they leave the demand curve for labor unchanged, and hence the equilibrium level of unemployment and the equilibrium wage are both increased. Increases in unemployment benefits have the same impact on the NSC curve, but they also reduce labor demand as workers become more expensive, so they cause unemployment to rise for two reasons.

Inward shifts in the labor demand schedule create more unemployment. Due to the NSC, wages cannot fall enough to compensate for the decreased labor demand. The transition to the higher unemployment equilibrium will not be immediate: wage decreases by individual firms will only become

attractive as the unemployment pool grows. This provides an explanation of wage sluggishness.

F. *Welfare Analysis*

In this section we study the welfare properties of the unemployment equilibrium. We demonstrate that the equilibrium is not in general Pareto optimal, when information costs are explicitly accounted for.

We begin with the case where the owners of the firms are the same individuals as the workers, and ownership is equally distributed among N workers. The central planning problem is to maximize the expected utility of the representative worker subject to the NSC and the resource constraint:

$$(12) \quad \max_{w, \bar{w}, L} \; (w - e)L + \bar{w}(N - L)$$

subject to $w \geq e + \bar{w} + (e/q)((bN$

$$/(N - L)) + r) \quad (NSC)$$

subject to $wL + \bar{w}(N - L) \leq F(L)$

$$(\text{Feasibility})$$

subject to $\bar{w} \geq 0$.

Since workers are risk neutral it is easy to check[16] that the optimum involves $\bar{w}$ at the minimum allowable level, which is assumed to be 0. The reason is that increases in $\bar{w}$ tighten the *NSC*, so all payments should be made in the form of w rather than $\bar{w}$.

Setting $\bar{w} = 0$, the problem simplifies to

$$(12') \quad \max_{w,\,L} (w - e)L$$

subject to $w \geq e + (e/q)((bN/(N-L)) + r)$;

and $\quad wL \leq F(L)$.

The set of points which satisfy the constraints is shaded in Figure 4. Iso-utility curves are rectangular hyperboles. So long as $F'(L) > e$, these are steeper than the average product locus, so the optimum occurs at point A where the *NSC* intersects the curve $w = F(L)/L$, that is, where wages equal the average product of labor. In contrast, the market equilibrium occurs at E where the marginal product of labor curve, $w = F'(L)$, intersects the *NSC* (Figure 2). Observe that in the case of constant returns to scale, $F'(L)L = F(L)$, so the equilibrium is optimal.

Wages should be subsidized, using whatever (pure) profits can be taxed away. An equivalent way to view the social optimum is a tax on unemployment to reduce shirking incentives; the wealth constraint on the un-

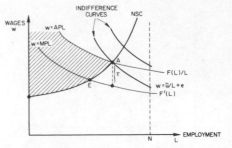

FIGURE 4. SOCIAL OPTIMUM AT A

employed requires that $\bar{w} \geq 0$, or equivalently that profits after taxes are nonnegative.[17] The optimum can be achieved by taxing away all profits and financing a wage subsidy of τ, shown in Figure 4. *The "natural" unemployment rate is too high.*

In the case where the workers and the owners are distinct individuals, the tax policy described above would reduce profits, increase wages, and increase employment levels. While it would increase aggregate output (net of effort costs), such a tax policy would *not* constitute a Pareto improvement, since profits would fall. For this reason, the equilibrium is Pareto optimal in this case, even though it fails to maximize net national product. We thus have the unusual result that the Pareto optimality of the equilibrium depends upon the distribution of wealth. The standard separation between efficiency and income distribution does not carry over to this model.

It should not be surprising that the equilibrium level of unemployment is in general inefficient. Each firm tends to employ too few workers, since it sees the private cost of an additional worker as w, while the social cost is only e, which is lower. On the other hand, when a firm hires one more worker, it fails to take account of the effect this has on V_u (by reducing the size of the unemployment pool). This effect, a negative externality imposed by one firm on others as it raises its

---

[16] Formally,

$$\mathcal{L} = (w - e)L + \bar{w}(N - L)$$

$$+ \lambda[w - e - \bar{w} - (e/q)(bN/(N-l) + r)]$$

$$+ \mu[F(L) - wL - \bar{w}(N - L)].$$

Differentiating with respect of w and $\bar{w}$ yields

$$\mathcal{L}_w = L + \lambda - \mu L \leq 0 \text{ and } = 0 \text{ if } w > 0.$$

$$\mathcal{L}_{\bar{w}} = (N - L) - \lambda - \mu(N - L) \leq 0 \text{ and } = 0 \text{ if } \bar{w} > 0.$$

We know $w > 0$ by the *NSC*, so $\mathcal{L}_w = 0$, i.e., $L(1 - \mu) + \lambda = 0$. Therefore, since $\lambda > 0$, $\mu > 1$. But then $\mathcal{L}_{\bar{w}} = (N - L)(1 - \mu) - \lambda < 0$. This implies that $\bar{w} = 0$.

[17] The constraint $\bar{w} \geq 0$ can be rewritten, using the resource constraint, as $F(L) - wL \geq 0$, i.e., $\pi \geq 0$.

level of employment, tends to lead to over-employment. In the simple model presented so far, the former effect dominates, and the natural level of unemployment is too high. This will not be true in more general models, however, as we shall see below.

II. Extensions

In this section we describe how the results derived above are modified or extended when we relax some of the simplifying assumptions. We discuss three extensions in turn: endogenous monitoring, risk aversion, and endogenous turnover. Detailed derivations of the claims made below are available in our earlier working paper.

A. *Endogenous Monitoring*

When employees can select the monitoring intensity q, they can trade off stricter monitoring (at a cost) with higher wages as methods of worker discipline. In general, firms' monitoring intensities will not be optimal, due to the externalities between firms described above. In general, it is not possible to ascertain whether the equilibrium entails too much or too little employment. In the case of constant returns to scale ($F(L) = L$), however (which led to efficiency with exogenous monitoring), the competitive equilibrium involves too much monitoring and too much employment.

The result is not as unintuitive as it first seems: each firm believes that the only instrument at its control for reducing shirking is to increase monitoring. There is, however, a second instrument: by reducing employment, workers are induced not to shirk. This enables society to save resources on monitoring (supervision). These gains more than offset the loss from the reduced employment.

It is straightforward to see how this policy may be implemented. If firms can be induced to reduce their monitoring, welfare will be increased. Hence a tax on monitoring, with the proceeds distributed, say, as a lump sum transfer to firms, will leave the no-shirking constraint/national-resource constraint unaffected, but will reduce monitoring.

B. *Risk Aversion*

With risk neutrality, the optimum and the market both involve $\overline{w} = 0$. Clearly $\overline{w} = 0$ cannot be optimal if workers are highly risk averse and may be separated from their jobs for exogenous reasons. Yet the market always provides $\overline{w} = 0$ (or the legal minimum). The proof above that $\overline{w} = 0$ carries over to the case of risk-averse workers.

When equilibrium involves unemployment, firms have no difficulty attracting workers and hence offer $\overline{w} = 0$, since $\overline{w} > 0$ merely reduces the penalty of being fired. When *other* firms offer $\overline{w} = 0$, this argument is only strengthened: unemployed workers are even easier to attract. It is striking that the market provides no unemployment benefits even when workers are highly risk averse. Clearly the social optimum involves $\overline{w} > 0$ if risk aversion is great enough. This may provide a justification for mandatory minimum benefit levels.

C. *Endogenous Turnover*

In general a firm's employment package will influence the turnover rate it experiences among its employees. Since the turnover rate b affects the rate of hiring out of the unemployment pool, and hence V_u, it affects other firms' no-shirking constraints. Because of this externality, firms' choices of employment packages will not in general be optimal. This type of externality is similar to search externalities in which, for example, one searcher's expected utility depends on the number or mix of searchers remaining in the market. In the current model, policies which discourage labor turnover are attractive as they make unemployment more costly to shirkers.

III. Alternative Methods for the Enforcement of Discipline

This paper has explored a particular mechanism for the enforcement of discipline: individuals who are detected shirking are fired, and in equilibrium the level of unemployment is sufficiently large that this threat serves as an effective deterrent to shirking. The question naturally arises whether there are alternative, less costly, or more effective discipline mechanisms.

A. *Performance Bonds*

The most direct mechanism by which discipline might be enforced is through the posting by workers of performance bonds. Under this arrangement the worker would forfeit the bond if the firm detected him shirking. One problem with this solution is that workers may not have the wealth to post bond.[18] A more fundamental problem with this mechanism is that the firm would have an incentive to *claim* that the worker shirked so that it could appropriate the bond. Assuming, quite realistically, that third parties cannot easily observe workers' effort (indeed, it is usually more costly for outsiders to observe worker inputs than for the employer to do so), there is no simple way to discipline the *firm* from this type of opportunism.

Having recognized this basic point, it is easy to see that a number of other plausible solutions face the same difficulty. For example, consider an employment package which rewards effort by raising wages over time for workers who have not been found shirking. This is in fact equivalent to giving the worker a level wage stream, but taking back part of his earlier payments as a bond, which is returned to him later. Therefore, by the above argument, the firm will have an incentive to fire the worker when he is about to enter the "payoff" period in which he recovers his bond. This is the equivalent to the firm's simply appropriating the bond. It is optimal for the firm to replace expensive senior workers by inexpensive junior ones.[19]

Clearly the firm's reputation as an honest employer can partially solve this problem; the employer is implicitly penalized for firing a worker if this renders him less attractive to prospective employees. Yet this reputation mechanism may not work especially well, since prospective employees often do not know the employer's record, and previous dismissals may have been legitimate (it is not possible for prospective employees to distinguish legitimate from unfair earlier dismissals, if they are aware of them at all). If the reputation mechanism is less than perfect, it will be augmented by the unemployment mechanism.

B. *Other Costs of Dismissal*

Unemployment in the model above serves the role of imposing costs on dismissed workers. If other costs of dismissal are sufficiently high, workers may have an incentive to exert effort even under conditions of full employment. Examples of such costs are search costs, moving expenses, loss of job-specific human capital, etc. In markets where these costs are substantial, the role of equilibrium unemployment is substantially diminished. The effect we have identified above will still be present, however, when effort levels are continuous variables: each firm will still find that employee effort is increasing with wages, so wages will be bid up somewhat above their full-employment level. The theory predicts that involuntary (as well as frictional) unemployment rates will be higher for classes of workers who have lower job switching costs.

---

[18] This is especially true if detection is difficult (low q) so that an effective bond must be quite large. Even if workers could borrow to post the bond, so long as bankruptcy is possible, the incentives for avoiding defaulting on the bond are not different from the incentives to avoid being caught shirking by the firm in the absence of a bond. Note once again the importance of the wealth distribution in determining the nature of the equilibrium. If all individuals inherit a large amount of wealth, then they could post bonds.

[19] In competitive equilibrium, the average (discounted) value of the wage must be equal to the average

(discounted) value of the marginal product of the worker. If there is a bonus for not shirking, *initially* the wage must be below the value of the marginal product. It is as if the worker were posting a bond (the difference between his marginal product and the wage), and as such this scheme is susceptible to precisely the same objections raised against posting performance bondings. The employer has an incentive to appropriate the bond. Since workers know this, this is not a viable incentive scheme. For a fine study in which firms' reputations are assumed to function so as to make this scheme viable, see Edward Lazear (1981).

C. *Heterogeneous Workers*

The strongest assumption we have made is that of identical workers. This assumption ruled out the possibility that firing a worker would carry any stigma. Such a stigma could serve as a discipline device, even with full employment.[20] In reality, of course, employers *do* make wage offers which are contingent on employment history. Such policies make sense when firms face problems of adverse selection.

We recognize that workers' concern about protecting their reputations as effective, diligent workers may provide an effective incentive for a disciplined labor force.[21] Shapiro's earlier (1983) analysis of reputation in product markets showed, however, that for reputations to be an effective incentive device, there must be a cost to the loss of reputation. It is our conjecture that, under plausible conditions, even when reputations are important, equilibrium will entail some use of unemployment as a discipline device for the labor force, at least for lower-quality workers. An important line of research is the study of labor markets in which adverse selection as well as moral hazard problems are present. In this context, our model should provide a useful complement to the more common studies of adverse selection in labor markets.

IV. Conclusions

This paper has explored the role of unemployment, or job rationing, as an incentive device. We have argued that when it is costly to monitor individuals, competitive equilibrium will be characterized by unemployment, but that the natural rate of unemployment so engendered will not in general be optimal. We have identified several forces at

work, some which tend to make the market equilibrium unemployment rate too high, and others which tend to make it too small. Each firm fails to take into account the consequences of its actions on the level of monitoring and wages which other firms must undertake in order to avoid shirking by workers. Although these externalities are much like pecuniary externalities, they are important, even in economies with a large number of firms.[22] As a result, we have argued that there is scope for government interventions, both with respect to unemployment benefits and taxes or subsidies on monitoring and labor turnover, which can (if appropriately designed) lead to Pareto improvements.

The type of unemployment studied here is not the only or even the most important source of unemployment in practice. We believe it is, however, a significant factor in the observed level of unemployment, especially in lower-paid, lower-skilled, blue-collar occupations. It may well be more important than frictional or search unemployment in many labor markets.

[20] See Bruce Greenwald (1979) for a simple model in which those who are in the "used labor market" are in fact a lower quality than those in the "new" labor market.

[21] This suggests once again that our results may be most significant in labor markets for lower-quality workers: in such markets employment histories are utilized less and workers already labeled as below average in quality have less to lose from being labeled as such.

[22] For a more general discussion of pecuniary, or more general market mediated externalities, with applications to economies with important adverse selection and moral hazard problems, see Greenwald and Stiglitz (1982).

REFERENCES

Alchian, Armen A. and Demsetz, Harold, "Production, Information Costs, and Economic Organization," *American Economic Review*, December 1972, *62*, 777–95.

Calvo, Guillermo A., "Quasi-Walrasian Theories of Unemployment," *American Economic Review Proceedings*, May 1979, *69*, 102–06.

———, "On the Inefficiency of Unemployment," Columbia University, October 1981.

——— and Wellisz, Stanislaw, "Hierarchy, Ability and Income Distribution," *Journal of Political Economy*, October 1979, *87*, 991–1010.

Diamond, Peter, "Mobility Costs, Frictional Unemployment, and Efficiency," *Journal of Political Economy*, August 1981, *89*, 798–812.

Greenwald, Bruce, C. N., *Adverse Selection in the Labor Market*, New York; London: Garland, 1979.

_____ and Stiglitz, Joseph E., "Pecuniary Externalities," unpublished, Princeton University, 1982.

Lazear, Edward P., "Agency, Earnings Profiles, Productivity, and Hours Restrictions," *American Economic Review*, September 1981, *71*, 606–20.

Salop, Steven C., "A Model of the Natural Rate of Unemployment," *American Economic Review*, March 1979, *69*, 117–25.

Shapiro, Carl, "Premiums for High Quality Products as Returns to Reputations," *Quarterly Journal of Economics*, November 1983, *98*, 658–79.

_____ and Stiglitz, Joseph E., "Equilibrium Unemployment as a Worker Discipline Device," Discussion Papers in Economics, No. 28, Woodrow Wilson School, Princeton University, April 1982.

Stiglitz, Joseph E., "Prices and Queues as Screening Devices in Competitive Markets," IMSSS Technical Report No. 212, Stanford University, 1976.

_____ and Weiss, Andrew, "Credit Rationing in Markets with Imperfect Information," *American Economic Review*, June 1981, *71*, 393–410.

Weiss, Andrew, "Job Queues and Layoffs in Labor Markets with Flexible Wages," *Journal of Political Economy*, June 1980, *88*, 526–38.

Wilson, Charles, "The Nature of Equilibrium in Markets with Adverse Selection," *Bell Journal of Economics*, Spring 1980, *11*, 108–30.

Involuntary Unemployment as a Principal-Agent Equilibrium

By James E. Foster and Henry Y. Wan, Jr.*

Whether and why involuntary unemployment exists with persistence are issues of continuing debate. Advocates of the natural rate hypothesis deny that unemployment can be involuntary in models having rational agents, and favor structural reforms rather than discretionary interventions in macroeconomic policies.[1] Keynesians would not so readily dismiss the presence of involuntary unemployment: instead they seek out microeconomic explanations and consider appropriate remedies for each separate source of the "malaise."[2]

Straightforward microeconomic explanations of involuntary unemployment, though, are not so easy to come by. As it is well known, the Walras equilibrium concept precludes persistent involuntary unemployment,[3] while search-theoretic explanations are usually identified with joblessness of a frictional and voluntary nature.[4] Explanations involving labor turnovers (for example,

wages are kept above equilibrium to help recruitment and discourage quitting) might also be regarded as frictional and not involuntary.[5] Critics of the implicit contract model argue that the unemployment predicted is not only voluntary, but is also preventable by efficient contracts.[6]

Other theories tracing inflexible, high wages to their beneficial effects on the morale and efforts of workers are confronted with the possibility that firms might adopt performance contracts (i.e., incentive wage systems), including the piece rate, to sidestep this issue altogether.[7] The merits of the various arguments lie beyond our present scope.

The purpose of this paper is to observe that, in a principal-agent model with performance contracts, there may exist unemployment that is both persistent and involuntary in nature.

We consider a simple principal-agent model based on Leonid Hurwicz and Leonard Shapiro (1978) and on Milton Harris and Robert Townsend (1981). Firms control the means of production and hire workers to produce a single good. The output of a worker depends on the number of workers employed by the firm, the worker's effort level, and the worker's "status" (for example, his health, mood, etc.). The status of each worker is assumed to be identically and independently distributed. The firm can observe a worker's output, but not his effort, nor his status.

The firm chooses the number of workers hired and a contract for each worker, stipu-

*Krannert School of Management, Purdue University, West Lafayette, IN 47907, and Department of Economics, Cornell University, Uris Hall, Ithaca, NY 14853, respectively. We thank Jack Barron, James Moore, Paul Thomas, and Andrew Weiss for helpful comments. Any errors or shortcomings are ours alone.

[1] For example, see Milton Friedman (1968) and Robert Lucas (1977,1978).

[2] See Robert Solow (1980) and the various contributions cited by him. On this view, if different causes of "wasteful" unemployment coexist, each should be separately analyzed and controlled; i.e., Occam's razor is inapplicable here. As an analogy, what were generically regarded as "fevers" in the last century are treated with different antidotes today.

[3] Lucas (1977), advocating an "equilibrium" theory of business cycles, would insist upon models that either are Walrasian or share many elements of the Walras framework. He cites Hayek: "By 'equilibrium theory' we here primarily understand the modern theory of general interdependence of all economic quantities, which has been most perfectly expressed by the Lausanne School of theoretical economics" (p. 7). Rationality of all individuals plays a central role in these models.

[4] We have in mind the important and numerous contributions evolved from the volume of Edmund Phelps et al. (1970).

[5] For example, see the penetrating analyses of George Akerlof (1976) and Andrew Weiss (1980).

[6] Unemployment in the implicit contract model of Costas Azariadis (1975), Martin Baily (1974), and Donald Gordon (1974) has been criticized by Robert Barro (1977) as preventable and by Oliver Hart (1983) as not being involuntary.

[7] Such explanations are discussed in Solow (1979), Roger Sparks (1982), Joseph Stiglitz (1982), and James Tobin (1972). Also see Wan (1973) for earlier literature and Takashi Negishi (1979) for an analytical review of the related issues. The criticism of such models was kindly provided to one of the authors by Walter Oi.

57

lating a (nonnegative) reward for each (nonnegative) output of the worker, possibly in some nonlinear manner.

Each worker has a utility function that depends positively on his reward and negatively on his efforts expended. He takes the number of coworkers and his contract as given, observes his status, and then chooses a utility-maximizing level of effort. So long as the worker's output is (continuously) increasing in effort, we can regard his "indirect" utility to be a function of his reward as well as his *output*, and parametrically dependent on the number of coworkers and his status.[8] With this in mind, we can regard the worker's choice variables to be his status-specific output levels instead of his effort levels.

The firm is assumed to know the worker's utility function and the underlying distribution of his status. The expected profit of a firm is the excess of outputs over rewards, averaged over all possible statuses and summed over all its workers. The problem facing a firm is to select the number of workers to hire and a contract for each worker, consistent with output responses maximizing its expected profit.

In Section I, profit-maximizing employment programs are explicitly derived for a parametric example with identical workers. Proposition 1 gives conditions under which there is an excess supply of labor when each firm adopts its profit-maximizing program. Moreover, the unemployment so obtained is "involuntary" in that each employed worker enjoys a strictly higher level of (expected) utility than every unemployed worker. The underlying reason for this is as follows. The profit-maximizing contract leaves a worker indifferent between working and shirking when in a less productive status, while inducing a strictly higher level of output (and utility) when the worker is in a more productive status. Thus the worker receives a strictly higher level of expected utility when employed. Yet the firm will not lower the wage schedule in response to an excess supply of labor. A wage cut at the level of output chosen in the less productive status would

induce the worker to produce zero output; a wage cut at the more productive output level would lead the worker to produce the output of the less productive status. A firm's profit would fall if it were to lower the wage schedule in response to an excess supply of labor, even though each employed worker is strictly better off than his unemployed twin.[9]

Section II shows that the intuition behind this result continues to hold in the more general model: under quite minimal conditions, any unemployment that arises must be of an involuntary nature (see Proposition 2). A brief discussion of the main results is given in Section III.

I. Example

To make our exposition as transparent as possible, we shall consider a simple example with specific functional forms similar to Hurwicz-Shapiro and Harris-Townsend.

There are m identical firms producing the same (numeraire) commodity, and a set I of workers each having the same nonlabor income, preference, and ability at work. The number of workers is denoted by L.[10] The assumption of identical workers is not strictly necessary for our results, but as stressed by Takashi Negishi (p. 30) in a related context, it ensures that labor heterogeneity is not the cause of the involuntary unemployment.

The von Neumann-Morgenstern utility index of each individual i from I is of the form $u(r^i, z^i) = r^i - (z^i)^2$ where $r^i \geq 0$ is the reward to the individual, and $z^i \geq 0$ is his effort level. Each worker has two possible statuses of productivity, $k^i = 1$ or $k^i = 2$, with corresponding probabilities $p_1 > 0$ and $p_2 > 0$. The common production technology for each worker is represented by

$$(1) \qquad y^i = f(z^i; k^i, N)$$
$$= a(k^i)e^{-bN}z^i,$$

where $a(k^i) > 0$ is the status-dependent pro-

---

[8] Compare with Hurwicz-Shapiro (p. 182).

[9] We are indebted to Andrew Weiss for this nice explanation.

[10] Strictly speaking, L is the measure of the set I. To avoid problems of indivisibilities, it is best to interpret I as the interval $[0, L]$.

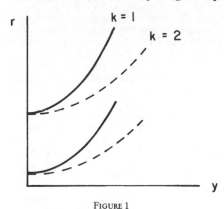

FIGURE 1

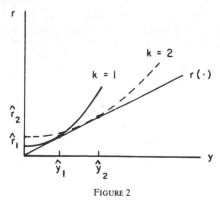

FIGURE 2

ductivity parameter, $N \geq 0$ is the number of workers hired by the firm, and $b > 0$ is a parameter representing scale diseconomies. Without loss of generality we take $a(1) < a(2)$; that is, status 2 is the more productive status.

Given k^i and N, we may invert f to obtain the effort-requirement function $g(y^i; k^i, N) = e^{bN}y^i/a(k^i)$, which indicates the amount of effort needed to produce a given output y^i. The "indirect" utility for individual i is then

$$(2) \quad v(y^i, r^i; k^i, N) = u(r^i, g(y^i; k^i, N))$$

$$= r^i - (e^{bN}y^i/a(k^i))^2.$$

Figure 1 depicts two sets of indifference curves for the indirect utility function, one set per status. The steeper slope of the status 1 indifference curves indicates that the worker must expend greater effort to produce the same output, hence must receive a higher reward to render him indifferent.

Being unable to observe a worker's status or monitor his effort level, the firm offers a performance contract $r^i(\cdot)$ which promises a nonnegative reward of $r^i(y^i)$ depending on the observed output y^i. A simple linear or "piece-rate wage" contract is depicted in Figure 2. The firm is assumed to choose an *employment program*, which specifies a level of employment N, and a performance con-

tract $r^i(\cdot)$ for each worker i hired by the firm.[11]

Once an individual is hired by a firm as part of an employment program, his status-dependent utility may be expressed as a function of y^i alone, namely,

$$(3) \quad w(y^i; k^i, N) = v(y^i, r^i(y^i); k^i, N)$$

$$= r^i(y^i) - (e^{bN}y^i/a(k^i))^2.$$

The worker then chooses output level $\hat{y}_1^i$ for status 1 and $\hat{y}_2^i$ for status 2 satisfying

$$(4) \quad w(\hat{y}_1^i; 1, N) \geq w(y^i; 1, N)$$

$$(5) \quad w(\hat{y}_2^i; 2, N) \geq w(y^i; 2, N)$$

for all $y^i \geq 0$. Examples of such status-dependent utility maxima are given in Figure 2: output $\hat{y}_1^i$ leads to a reward of $\hat{r}_1^i$ where the contract touches the highest possible indifference curve in status 1, and similarly for $(\hat{y}_2^i, \hat{r}_2^i)$.

The status-dependent output responses of worker i lead to a level of expected profit (due to worker i) of

$$(6) \quad p_1(\hat{y}_1^i - r^i(\hat{y}_1^i)) + p_2(\hat{y}_2^i - r^i(\hat{y}_2^i))$$

---

[11]Implications of this assumption are discussed in Section III. Note that it is *not* assumed that all performance contracts offered by the firm are identical, although this may typically hold at equilibrium.

for the employer. The total expected profit associated with an employment program is found by summing (6) over all workers employed by the firm. An employment program which leads to the highest level of total expected profit is called a *profit-maximizing program* for the firm. We have the following result.

PROPOSITION 1: *If $m/2b < L$, then there will be unemployment when each firm chooses its profit-maximizing program. Further, the expected utility of each unemployed worker will be strictly less than the expected utility of every employed worker.*

To show this we will explicitly determine a profit-maximizing program for each firm. First, let us assume that an arbitrary employment level of $N > 0$ is given for a firm. Notice that the contracts or outputs of a worker's coworkers have no effect on the contract or output for that worker. Thus we can maximize total expected profit by maximizing the expected profit of each worker independently.

LEMMA 1: *Suppose N and the contracts $r^j(\cdot)$ of all workers $j \neq i$ at a firm are given. Then the contract $r_N(\cdot)$ defined by*

$$(7) \quad r_N(y)$$

$$= \begin{cases} 0 & \text{for } 0 \leq y < \hat{y}_1(N) \\ \hat{r}_1(N) & \text{for } \hat{y}_1(N) \leq y < \hat{y}_2(N) \\ \hat{r}_2(N) & \text{for } \hat{y}_2(N) \leq y; \end{cases}$$

$$(8) \quad \hat{y}_1(N) = \alpha_1 e^{-2bN}, \quad \hat{y}_2(N) = \alpha_2 e^{-2bN},$$

$$\hat{r}_1(N) = \beta_1 e^{-2bN}, \quad \hat{r}_2(N) = \beta_2 e^{-2bN};$$

(where $\alpha_1, \alpha_2, \beta_1, \beta_2 > 0$ are terms involving $a_1 = a(1)$, $a_2 = a(2)$, p_1, and p_2 as specified in the Appendix) leads to the highest expected profits from worker i. (For the proof of Lemma 1, see the Appendix.)

Since $r_N(\cdot)$ yields the highest profit from a given worker irrespective of the contracts of all other workers at the firm, it is clear that a program in which all contracts are $r_N(\cdot)$

must be profit maximizing for that N. By a simple calculation, the maximum total expected profit that can be achieved with N workers is $Ne^{-2bN}K$, where $K = p_1(\alpha_1 - \beta_1) + p_2(\alpha_2 - \beta_2) > 0$. Since this function achieves a unique maximum at $\hat{N} = 1/2b$, the employment program having $\hat{N}$ workers and identical contracts $\hat{r}(\cdot) = r_{\hat{N}}(\cdot)$ for all employees is a profit-maximizing program. Clearly, then, the total number of workers employed at all m identical firms is $m\hat{N} = m/2b$, when each adopts its profit-maximizing program. Hence, if $m/2b < L$ as assumed above, then $L - m/2b > 0$ of the workers must be unemployed.

Now an unemployed worker i receives the utility level associated with the pair $(r^i, z^i) = (0,0)$ in both statuses, namely $u(0,0) = 0$. An employed worker, by contrast, enjoys

$$(9) \quad v(\hat{y}_1, \hat{r}_1; 1, \hat{N}) = \hat{r}_1 - e\hat{y}_1^2/a_1^2$$

$$v(\hat{y}_2, \hat{r}_2; 2, \hat{N}) = \hat{r}_2 - e\hat{y}_2^2/a_2^2$$

in statuses 1 and 2, respectively, where $\hat{r}_k = \hat{r}_k(\hat{N})$ and $\hat{y}_k = \hat{y}_k(\hat{N})$ for $k = 1, 2$. By evaluating (4) and (5) at $y^i = 0$ and $y^i = \hat{y}_1$, respectively, we obtain

$$(10) \quad \hat{r}_1 - e\hat{y}_1^2/a_1^2 \geq 0,$$

$$\hat{r}_2 - e\hat{y}_2^2/a_2^2 \geq \hat{r}_1 - e\hat{y}_1^2/a_1^2.$$

Since $a_1 < a_2$, it follows that $\hat{r}_2 - e\hat{y}_2^2/a_2^2 > 0$ which by $p_2 > 0$ implies that the expected utility of an employed worker is strictly greater than that of an unemployed worker. This establishes Proposition 1.

Figure 3 depicts the contract $\hat{r}(\cdot)$ from the above profit-maximizing program, and the status-dependent responses $\hat{y}_1$ and $\hat{y}_2$ of the worker. The contract offers a "base pay" of $\hat{r}(\hat{y}_1)$ when an output at least as great as $\hat{y}_1$ is achieved, with a "bonus" of $\hat{r}(\hat{y}_2) - \hat{r}(\hat{y}_1)$ for reaching $\hat{y}_2$. The class of profit-maximizing contracts consists of all contracts that (i) pass through $(\hat{y}_1, \hat{r}(\hat{y}_1))$ and $(\hat{y}_2, \hat{r}(\hat{y}_2))$, and (ii) lie nowhere above the status 1 and 2 indifference curves through $(\hat{y}_1, \hat{r}(\hat{y}_1))$. Note that there is a slight ambiguity in the definition of profit since the best responses of the workers are not unique; the worker may

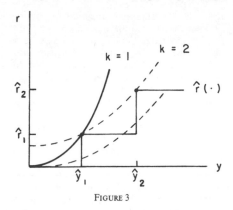

choose an output level of 0 in status 1, or $\hat{y}_1$ in status 2, without lowering his expected utility. To avoid this prospect, the firm can offer an "ε-optimal" contract in which a small amount of profit is forfeited to ensure that the unique response in status k is $\hat{y}_k$.

Remark: In the terminology of Harris-Townsend, the pairs $(\hat{y}_1, \hat{r}_1)$ and $(\hat{y}_2, \hat{r}_2)$ comprise a "parameter-contingent ($p.c.$) outcome" for the environment, satisfying the "self-selection" constraints

(SS) $v(\hat{y}_1, \hat{r}_1; 1, \hat{N}) \geq v(\hat{y}_2, \hat{r}_2; 1, \hat{N})$

$v(\hat{y}_2, \hat{r}_2; 2, \hat{N}) \geq v(\hat{y}_1, \hat{r}_1; 2, \hat{N})$

and the "individual rationality" constraints

(IR) $v(\hat{y}_1, \hat{r}_1; 1, \hat{N}) \geq 0$

$v(\hat{y}_2, \hat{r}_2; 2, \hat{N}) \geq 0.$

This can be seen in Figure 3 since $(\hat{y}_1, \hat{r}_1)$ lies on a status 1 indifference curve that is above $(\hat{y}_2, \hat{r}_2)$, and $(\hat{y}_2, \hat{r}_2)$ lies on the same status 2 indifference curve as $(\hat{y}_1, \hat{r}_1)$, verifying the (SS) constraints; while $(\hat{y}_1, \hat{r}_1)$ and $(\hat{y}_2, \hat{r}_2)$ lie on or above their respective state-dependent indifference curves passing through the origin, verifying the (IR) constraints.

II. A General Result

The above example illustrates a situation in which there exists persistent unemploy-

ment that is neither voluntary nor frictional. "Not frictional" is a by-product of the steady-state nature of the model. The employed and unemployed never change positions, and there are no workers caught between jobs. By "not voluntary," we mean that there are two identical individuals, one employed and the other jobless, where the former is better off than the latter in expected utility terms.

The two salient features of the example reinforce each other. On one hand, the persistence of the terms and levels of unemployment admits no tendency for change. On the other hand, identical persons enjoy different expected utility with "on-the-job" being favored over "on-the-dole."

Persistence of unemployment reflects adherence to profit-maximizing programs by firms. Barring wage concessions, firms would never hire more workers because of diminishing returns to employment. Further, any wage concession which might be offered by the jobless would always be resisted by firms. In a profit-maximizing program, a firm offers the lowest reward for each output response, until it becomes irreducible due to either the individual rationality or the self-selection constraints. Individuals never offer wage concessions which violate individual rationality: the utility of reward must at least cover the disutility of effort. Firms would never accept wage concessions that violate self-selection: such offers would be illusory as it would be incentive incompatible for workers to produce the particular outputs to which the concessions apply. Hence, any offered concession must be incredible while any credible concession would never be offered.

These conclusions are not limited to the simple two-status example presented above. Let us return to the general framework presented in the introduction, and assume that each identical worker has $s \geq 2$ possible statuses, where $p_k > 0$ for $k = 1, \ldots, s$. Then employing the notation of Section I, the following proposition can be shown.

PROPOSITION 2: *Suppose that there exists a profit-maximizing program $(\hat{r}(\cdot), \hat{N})$ with status dependent responses $\hat{y}_1, \ldots, \hat{y}_s$. If an output $\hat{y}_{k'}$ can be produced in an alternative* *status* $k'' \neq k'$ *using less effort, then any unemployment must be involuntary.*

PROOF:

Denote the utility level of the unemployed by w_0. Since rewards are nonnegative, $w(0; k, \hat{N}) \geq w_0$, and since $\hat{y}_k$ is a utility-maximizing response in status k, we have $w(\hat{y}_k; k, \hat{N}) \geq w_0$, for each k.

Now suppose that $\hat{y}_{k'}$ can be produced in status $k'' \neq k'$ using less effort. Then since effort causes disutility,

$$(11) \quad w(\hat{y}_{k'}; k'', \hat{N}) > w(\hat{y}_{k'}; k', \hat{N}).$$

And since $\hat{y}_{k''}$ is a best response in status k'',

$$(12) \quad w(\hat{y}_{k''}; k'', \hat{N}) \geq w(\hat{y}_{k'}; k'', \hat{N}).$$

Thus, an employed worker obtains strictly higher utility than w_0 in status k'', and at least w_0 in every other status, so that the expected utility of the employed worker exceeds that of the unemployed.

Remark: Suppose that the worker is uniformly more productive in some status k'' than k', in that he can produce strictly more output at each positive effort level (see the above example). If the profit-maximizing program leads to a positive output in status k', then the hypothesis of Proposition 2 is satisfied.

The crucial aspect of our model is the presence of asymmetric information between worker and firm *favoring the worker*. This may be seen most clearly in terms of the individual rationality and self-selection constraints that must hold for a profit-maximizing contract. The individual rationality constraint implies that in any given status k, the worker's status-dependent response $\hat{y}_k$ is no worse than not working. By assumption, there are two statuses k' and k'' such that the output $\hat{y}_{k'}$ may be produced with less effort, and hence higher utility, in status k'' than in status k'. Since the firm is unable to observe

the worker's status, it must abide by the self-selection constraint in status k'': the utility derived from producing $\hat{y}_{k''}$ must be at least as great as from producing $\hat{y}_{k'}$ in status k''. Thus, as compared to being unemployed, an employed worker receives strictly more utility in status k'', and no less utility in all other statuses, so that the expected utility of an employed worker is strictly higher than that of an unemployed worker.

III. Conclusion

We have shown that under certain circumstances it may be rational for a firm to pay its workers more than required to cover the disutility of labor effort, despite the presence of identical unemployed workers. That the accompanying unemployment is involuntary in nature is evident from the above discussion; yet we are not claiming to have obtained "Keynesian" unemployment. There remains a great deal of controversy surrounding the *General Theory*, and the chapter on involuntary unemployment is no exception. For instance, Robert Lucas (1978) dismisses Keynes' treatment of unemployment as "evasion and wordplay"; while Negishi infers from Chapter 2 a definition of involuntary unemployment similar to the one presented above. It is surely not our purpose to offer a novel interpretation of Keynes, nor to claim that the above model in any way captures the richness of the Keynesian "family of models" (Robert Clower and Axel Leijonhufvud, 1975, p. 182). Instead we have addressed the question of whether involuntary unemployment is a priori inconsistent with rational firms and workers. We have presented a preliminary answer in the form of a model with asymmetric information that admits involuntary unemployment in equilibrium.

Of course, our results may be sensitive to the precise form of the model we have adopted. For instance, we have assumed that a worker observes his status *after* being hired by the firm as part of an employment program. If the order of events were switched around so that the worker learned his status *before* being hired (or if renegotiation were allowed), intriguing questions would arise as to whether there are "rationing schemes" or other mechanisms which might better sort out high productivity workers from low, and lead to a higher expected profit for the firm. In the present paper, this is explicitly ruled out by an assumption which restricts the strategy of a firm to be an employment program.[12] It would be interesting to see how changing the model in this way, and allowing a richer strategy set for firms, might affect our results.

Another feature that should be noted is our requirement that contracts give ,a nonnegative reward for each output level. If firms are able to punish workers or force them to pay a penalty when output falls below a certain level, then one might find that the expected utility of those with jobs would be lowered to that of the jobless. Equivalently, involuntary unemployment in our sense may disappear if a firm can exact an "application fee" of such magnitude that any unemployed worker would be indifferent about whether he is hired or not.[13] Of course, this leads to serious questions about the enforceability of such labor contracts, both legally and practically, and in particular about what happens if a worker is forced below his budget constraint. In addition, one would expect the "reservation" level of utility (fixed at zero in our example) to be an endogenous variable of the model, determined by competition among firms and the relative scarcity of labor. Further work along these lines would surely be of interest.

---

[12]Under this assumption, Proposition 1 holds in the latter model as well, and has an interesting interpretation brought to our attention by Weiss. Since a worker observes his status before being hired by the firm, it is natural in this context to call the status of a worker his "type." Then there are two types of workers that the firm could hire, less productive and more productive, with the firm unable to identify a given worker's type. Proposition 1 shows that at the profit-maximizing employment program, the first type of worker is indifferent between working and being unemployed, while the second more productive type is strictly better off.

[13]For a discussion of application fees (or collateral requirements) in several related contexts, see Stiglitz and Weiss (1981; 1983, fn. 27).

APPENDIX

PROOF of Lemma 1:

Let N and the contracts of all other workers be given. Consider the contract $r_N(\cdot)$ defined in equations (7) and (8), where

$$(A1) \quad \alpha_1 = \frac{p_1 a_1^2 a_2^2}{2(a_2^2 - p_2 a_1^2)}, \qquad \alpha_2 = \frac{a_2^2}{2};$$

$$(A2) \quad \beta_1 = \left[\frac{p_1 a_1 a_2^2}{2(a_2^2 - p_2 a_1^2)}\right]^2,$$

$$\beta_2 = \left(\frac{a_2}{2}\right)^2 + (a_2^2 - a_1^2)\left[\frac{p_1 a_1 a_2}{2(a_2^2 - p_2 a_1^2)}\right]^2.$$

For simplicity of notation, we denote $\bar{y}_k = \hat{y}_k(N)$ and $\bar{r}_k = \hat{r}_k(N)$ for $k = 1, 2$, and drop the superscript i in what follows. It is an easy matter to verify that $0 < \alpha_1 < \alpha_2$, and so $0 < \bar{y}_1 < \bar{y}_2$. Note that $\beta_1 = (\alpha_1/a_1)^2$ and $\beta_2 = (\alpha_2/a_2)^2 + (a_2^2 - a_1^2)(\alpha_1/(a_1 a_2))^2$, so that $\bar{r}_1$ and $\bar{r}_2$ are strictly positive. The inequalities $\bar{r}_1 < \bar{r}_2$ and $\beta_1 < \beta_2$ will follow from Claim 3, below.

We shall show first that $\bar{y}_1$ is an optimal response in status 1, and $\bar{y}_2$ is an optimal response in status 2. Note that the contract $r_N(\cdot)$ specifies a constant reward on each of the intervals $[0, \bar{y}_1)$, $[\bar{y}_1, \bar{y}_2)$, and $[\bar{y}_2, \infty)$. Since effort generates disutility, the left endpoint in each interval is strictly preferred to the remaining points in the interval, irrespective of the status. Thus, we need only show $w(\bar{y}_1; 1, N) \geq 0$ and $w(\bar{y}_1; 1, N) \geq w(\bar{y}_2; 1, N)$ to verify that $\bar{y}_1$ is an optimal response in status 1; and $w(\bar{y}_2; 2, N) \geq 0$ and $w(\bar{y}_2; 2, N) \geq w(\bar{y}_1; 2, N)$ to show that $\bar{y}_2$ is an optimal response in status 2. This is done in the following four claims.

Claim 1: $w(\bar{y}_1; 1, N) = 0$.

$$w(\bar{y}_1; 1, N) = \beta_1 e^{-2bN} - \left(e^{bN}\alpha_1 e^{-2bN}/a_1\right)^2$$

$$= e^{-2bN}(\alpha_1/a_1)^2 - \left(e^{-bN}\alpha_1/a_1\right)^2.$$

Claim 2: $w(\bar{y}_1; 1, N) > w(\bar{y}_2; 1, N)$.

$$w(\bar{y}_2; 1, N) = \beta_2 e^{-2bN} - \left(e^{bN}\alpha_2 e^{-2bN}/a_1\right)^2$$

$$= \left[\left(\frac{\alpha_2}{a_2}\right)^2 + \left(a_2^2 - a_1^2\right)\left(\frac{\alpha_1}{a_1 a_2}\right)^2\right.$$

$$\left. - \left(\frac{\alpha_2}{a_1}\right)^2\right]e^{-2bN}$$

$$= \left[\alpha_2^2 a_1^2 + \left(a_2^2 - a_1^2\right)\alpha_1^2 - \alpha_2^2 a_2^2\right]$$

$$\times e^{-2bN}/\left(a_1^2 a_2^2\right)$$

$$= \left(a_2^2 - a_1^2\right)\left(\alpha_1^2 - \alpha_2^2\right)$$

$$\times e^{-2bN}/\left(a_1^2 a_2^2\right).$$

Since $a_2^2 > a_1^2$ and $\alpha_1^2 < \alpha_2^2$ we have $w(\bar{y}_2; 1, N) < 0$, which along with Claim 1 establishes the result.

Claim 3: $w(\bar{y}_2; 2, N) = w(\bar{y}_1; 2, N)$.

$$w(\bar{y}_2; 2, N)$$

$$= \left[\left(\frac{\alpha_2}{a_2}\right)^2 + \left(a_2^2 - a_1^2\right)\left(\frac{\alpha_1}{a_1 a_2}\right)^2\right]e^{-2bN}$$

$$- \left(e^{bN}\alpha_2 e^{-2bN}/a_2\right)^2$$

$$= \left(a_2^2 - a_1^2\right)\left(\frac{\alpha_1}{a_1 a_2}\right)^2 e^{-2bN}$$

$$= \left(\frac{\alpha_1}{a_1}\right)^2 e^{-2bN} - \left(e^{bN}\alpha_1 e^{-2bN}/a_2\right)^2$$

$$= w(\bar{y}_1; 2, N).$$

Claim 4: $w(\bar{y}_2; 2, N) > 0$.

$$w(\bar{y}_2; 2, N) = w(\bar{y}_1; 2, N)$$

$$= \bar{r}_1 - \left(e^{bN}\bar{y}_1/a_2\right)^2 > \bar{r}_1 - \left(e^{bN}\bar{y}_1/a_1\right)^2$$

$$= w(\bar{y}_1; 1, N) = 0,$$

since $\bar{y}_1 > 0$ and $a_2 > a_1$.

Now let $r(\cdot)$ be an alternative contract, with optimal responses y_1 and y_2. Denote $r_1 = r(y_1)$ and $r_2 = r(y_2)$. We shall show that the expected profit associated with $r(\cdot)$ can be no larger than the expected profits from $r_N(\cdot)$.

To be sure, the worker must find y_1 to be at least as preferred as 0 in state 1 under contract $r(\cdot)$, so that

(A3) $r_1 \geq e^{2bN}y_1^2/a_1^2$.

Further, y_2 must be at least as preferred as y_1 in status 2 under $r(\cdot)$, so that

(A4) $r_2 - e^{2bN}y_2^2/a_2^2 \geq r_1 - e^{2bN}y_1^2/a_2^2$,

and so

(A5) $r_2 \geq e^{2bN}\left(y_2^2/a_2^2 + y_1^2/a_1^2 - y_1^2/a_2^2\right)$.

In addition, recall that

(A6) $\bar{r}_1 = e^{2bN}\bar{y}_1^2/a_1^2$,

(A7) $\bar{r}_2 = e^{2bN}\left(\bar{y}_2^2/a_2^2 + \bar{y}_1^2/a_1^2 - \bar{y}_1^2/a_2^2\right)$.

For $k = 1, 2$, denote $h_k = \bar{y}_k - y_k$ and $\mu_k = \bar{y}_k^2 - y_k^2$, and note that $\mu_k = 2h_k\bar{y}_k - h_k^2$. Then,

(A8) $p_1(\bar{y}_1 - \bar{r}_1) + p_2(\bar{y}_2 - \bar{r}_2)$

$$- p_1(y_1 - r_1) - p_2(y_2 - r_2)$$

$$= p_1 h_1 + p_2 h_2 + p_1(r_1 - \bar{r}_1) + p_2(r_2 - \bar{r}_2)$$

$$\geq p_1 h_1 + p_2 h_2 - p_1 e^{2bN}\mu_1/a_1^2$$

$$- p_2 e^{2bN}\left(\mu_2/a_2^2 + \mu_1/a_1^2 - \mu_1/a_2^2\right)$$

$$= p_1 h_1 - e^{2bN}\mu_1/a_1^2 + e^{2bN}\mu_1 p_2/a_2^2$$

$$- p_2 e^{2bN}\mu_2/a_2^2 + p_2 h_2$$

$$= p_1 h_1 - e^{2bN}\mu_1\left(\frac{p_1}{2\alpha_1}\right)$$

$$- p_2 e^{2bN}\mu_2/a_2^2 + p_2 h_2$$

$$= p_1 h_1 - e^{2bN}h_1\bar{y}_1\left(\frac{p_1}{\alpha_1}\right) + e^{2bN}h_1^2\left(\frac{p_1}{2\alpha^1}\right)$$

$$+ e^{2bN}\left(\frac{p_2}{2\alpha_2}\right)h_2^2 - p_2 h_2 \frac{e^{2bN}}{\alpha_2}\bar{y}_2 + p_2 h_2$$

$$= e^{2bN}\left(\frac{p_1}{2\alpha_1}h_1^2 + \frac{p_2}{2\alpha_2}h_2^2\right) \geq 0.$$

Thus, the expected profit associated with $r_N(\cdot)$ is highest among all contracts.

REFERENCES

Akerlof, George, "The Economics of Caste and of the Rat Race and Other Woeful Tales," *Quarterly Journal of Economics*, November 1976, *90*, 591–617.

Azariadis, Costas, "Implicit Contracts and Underemployment Equilibria," *Journal of Political Economy*, December 1975, *83*, 1183–202.

Baily, Martin N., "Wages and Employment Under Uncertain Demand," *Review of Economic Studies*, January 1974, *41*, 37–50.

Barro, Robert J., "Long-term Contracting, Sticky Prices and Monetary Policy," *Journal of Monetary Economics*, July 1977, *3*, 305–16.

Clower, Robert and Leijonhufvud, Axel, "The Coordination of Economic Activities: A Keynesian Perspective," *American Economic Review Proceedings*, May 1975, *65*, 182–88.

Friedman, Milton, "The Role of Monetary Policy," *American Economic Review*, March 1968, *58*, 1–17.

Gordon, Donald F., "A Neo-classical Theory of Keynesian Unemployment," *Economic Inquiry*, December 1974, *12*, 431–59.

Hart, Oliver D., "Optimal Labour Contracts Under Asymmetric Information: An Introduction," *Review of Economic Studies*, January 1983, *50*, 3–35.

Harris, Milton and Townsend, Robert M., "Resource Allocation Under Asymmetric Information," *Econometrica*, January 1981, *49*, 33–64.

Hurwicz, Leonid and Shapiro, Leonard, "Incentive Structures Maximizing Residual Gain Under Incomplete Information," *Bell Journal of Economics*, Spring 1978, *9*, 180–91.

Keynes, John M., *The General Theory of Employment Interest and Money*, New York 1936.

Lucas, Robert E., Jr., "Understanding Business Cycles," in Karl Brunner and Allan H. Meltzer, eds., *Stabilization of the Domestic and International Economy*, Vol. 5, Carnegie-Rochester Conferences on Public Policy, *Journal of Monetary Economics*, Suppl. 1977, 7–29.

_____, "Unemployment Policy," *American Economic Review Proceedings*, May 1978, *68*, 353–57.

Negishi, Takashi, *Microeconomic Foundations of Keynesian Macroeconomics*, Amsterdam: North-Holland, 1979.

Phelps, Edmund S. et al., *Microeconomic Foundations of Employment and Inflation Theory*, New York: Norton, 1970.

Solow, Robert M., "Another Possible Source of Wage Stickiness," *Journal of Macroeconomics*, Winter 1979, *1*, 79–82.

_____, "On Theories of Unemployment," *American Economic Review*, March 1980, *70*, 1–10.

Sparks, Roger W., "A Model of Unemployment and Wage Rigidity," unpublished paper, University of California-Davis, 1982.

Stiglitz, Joseph E., "The Wage-Productivity Hypothesis: Its Economic Consequences and Policy Implications," paper presented at the annual meeting of the American Economic Association, 1982.

_____ and Weiss, Andrew, "Credit Rationing in Markets with Imperfect Information," *American Economic Review*, June 1981, *71*, 393–410.

_____ and _____, "Incentive Effects of Terminations: Applications to the Credit and Labor Markets," *American Economic Review*, December 1983, *73*, 912–27.

Tobin, James, "Inflation and Unemployment," *American Economic Review*, March 1972, *62*, 1–18.

Wan, Henry Y., Jr., "A General Theory of Wages, Employment, and Human Capital —An Application of Semi-Competitive Equilibrium," Department of Economics Working Paper No. 51, Cornell University, 1973.

Weiss, Andrew, "Job Queues and Layoffs in Labor Markets with Flexible Wages," *Journal of Political Economy*, June 1980, *88*, 526–38.

LABOR CONTRACTS AS PARTIAL GIFT EXCHANGE*

GEORGE A. AKERLOF

This paper explains involuntary unemployment in terms of the response of firms to workers' group behavior. Workers' effort depends upon the norms determining a fair day's work. In order to affect those norms, firms may pay more than the market-clearing wage. Industries that pay consistently more than the market-clearing wage are primary, and those that pay only the market-clearing wage are secondary. Thus, this paper also gives a theory for division of labor markets between primary and secondary.

I. INTRODUCTION

In a study of social relations among workers at a utility company in the eastern United States, George Homans [1953, 1954] observed that a small group of young women (doing a job called "cash posting") exceeded the minimum work standards of the firm by a significant margin (i.e., on average by 15 percent). Most of these women neither desired nor expected promotion in the firm in return for their troubles. Why did they do it?

Section II shows that the standard neoclassical model cannot simultaneously explain both the behavior of the firm and the behavior of the cash posters. But, as shown in Section III, application of a standard sociological model does explain the behavior of both the young women and their employer. According to this model, in their interaction workers acquire sentiment for each other and also for the firm. As a consequence of sentiment for the firm, the workers acquire

* The author would like to thank William Dickens, Brian Main, Hajime Miyazaki, Janet L. Yellen, and two referees for invaluable help. He would also like to thank the National Science Foundation for generous financial support under Research Grant SOC 79-05562, administered by the Institute of Business and Economic Research of the University of California, Berkeley.

utility for an exchange of "gifts" with the firm—the amount of utility depending upon the so-called "norms" of gift exchange. On the worker's side, the "gift" given is work in excess of the minimum work standard; and on the firm's side the "gift" given is wages in excess of what these women could receive if they left their current jobs. As a consequence of worker sentiment for one another, the firm cannot deal with each worker individually, but rather must at least to some extent treat the group of workers with the same norms, collectively.

Norm–gift-exchange models have been used in many sociological studies to explain the behavior of workers. And these explanations are simple; properly understood, they are in tune with everyone's personal experiences of human behavior, so that they can be taken to have considerable generality. For that reason I feel confident in extrapolating such behavior beyond the narrow and particular instance of the "cash posters" to concern wage bargains and work conditions in some generality. Sections IV and V verbally explore the consequences of such behavior for wage determination; Sections VI and VII build formal mathematical models; and Section VIII gives conclusions.

This model of the microeconomics of the labor market is used to explain two phenomena that have not been successfully analyzed by more conventional economic theory. First, in most other analyses of unemployment, such as that of search theory [Phelps *et al.*, 1970], all unemployment is voluntary. In my analysis there are primary labor markets in which unemployed workers are unable to obtain jobs at the prevailing market wages. Second, the theory of dual labor markets [Doeringer and Piore, 1971] brings up the question as to which markets will be primary and which markets secondary. In the formal models developed in this paper, it is endogenously determined whether a market will be primary or secondary. Primary markets are those in which the gift component of labor input and wages is sizeable, and therefore wages are not market-clearing. Secondary labor markets are those in which wages are market-clearing.

The major feature of the usual model of implicit contracts due to Azariadis [1975] and Baily [1974] is risk-sharing agreements by the contracting agents over a span of time. These models have been taken as a vehicle for Okun's [1981, p. 133] description of labor and customer markets. This paper offers an alternative microfoundation for implicit contracts. Its emphasis is sociological. It focuses on the gift-exchange nature of employment arrangements, where the exchange is based partially on norms of behavior that are endogenously determined. This dependence of implicit contracts on *norms* of behavior (rather than on risk sharing) captures important aspects of Okun's description [1975, 1981] that have not been analyzed in the Azariadis-Baily framework.

According to this paper, norms of work effort are a major determinant of output. In emphasizing effort, it carries further the work of Leibenstein [1976] on X-efficiency. The focus on effort could also be expressed in Marxian terminology via the distinction between *labor power* and *labor* as in Edwards' recent book [1979] on the inevitable conflict between labor and management over the use of labor power.[1] In Edwards' terms this paper gives equilibrium models of the resolution of this conflict. Finally, it should be mentioned, Hirschman's concepts of *Exit*, *Voice*, and *Loyalty* [1970] can be expressed in terms of norms and gift exchange.

II. The Nonneoclassical Behavior of the Cash Posters or of the Eastern Utilities Co.

Economists usually assume that labor is hired as a factor of production and is put to work like capital. There is, however, one fundamental difference between labor and capital that is ignored by this assumption. Once a capitalist has hired capital, he is, over a fairly wide latitude, free to use it (or abuse it) as he wishes. However, having hired a laborer, management faces considerable restriction on how it can use its labor. Not only are there legal restrictions (such as OSHA regulations, child labor laws, etc.), but the willing cooperation of labor itself must usually be obtained for the firm to make the best use of the labor services.

Of course, standard economic theory does describe the nature of contracts when there are many possible standards of performance. According to standard theory, when a firm hires a laborer, there is an understanding by both parties that certain minimum standards of performance must be met. Furthermore, the contract may be *implicit* in the sense that workers need not be currently rewarded for their current performance but may earn chances for promotion with higher pay in the future in return for good performance in their current jobs. If this is the case, the firm need not have tight rules regarding work and compensation that very carefully specify the *quid pro quo* of pay for work, since injustices in the present can be compensated later. So standard theory can serve as a good approximation to reality even

---

1. For a review of the Marxian literature on this distinction, also see Edwards [1979].

TABLE I

WORK PERFORMANCE OF INDIVIDUAL CASH POSTERS

	Age in years	Time on job in years-months	Mean cards per hour	Mean errors per hour
Asnault	22	3–5	363	0.57
Burke	26	2–5	306	0.66
Coughlin	20	2–0	342	0.40
Donovan	20	1–9	308	0.79
Granara	21	1–3	438	0.65
Lo Presti	25	–11	317	0.03
Murphy	19	–7	439	0.62
Rourke	17	–4	323	0.82
Shaugnessy	23	–2	333	0.44
Urquhart	18	–2	361	0.49
Average	21.1	1–4	353	0.55

where very specific contracts relating effort or output to compensation would be quite expensive.

Against this background let us consider the study by Homans of "The Cash Posters." In this study a group of ten young women working as cash posters for a utility company in a New England city were interviewed and closely observed over a period of six months. The duty of a cash poster at Eastern Utilities was to record customers' payments on ledger cards at the time of receipt. The company's standard for such cash posting was 300 per hour, and careful records were made of the speed at which individual cash posters variously worked. Anyone who worked below the rate of 300 per hour received a mild rebuke from the supervisor. Table I adapted from Homan's article, "The Cash Posters," shows both the number of cash postings per hour of different workers and their rate of error.

Note from Table I that the average number of cash postings per hour (353) was 17.7 percent greater than the standard set by the company. The simple neoclassical theory of contracts cannot simultaneously explain why the faster persons did not reduce their speed to the standard; or, alternatively, why the firm did not increase the speed expected of its faster workers. The possibility that the faster workers worked harder than the standard for either increased pay or promotion was belied by the uniformity of wage for all cash posters and by the refusal of promotion by two cash posters. When promotion did occur, it was normally to a job considered more responsible than cash posting, but nevertheless paying the same wage. In addition, voluntary quits among the cash posters were quite frequent (with most of the young women leaving to be married), so that in most cases promotion was not a relevant consideration. Since pay was not dependent on effort and promotion was rarely a consideration, the standard economic model of contract would predict that workers set their work habits to meet the company's minimum standards of performance as long as they have marginal disutility for work at that level. On the other hand, if workers do have positive utility for work at this level, the lack of incentives for effort given by the firm should lead them to choose to work to the point where the marginal disutility of additional effort is just zero. But in that case the firm could increase its profits by increasing work standards for the faster workers. Unless their utility function is discontinuous, they would still prefer their current jobs to what they could obtain elsewhere at somewhat faster speeds of work.

Since output is easily observable, it is at least a bit surprising from the point of view of the neoclassical theory of contracts that workers are not paid wages proportional to their outputs. This constitutes another puzzlement regarding the system of industrial relations among the cash posters at Eastern Utilities, although a potential answer has been suggested by Etzioni [1971]. According to Etzioni, workers find pecuniary incentives, such as piece rates, "alienating."

The mysterious behavior of the cash posters and of Eastern Utilities in terms of neoclassical theory can be posed a bit more formally. Suppose for whatever reason (perhaps Etzioni's) that the firm has decided to pay the same wage $w = \overline{w}$ to all cash posters. Further, suppose that workers have a utility function $u(w,e)$, where w is the wage rate and e is effort. Workers, mindful of the firm's work rules, should choose their effort e to maximize

(1) $u(w,e)$,

subject to the constraints,

(2) $w = \overline{w}$

(3) $e \geqq e_{\min}$,

where $\overline{w} = \$1.05$ per hour, the wage fixed for all cash posters, and $e_{\min}$ is the minimum effort necessary to accomplish the required 300 cash postings per hour.

Solution of this trivial maximization problem yields

(4) $e = e_{\min}$

as long as $u_e < 0$ for $e \geqq e_{min}$. On the assumption that utility is convex, there are two potential types of solutions. Each poses an empirical problem. If $u_e(\overline{w}, e_{min}) < 0$, the question arises—why did the workers not reduce their effort to 300 per hour? On the other hand, if $u_e(\overline{w}, e_{min}) > 0$, so that workers choose $u_e = 0$, why did the firm not raise the minimum standards for different workers above the point where $u_e = 0$? In either case the observation obtained is inconsistent with the neoclassical model.[2]

Of course, each cash poster may have a different utility function, and for some reason the firm may find it optimal to set the same minimum standard for all workers. For example, the rate perhaps cannot be set higher than 300 per hour in deference to the two workers who find the standard a bit onerous (as shown by Burke's and Donovan's performance in Table I, only 2 percent above the 300 minimum). But the question of why the same standard should be set for all workers can be answered only in terms of the interactions of workers among themselves and also with the firm. It is precisely in such terms that the next section poses the solution to the cash poster mystery.

Other potential objections such as the nonobservability of output and risk aversion by workers can be all but ruled out. Workers kept records of their outputs so output was easily observable; and workers did not work faster than the minimum out of fear of being sacked for falling below the minimum; as already mentioned, falling below the minimum occasioned no more than mild rebuke.

An explanation for either the firm's behavior or the workers' behavior must depend either on maximization of something other than profits by the firm or on interaction of the workers with each other and with the firm that alters their utility functions. It is to such a theory that we now turn.

III. SOCIOLOGICAL EXPLANATION OF CASH POSTERS'– EASTERN UTILITIES' BEHAVIOR

The previous section showed behavior by the cash posters inconsistent with a simple neoclassical theory of worker utility maximization and firm profit maximization. I do not doubt that there is some neoclassical model involving turnover costs or difficulty of ob-

2. The argument is just a bit subtle. If a worker with convex utility and positive marginal product for effort has a positive utility for wage income and zero disutility for added effort, the firm can increase his compensation and force him to work harder, to the advantage of both. If the worker was satisfied with his job before this additional trade, he will be even more satisfied afterwards, and therefore less willing to quit.

servation[3] which can explain the behavior of the firm and the cash posters, but given the failure of the simple model, the adequate model must of necessity be complicated. In contrast, this section presents a simple sociological explanation of the joint behavior of the cash posters and the Eastern Utilities Company.

According to a prominent school of sociological thought, the determinant of workers' effort is the norm of the work group. According to Elton Mayo [1949, p. 70], referring to the famous studies at the Hawthorne plant in the Bank Wiring Observation Room, "the working group as a whole actually determined the output of individual workers by reference to a standard, predetermined but clearly stated, that represented the group's conception of a fair day's work. The standard was rarely, if ever, in accord with the standards of the efficiency engineers."

According to an alternative, but equivalent, view of the cash posters' performance, they give a *gift* to the firm of work in excess of the minimum work required of 300 per hour. Offhand, it may seem absurd to view the worker as giving the firm a gift of any part of his work. Of course, the worker does not strictly give his labor as a gift to the firm; he expects a wage in return and, if not paid, will almost certainly sue in court. Likewise, the firm does not give the wage strictly as a gift. If the worker consistently fails to meet certain minimum standards, he will almost surely be dismissed. But above these minimum standards the worker's performance is freely determined. The norm (or "standard" as Mayo termed it) for the proper work effort is quite like the norm that determines the standards for gift giving at Christmas. Such gift giving is a trading relationship—in the sense that if one side of the exchange does not live up to expectations, the other side is also likely to curtail its activities.

The classic anthropological literature on the gift, particularly the essay by Marcel Mauss [1954], emphasizes this reciprocal nature of gift giving.[4] Mauss points out that, in the two major branches of Western European languages, the root for *poison* is the same as the root for *gift*, since in ancient German the word *gift* means both gift and poison, and the Greek word δόσισ for poison, which is the root of the English *dose*, has the same root as the Greek word to *give*. The reason for the close association of the words for *gift* and *poison* in these ancient languages comes from the obligatory nature of reci-

3. For an interesting explanation of unemployment due to imperfect information, see Stoft [1980]. Solow [1980] supports the view that involuntary unemployment must be explained by sociological models of behavior.

4. A good, although not recent, review of the anthropology and sociology of gift exchange is Belshaw [1965]. See also Titmuss [1971].

procity of a gift, or, equivalently, the threat of harm that was believed to befall a recipient who failed to reciprocate. Although the magic has gone out of the sanctions behind repayment of most gifts, there are probably few in modern times who have never received a gift they did not want or who have not given a gift they considered to be inadequately appreciated.[5]

Why should there be any portion of labor that is given as a gift by the firm or of treatment of the worker by the firm that can be considered a gift? The answer to this question is at once trivial and profound. Persons who work for an institution (a firm in this case) tend to develop sentiment for their co-workers and for that institution; to a great extent they anthropomorphize these institutions (e.g., "the friendly bank"). For the same reasons that persons (brothers, for example) share gifts as showing sentiment for each other, it is natural that persons have utility for making gifts to institutions for which they have sentiment. Furthermore, if workers have an interest in the welfare of their coworkers, they gain utility if the firm relaxes pressure on the workers who are hard pressed; in return for reducing such pressure, better workers are often willing to work harder.

The giving of gifts is almost always determined by norms of behavior. In most cases the gift given is approximately in the range of what the recipient expects, and he reciprocates in kind. The norms of gift giving are determined by the relationship between the parties; thus, for example, it is expected that an increase in workers' productivity will be rewarded by increased wages to the workers. Much of union wage negotiations concerns the question of what constitutes a *fair* wage. To an economist who believes that wages are market-clearing or only determined by the relative bargaining power of the contractual parties, long discussions about the "fair wage" should have no bearing on the final settlement. But this notion neglects the fact that the average worker works harder than necessary according to the firm's work rules, and in return for this donation of goodwill and effort, he expects a fair wage from the firm.

This view of wages-effort as mutually reciprocal *gifts* leaves several unanswered questions. The firm decides not only work rules but also wages for each and every worker. Why should not Eastern Utilities set high standards of minimum effort and terminate all workers who are not capable of meeting or who are not willing to meet

5. It has been suggested to me by one referee that the analysis of labor contracts as partial gift exchange relates to the Freeman-Medoff argument [1979] on trade unions as collective voice. Reciprocal gift giving induces union formation because discontented workers find it more difficult to quit and find another job with gift giving than without. As in Mauss's analysis it is suggested that reciprocal gift giving i.e., mutual benevolence and dependence, go together with mutual hostility and militancy.

that standard (for example, Burke and Donovan in Table I)? Again there is a simple answer. In working together, workers acquire sentiment for each other. An increase in minimum standards that would put pressure on Burke and Donovan might easily be considered by the group as a whole as failure by the firm to reciprocate the group's collective donation of productivity 17.7 percent in excess of the minimum requirements. Indeed, although the details are unclear in Homans' account, there is indication that such a situation had arisen with respect to the cash posters. As Homans reports, "a couple of years before, when relations between the posters and a former division head were strained, there may have been some restriction on output."

In a different context, that of a soldier in basic training in World War II, it is revealed most clearly why better workers come to the aid of their fellows:

> If one is so favored by nature or training that he gets much more done, or done better, than his neighbor, he shows up that neighbor. The neighbor then gets rebukes or extra work. One cannot do this to any decent fellow who is trying his best, especially when you have to live side by side with him and watch his difficulties and sufferings. Therefore, the superior person—if he has any heart at all and if he is sensitive to the attitudes of his barracks mates—will help his less able neighbor to get along [Stouffer et al., 1949, Vol. 2, p. 414].

Of course the cash posters were working under less extreme conditions. Nevertheless, they undoubtedly could have expressed their own reasons for helping each other in similar terms.

I have indicated the nature of the trade between firms and workers that is exemplified in the case study of the cash posters and that gives a consistent and plausible explanation for the behavior of both the firm and the workers; this explanation tells why workers exceed the minimum standards of work on the one hand, and why the firm does not raise these minimum standards on the other hand. But work standards are only one dimension of the treatment of workers. Another dimension is wages. For reasons similar to why minimum work standards are not necessarily set at the limit that workers will bear before leaving the firm, the optimal contract may not set wages at the minimum acceptable: if part of worker effort is a *gift*, likewise, part of wages paid should be a *gift*.

IV. REFERENCE GROUPS

With the cash posters (or any other work group whose effort is determined not by the work rules but by the group's norms) the question arises: What does the group receive in return for working more than prescribed by the work rules? In the first place the worker may receive leniency in the work rules. Even if the worker habitually works at a speed in excess of work rules, he still benefits from leniency in two ways. First, he derives positive utility from the *gift* by the firm of potential leniency should he slacken his pace; second, as already mentioned, if he has sympathy for other members of the work group, he derives utility from the firm's generous treatment of other members of the group for whom the work rules are a binding constraint. Additionally, the firm may give remuneration in excess of that needed to obtain another worker of similar skills. Thus, excess remuneration and leniency of work rules constitute the major gifts by the firm to its workers.

Presumably, the gift of the worker to the firm, effort in excess of the work rules is linked to the gift of the firm to the worker. Following Mauss and others, reciprocity is a major feature of gift exchange (as also of market exchange).

The *quid pro quo* in gift exchange is, however, established at least slightly differently from market exchange. The norms for effort are established according to the conception of a fair day's work. (Note that Mayo described the work standard in precisely those terms.) In return the workers expect to be treated "fairly" by the firm. The conception of fair treatment has been the subject of considerable work by social psychologists and sociologists. For the most part it is not based on absolute standards, but, rather, on comparison of one's own situation with that of other persons.

According to Festinger [1954], persons have an innate psychological need to compare their actions and treatment with those of others. Persons use comparison with others as a guide to how they ought to behave or how they ought to be treated. The point should be clear to any parent with a young child. Consider the young child who has fallen but not hurt himself/herself. Such situations usually produce that momentary pause before the child decides whether s/he should cry. If the surrounding adults act as if the situation calls for crying, the child is likely to behave accordingly; however, if adults act as if s/he should not cry, the child is likely not to do so. In the context of this paper I wish to note that the child's behavior is not determined by the real phenomenon of being hurt, but rather by the social definition of the situation given by the norms of the surrounding adults. In this way the child calibrates his/her actions by the social standards set by others.[6]

6. For this point of view of social interaction, see Coser [1971] on Park, Mead, and Cooley. The idea of the "definition of the situation" is due to William I. Thomas.

How do people decide that they are fairly treated? There is no natural measure (just as there is no natural language). Merton [1957] has constructed a theory of how people determine the fairness of their treatment by reference to the treatment of reference individuals and treatment of reference groups.

In World War II the Research Branch of the Information and Education Division of the U.S. Department of War conducted a large number of surveys of soldiers' attitudes. Some of these attitudes appear paradoxical from a purely individualistic, utilitarian point of view. For example, in the Army Air Force, in which promotion rates were much higher than in the rest of the army, soldiers were much less satisfied with their chances of promotion than elsewhere. Or, as a second example, although all soldiers abroad showed strong desire to return to the United States, noncombat soldiers abroad showed little more dissatisfaction with army life than soldiers stationed in the United States. Merton [1957] explains these seemingly paradoxical findings (as well as many others) with the concept of the reference group. The soldier in the Air Force felt unsatisfied with his chances of promotion precisely because the promotion rate was high in the Air Force, thereby enabling him to compare himself with other personnel who had been promoted (and causing him to feel relatively deprived). Noncombat soldiers abroad felt relatively satisfied given their objective conditions because they compared their lot to that of combat soldiers abroad, whereas the soldiers in the United States felt relatively unsatisfied (relative to their objective conditions) because they compared their lot to that of civilians at home. In each of these cases the seemingly paradoxical behavior is quite natural when the soldiers' attitudes are explained in terms of their deprivation relative to that of the appropriate reference group.

At the same time that *The American Soldier* [1949, Volumes 1 and 2] shows how attitudes toward fairness are formed (e.g., through reference to the relative deprivation of the appropriate reference group), it also contains evidence consistent with our hypothesis that *group norms* determine performance (as we have suggested is the case with respect to the cash posters and had been found earlier in the studies by Mayo [1949] and Roethlisberger and Dickson [1947]). In this regard three specific findings are worthy of particular note.

First, the Research Branch chose to measure performance of combat units by the percentage of *nonbattle casualties*. This statistic is equivalent to the percentage of combat men who became ineffective for reasons other than wounds or other battle injuries. This statistic was chosen as the best proxy for the quality of the unit, since it is almost independent of the group's battle environment. It is, as well, unambiguously related to the quality of discipline in the unit: presumably, better organized units would lose smaller fractions of persons outside of battle. An excellent correlation was obtained [Stouffer, 1949, Vol. 2, p. 11] on a company-by-company basis between relatively favorable attitudes toward army life in interviews taken before the Normandy landing and the rate of nonbattle casualties following the Normandy landing in the three tested army divisions. This correlation of performance and attitude is a useful indicator that satisfaction in the job leads to improved job performance, justifying one aspect of our view that the firm will be willing to give a *gift* to the worker to increase his job satisfaction, so as, in turn, to increase his job performance.

There is one other noteworthy statistic from the same study. For one regiment (the Thirty-seventh Regiment of the Ninth Division) a graph was made plotting the percentage of nonbattle casualties of soldiers with and without previous combat experience in the same company. The graph shows a clear relation: in those companies in which the combat veterans had high rates of nonbattle casualties, the new recruits also had high rates (and vice versa). The correlation between the two statistics (taken across companies) was 80 percent [Stouffer, 1949, Vol. 2, p. 27]. This statistic is consistent with the hypothesis that members of a work group tend to take on the *group* norms, the companies with group norms more favorable to army life having fewer casualties among both new recruits and veterans. However, this conclusion follows of necessity only if the Research Branch was correct in its judgment that nonbattle casualties were independent of the environment; otherwise, such a correlation could be obtained because veterans and new recruits respond alike in their nonbattle casualties to changes in the environment.

Finally, there is the study by the Research Branch on the attitudes of soldiers in the Caribbean. It was hypothesized that there would be correlation between dissatisfaction and comfort. Perhaps surprisingly, at least to a very utilitarian view of motivations, the evidence showed at most only weak relation between dissatisfaction and the quality of soldiers' living conditions. This finding is useful in supporting our view that the morale of the working group (and indirectly its norms of work behavior) will depend largely on deprivation relative to that of reference individuals and reference groups, rather than depending on objective conditions alone.

This behavior of the American soldier is exactly consistent with our hypotheses concerning the behavior of the cash posters. We hypothesized (1) that the cash posters worked harder than required because of favorable work attitudes; (2) these attitudes, following Mayo *et al.*, were not just individual but also attitudes of the work group; (3) these attitudes depended in part upon workers' sense of fair treatment, where fairness was measured by comparison with persons similarly situated. In exact parallel *The American Soldier* shows (1) favorable attitudes were correlated with lower percentages of nonbattle casualties, both on a group-by-group basis and also on an individual basis. (2) The company-by-company correlation between performances of recruits and combat veterans demonstrates that performances were not randomly distributed over individuals but in fact varied systematically over groups. (There is considerable research in social psychology that shows how such patterns occur.) (3) Finally, attitudes of groups of soldiers toward the army can be systematically explained under the hypothesis that soldiers form their attitudes by comparing their situations to that of reference individuals or reference groups. I take the fact that the same model seems to apply to both the cash posters and the American soldier to be an indication of its universality.

V. THE FAIR WAGE

The gift of the firm to the worker (in return for the worker's gift of hard work for the firm) consists in part of a wage that is fair in terms of the norms of this gift giving. Using reference-individual–reference-group theory, the fairness of this wage depends on how other persons in the worker's reference set are similarly treated. Although, persons do sometimes have reference groups, or reference individuals who are dissimilar [Hyman, 1942], in matters of fairness it is probably safe to suppose that most persons compare themselves to persons who are *similar*. In that case one argument of the perceived fairness of the wage will be the wages received by other similar workers. Such workers, of course, include workers who are employed; but, in addition, it includes workers in the reference set who are unemployed. While empirically unemployment at any moment is a fairly small fraction of the labor force, flows in and out of unemployment are large, and most workers have many friends and close relatives. The probability that a whole reference set be free of unemployment for a significant period (say a year) is not large for most persons.

There is one other argument to the reference wage. To the psychologist or sociologist, to say that persons compare their own behavior or treatment with that in the past is probably neither useful nor profound. But persons certainly do that, and some economic theory (for example, the Modigliani-Duesenberry peak income hypothesis) does depend on such behavior. Thus, one additional argument to the reference wage, in addition to the remuneration of similar employed and unemployed persons and their respective weights in the reference set, is past wages.

Consistent with this observation is the role of past wages in all labor negotiations. Labor disputes often concern the level of past wages, which are the benchmark for current negotiations. To cite a case in point, consider the General Motors strike of 1970. In the 1967–1970 contract wages were indexed, but an eight-cent-per-hour limit was placed on raises due to increases in the cost of living. The cost of living increased relative to wages by considerably more than eight cents per hour with a resultant level of wages twenty-six cents below the fully indexed level [Pearlstine, 1970]. The union claimed that the corporation had already received a windfall gain for the three years of the contract during which period wages were not fully indexed, and the negotiations should concern growth of the real wage from the fully indexed level; the company claimed negotiations should concern growth from the actual 1970 level. This matter was the most contentious issue in the settlement of a long strike.

Summing up all our discussion of the fair wage, the fair wage received by the worker depends on the effort he expends in excess of the work rules, the work rules themselves, the wages of other workers, the benefits of unemployed workers, as well as the number of such workers, and the worker's wages received in previous periods. Our theory of reference-group behavior thus yields a fair wage that looks very much like the wage paid in a Phillips curve:

$$(5) \qquad w^f_{i,t+1} = f(w_{i,t}, w_0, b_u, u, e_i, e_0)$$

where

$w^f_{i,t+1}$ is the perceived fair wage of individual i at $t + 1$

$w_{i,t}$ is the actual wage of individual i in previous period(s)

w_0 is the wage paid of others in the individual's reference set in current and previous periods

b_u is unemployment benefits of individuals in the reference set in current and previous periods

u is the number of unemployed in the reference set in current and previous periods

e_i is the individual's work rules in current and previous periods

e_0 is the work rules of persons in the individual's reference set in current and previous periods.

Equation (5) is, of course, the basis for a Phillips curve of the traditional sort. It is important to note, however, that contrary to the Phillips relations obtained from search theory [Phelps *et al.*, 1970], (5) is not derived from market-clearing considerations. In general, there can be workers willing to enter gift relations with a firm, but no firms willing to enter gift relations with the workers. The next two sections model this occurrence. Our models are based upon the preceding discussion of reference groups and of the cash posters.

VI. A MODEL

This section and the next develop formal models that capture to some degree of accuracy most of the gift-giving idea in wage contracts. The ingredients of this model are spelled out in this section as follows.

1. *Norms* of effort on the part of workers in the work group. These norms depend on the work rules of the firm, the average wage paid by the firm, the incentive system of the firm (in terms of the different wages paid for different levels of output or effort), and the utility of co-workers in the firm who are part of the work group and for whom each worker has sympathy. All of these variables are endogenous to the firm. Exogenous to the firm, the norms depend on the returns to other persons in the workers' reference sets. In terms of our model these variables can be summarized by wages received by workers at other firms, the unemployment rate, and unemployment benefits. The model is considerably simplified by assuming only one time period. I do not see that this assumption takes anything away from the argument; it can be easily modified.

We thus summarize norms by the equation,

$$(6) \qquad e_n = e_n(\{w(e,\epsilon)\}, e_{\min}, u_1, \ldots, u_J; w_0, u, b_u),$$

where

$\{w(e,\epsilon)\}$ is the function that relates wages of a worker of type ϵ to his effort; this is the remuneration system of the firm
$e_{\min}$ is the work rules
u_j is the utility of the jth worker in the firm
w_0 is the wage paid by other firms (perhaps a vector)
u is the unemployment rate
b_u is the unemployment benefit.

2. *Workers.* Each worker has a utility function. A worker who has been offered employment must decide on his level of effort and whether or not to accept employment at the terms offered. The utility of each worker depends on the norms for effort, the effort itself, and the wage rate if employed; it depends on the unemployment benefit if unemployed. A worker makes two choices. If offered employment (i.e., if the firm offers to "exchange gifts"), he must decide whether or not to accept the offer, and, if accepted, he must decide the size of the reciprocal gift. Thus, a worker of trait ϵ has a utility of working for the firm of

(7) $$u(e_n, e, w, \epsilon),$$

and if not working for the firm, of

$$u(b_u, \epsilon).$$

If working for the firm, the worker chooses the level of effort e, which maximizes utility u, subject to the condition necessary to maintain his employment, that effort should exceed the firm's minimum requirement, $e \geqq e_{min}$. Accordingly, the worker chooses a job, if offered, in preference to unemployment accordingly as

(8) $$\max_{e \geqq e_{min}} u(e_n, e, w, \epsilon)$$

is greater than or less than

(9) $$u(b_u, \epsilon).$$

If a worker has more than one offer from different firms, he chooses the offer that maximizes his utility.

Across workers there is a distribution of tastes ϵ; we call this distribution function $f(\epsilon)$.

3. *Firms.* We are, finally, left with firm behavior. Firms have an output that depends on the work effort of the workers. This output q is

(10) $$q = f(e_1, e_2, \ldots, e_J),$$

where J is the number of workers hired. e_j is the effort of worker j.

Firms pay wages in general according to type of worker ϵ and effort, so that $w = w(e, \epsilon)$.

Thus, wage cost is, accordingly,

$$\sum_{j=1}^{J} w(e_j, \epsilon_j),$$

where e_j is the effort of worker j and ϵ_j is the tastes of worker j.

82   George A. Akerlof

The firm chooses the wage function $w(e,\epsilon)$, work rules, $e_{\min}$, and the number of workers it wishes to hire to maximize profits, which are

$$(11) \qquad pf(e_1,\dots,e_J) - \sum_{j=1}^{J} w(e_j,\epsilon_j),$$

where p is the price of output. The firm's behavior is subject to the constraint that a worker chooses whether or not to join the firm according to whether or not the firm is making the worker his best offer (including unemployment as an alternative); the firm also views e_n as endogenously determined.

Models may differ regarding the firm's knowledge of workers' tastes ϵ; in the models of the next section, where this is relevant, we assume that the probability that it chooses a worker of given tastes ϵ from the unemployment pool is random. That assumption, while convenient, could be modified.

The general model just described of norms-workers-firms is enough taken across all workers and firms to describe aggregate supply for a whole economy. Two such examples are explored in some detail in the next section. These examples describe major features of models with such norm-determined firm-worker interaction.

VII. Two Examples

According to the standard neoclassical model of the labor market, the firm purchases labor services in an optimal amount, *given the market wage*. This statement does not completely describe the firm's choice set, although in the *neoclassical* model the inaccuracy is of no importance. The neoclassical firm can purchase all the labor services it wishes if it pays a wage *at least as great as* the market wage. The firm chooses the wage and its purchases of labor services subject to this constraint. If the firm chooses a wage below the market-clearing level, it receives no labor. As far as its choice is concerned, it would be making the same decision if it demanded no labor and paid the market wage; and there is no advantage to choosing a wage in excess of the market rate. The firm's choice of wage therefore is always at the boundary: it will choose the optimal quantity of labor at the market-clearing wage.

However, once labor contracts are viewed in the context of gift exchange, it is not necessarily true that the firm will always choose wages on the boundary. In gift exchange the usual norm is that gifts should be more than the minimum required to keep the other party in the exchange relationship. In terms of the labor market this means that the worker who does no more than necessary to keep his job is the subject of at least some slight loss of reputation; reciprocally, the firm that pays its workers no more than the minimum necessary to retain them will also lose some reputation. In the neoclassical model the firm *never* chooses to pay more than the market-clearing wage because there is no advantage to doing so. In the gift-exchange model, however, the interior solution, in which the firm finds it advantageous to pay a wage in excess of the one at which it can acquire labor, may occur because there are some benefits (as well as costs) from paying a higher wage. Doubtless, this interior solution need not occur. Where it does occur, the labor market is primary. A worker entering the labor market will not automatically find work at the wage received by equally qualified employed persons. If the boundary solution occurs, in contrast, the labor market clears; the market is secondary, and a person in that market can readily obtain work at the wage received by current employees of similar qualifications. ·

The purpose of this section is to demonstrate by two specific examples the characteristics of the labor market in which gift exchange occurs in the sense that the workers' norm for effort depends upon their treatment by the firm. One example assumes that the firm's work rules are fixed, and with this assumption the equilibrium wage and unemployment are derived. The second example assumes that the real wage is fixed and demonstrates that work rules do not equilibrate supply and demand for labor in the sociological model (with norms) as they do in the neoclassical model. This model is specifically constructed with the behavior of the cash posters in mind.

Example I. Wages

Rather than present a model and show that there will be equilibrium unemployment, we work in reverse. All the parameters and functions of the model are chosen with the exception of the size of the labor force. It is then shown that appropriate particular choice of the size of the labor force will yield an equilibrium with unemployment rate u_0.

Let $\bar{l}$ workers per firm be the supply of labor. $\bar{l}$ will later be chosen to have a particular value to conform to the unemployment rate u_0, but that choice is at the end, not at the beginning of the story.

Let output q be a function of effort e and labor n according to the production function,

(12) $$q = (en)^{\alpha}.$$

Let effort e of all workers be at the norm e_n. And let all workers be the same so that

(13) $$e = e_n.$$

Let the effort norm be a function of the wage of the firm relative to the reference wage as

(14) $$e_n = -a + b(w/w_r)^\gamma, \qquad \gamma < 1.$$

(Two considerations explain the particular choice of $e_n - w$ function (14). First, the firm chooses w to maximize the number of labor efficiency units per dollar spent. Solow [1979] has shown that such an internal maximum occurs where the elasticity of w with respect to e is equal to unity. And to insure that this choice of w yields the maximum effort per dollar of expenditure, the $e_n - w$ elasticity must be declining. The function (14) has been chosen accordingly with a declining $e_n - w$ elasticity. A second consideration is responsible for the negative intercept of $-a$. If positive effort is obtained at a 0 wage, a 0 wage [with infinite effort per dollar] is optimal.)

Let the reference wage w_r be the geometric mean,

(15) $$w_r = w_0^{1-u} b_u^u,$$

where

u is the unemployment rate,
w_0 is the wage paid by other firms, and
b_u is the level of unemployment benefits.

Since the firm in question is the typical firm, it also follows that the employment by the firm n is the average number of employed persons per firm, or

(16) $$n = (1 - u)\bar{l}.$$

Furthermore, again because the firm in question is the typical firm, its wage is the same as the wage of other firms, or

(17) $$w = w_0.$$

Suppose that u is u_0. It will be shown that with appropriate choice of the parameter $\bar{l} = l_0$, the profit-maximizing firm will choose to hire an amount of labor $n = (1 - u_0)\bar{l}$ if its wage w is the same as the wage of other firms w_0. Consequently, u_0 is an equilibrium rate of unemployment with labor supply l_0.

The firm behaves in the following fashion. With unemployment at $u_0 > 0$, it can obtain all the workers it wants at any wage. Consequently, it chooses n and w to maximize profits, or

$$(18) \qquad \qquad \Pi = (en)^\alpha - wn$$

subject to the constraints

$$(19) \qquad \qquad e = e_n$$

$$(20) \qquad \qquad e_n = -a + b(w/w_r)^\gamma$$

$$(21) \qquad \qquad w_r = w_0^{1-u} \, b_u^u.$$

This maximization problem together with the condition $w = w_0$ yields the demand for labor n^d as a function of the unemployment rate u_0:

$$(22) \qquad n^d = \left(\alpha^{-1} b_u \left(\frac{a\gamma}{1-\gamma} \right)^{-\alpha} \left(\frac{a}{b(1-\gamma)} \right)^{1/\gamma u_0} \right)^{1/(\alpha-1)}.$$

If n^d is consistent with the unemployment rate, then the supply of labor, which is as yet an unchosen parameter of our model, must be

$$(23) \quad \bar{l} = l_0 = \frac{n^d}{1-u_0} = (1-u_0)^{-1} \left(\alpha^{-1} b_u \left(\frac{a\gamma}{1-\gamma} \right)^{-\alpha} \right.$$
$$\left. \times \left(\frac{a}{b(1-\gamma)} \right)^{1/\gamma u_0} \right)^{1/(\alpha-1)}.$$

With $\bar{l}$ chosen in this fashion according to the right-hand side of (23), our model has an equilibrium at the rate of unemployment u_0, where $0 < u_0 < 1$. Note that the unemployed would be willing to work at the wage paid employed workers, but firms will be unwilling to hire them at that wage, or one which is lower.

Moreover, it is also easy to construct an example in which the firm's choice of w is not interior. After all, if the coefficient $b = 0$ and $a < 0$, the example exactly corresponds to the neoclassical model verbally analyzed at the beginning of this section in which all markets cleared. In our analysis the property, whether or not markets clear, or, alternatively stated, whether labor markets are secondary or primary is endogenous.[7]

Example 2. Work Standards

The first example illustrated the possibility (and the accompanying discussion partially characterized that possibility) that the

---

7. Just because some markets clear does not mean that there is no unemployment. Unemployed workers may be waiting for an opportunity to take a primary sector job. See Hall [1975].

relation between work norms and wages will cause an economy-wide (or labor-market-wide) equilibrium with nonmarket-clearing prices because firms themselves find it advantageous to set wages above the minimum at which they can freely obtain labor.

Our discussion of the cash posters, however, was not concerned with wages but rather with work rules. According to the standard neoclassical model, even if for some reason wages are not fixed at market-clearing levels, still firms should adjust work rules to the point where supply and demand for labor are equal (*even at a nonequilibrial wage*). This section gives an example, in which the work rules will not equilibrate labor supply and demand. It is not the simplest example—partly because of our desire to make the model a faithful representation of the cash posters, and partially also because the reaction of workers to norms inherently involves a great deal of behavior that cannot easily be represented by simple linear functions.

Because in the standard neoclassical model work standards would equate demand and supply for labor even at a fixed nonequilibrating wage rate, we start with the assumption that the wage rate $\overline{w}$ is fixed. Although artificial, we could assume that the government has controlled wages. Certainly this occasionally happens when the government imposes certain forms of incomes policy.

Recall that among the cash posters some workers worked much above the work standard set by the firm (45 percent for Granara and Murphy) while some workers were quite close to the margin (only 2 percent above for Burke and Donovan).

To represent a model in which some workers are above the margin while other workers are at the margin, it is necessary to have at least two types of workers. For that reason our model has two groups of workers with different tastes. Poor workers form a fraction p of the work force. Good workers form a fraction $1 - p$.

In the story behind our model the firm is capable of identifying the tastes of workers only after they have joined the firm, but not before. In terms of the cash posters, who could have predicted that the almost equally outgoing and gregarious Murphy and Burke would have work records which were polar opposites? Homans hints that this difference may have occurred in part because Burke socialized primarily with a group of "ledger posters," while the rest of the cash posters socialized mainly among themselves. Certainly no personnel officer could have predicted such an occurrence.

Although the firm can measure performance easily once workers are hired, it is assumed that it cannot fire them without a reduction in the work norms. As a result, in the model constructed labor effort is observable ex post but not predictable ex ante.

Worker Behavior

Among the two types of workers, good workers who work for the firm have utility, denoted U^+, where

(24) $$U^+ = A - B(e - (e_n + \epsilon))^2.$$

The parameter A depends on wages, but since they are assumed fixed, we have suppressed that dependency. Poor workers who work for the firm have utility, denoted U^-, where

(25) $$U^- = A - B(e - (e_n - \epsilon))^2.$$

The parameters A and B are both positive, e_n is the norm of work effort, e is actual effort by the individual worker, and ϵ is a parameter reflecting the type of worker. U^+ and U^- are the utilities of good workers and bad workers, respectively, when working for the firm. Workers have the option of working for the firm with effort e and also the option of quitting and being unemployed. In that case their utility is assumed to be 0.

A worker who works for a firm maximizes his utility subject to abiding by the work rules of the firm. Thus, a good worker with utility function U^+ chooses e to maximize

(26) $$A - B(e - (e_n + \epsilon))^2,$$

subject to the constraint

(27) $$e \geqq e^+_{min},$$

where e^+_{min} is the minimum work standard set by the firm for good workers. Accordingly, for such a worker if U^+ working for the firm is positive, the worker chooses to work with effort e^+:

(28) $$e^+ = \max(e^+_{min}, e_n + \epsilon).$$

Similarly, if U^- working for the firm is positive, a poor worker chooses to work with effort e^-:

(29) $$e^- = \max(e^-_{min}, e_n - \epsilon).$$

Norms

The norms of behavior depend upon the work rules,

(30) $$e_n = e_n(e^-_{min}, e^+_{min}).$$

Later it will be assumed that e^-_{min} and e^+_{min} have an effect on norms only insofar as they are a binding constraint on workers' effort.

Firm Behavior

On its side, the firm takes into account the reaction of the workers' effort to the norms and the reaction of the norms to work rules. In the case of excess supply of labor, where labor is freely available as long as U^+ and U^- are positive, the firm chooses e_{min}^+, e_{min}^-, and n to maximize profits, or

$$(31) \qquad (\bar{e}(e_{min}^-, e_{min}^+)n)^\alpha - \bar{w}n,$$

where $\bar{e}(\ )$ is the function combining (28), (29), and (30) with the appropriate weights to account for the dependence of average effort on work rules.

Accordingly, at an interior maximum the firm that can obtain all the labor it wishes will choose e_{min}^- and e_{min}^+ to maximize $\bar{e}(e_{min}^-, e_{min}^+)$, and its demand for labor according to the marginal product condition,

$$(32) \qquad \alpha \bar{e}(e_{min}^{-*}, e_{min}^{+*})^\alpha n^{\alpha - 1} = \bar{w}.$$

As long as n so chosen by the typical firm is less than $\bar{l}$, the demand for labor is less than the supply, and the assumption that the firm can obtain all the labor it wishes is justified.

Problems with obtaining an interior maximum. The question, however, arises, how there can be an interior maximum for e_{min}^+ or e_{min}^-. After all, why should the firm not increase e_{min}^+ just up to the point where all good workers are on the verge of quitting? (In so doing, it also may have the added dividend of screening out the poorer workers.) In the real world workers usually apply sanctions against such behavior by the firm. For example, in the case of the cash posters, remember that Homans recorded a work slowdown in a previous dispute with a supervisor. In our model this is represented by the fact that as the work rules force workers to work sufficiently in excess of the norms, they quit.

Let the fraction p of poor workers be $\frac{1}{2}$. Let the tastes parameter ϵ be 1. And let the parameters A and B in (24) and (25) be 2 and $\frac{1}{2}$, respectively, so that

$$(33) \qquad U^+ = 2 - \frac{1}{2}(e - (e_n + \epsilon))^2$$

$$(34) \qquad U^- = 2 - \frac{1}{2}(e - (e_n - \epsilon))^2.$$

Good workers, who maximize U^+, will choose

$$(35) \qquad e = e_n + \epsilon$$

as long as they are unconstrained by the work rules. Similarly, if unconstrained, poor workers, who maximize U^-, will choose

$$(36) \qquad\qquad e = e_n - \epsilon.$$

We assume that the work rules have an effect on the effort norm if and only if they are binding. Accordingly, the norm depends on $\max(e^+_{min} - (e_n + \epsilon),0)$ and $\max(e^-_{min} - (e_n - \epsilon),0)$. Furthermore, it is assumed that the norms are egalitarian in that a difference between the work rules for the two types of workers will have a negative effect on the norms.

Accordingly, the norm in this example follows the formula,

$$(37) \quad e_n = 6 - 0.8 \max(e^+_{min} - (e_n + \epsilon), e^-_{min} - (e_n - \epsilon),0)$$
$$- 20|e^+_{min} - e^-_{min}|.$$

The second term of (37) reflects the decline in the norm of effort as the work rules become increasingly binding on the workers' choice of effort. The third term reflects the effect on the norm of an inequality in the treatment of the two types of workers.

It is easy to check that the firm which wishes to maximize $\bar{e}$ will choose

$$(38) \qquad\qquad e^+_{min} = e^-_{min} \leqq 5,$$

and at this maximum $\bar{e} = 6$.

I will sketch the proof. First, inequality in e^+_{min} and e^-_{min} causes such a large reduction in e_n (the coefficient of the last term of (37) being 20) that the firm always finds it advantageous to set $e^+_{min} = e^-_{min}$. In that case the formula for e_n (37) can be simplified to

$$(39) \qquad\qquad e_n = 6 - 0.8 \max(e_{min} - (e_n - \epsilon),0).$$

A bit of algebra shows that with $\epsilon = 1$ (39) can be rewritten as

$$(40A) \qquad\qquad e_n = 6 \qquad\qquad e_{min} \leqq 5$$

$$(40B) \qquad\qquad e_n = 30 - 4e_{min} - 4 \qquad\qquad e_{min} \geqq 5.$$

It is easy to check using (34), (40A), (40B) and the value of $\epsilon = 1$ that U^- is positive if $e_{min} < 5.4$ and negative if $e_{min} > 5.4$. Similarly, U^+ is positive if $e_{min} < 5.8$ and is negative for $e_{min} > 5.8$.

Thus, in the range $0 \leqq e_{min} < 5.4$ both good and bad workers are working. For $0 \leqq e_{min} \leqq 5$ work rules are binding on neither good nor bad workers, and therefore

$$(41) \quad \bar{e} = \tfrac{1}{2}(e_n + \epsilon) + \tfrac{1}{2}(e_n - \epsilon) = e_n = 6, \qquad 0 \leqq e_{min} \leqq 5.$$

For $5 < e_{\min} < 5.4$ work rules are binding on poor workers but not on good workers. U^- and U^+ are both positive so both good and bad workers are at work. Hence

(42) $\bar{e} = \frac{1}{2}(e_n + \epsilon) + \frac{1}{2}e_{\min}$ $5 < e_{\min} < 5.4$

(43) $= 13.5 - 1.5e_{\min} < 6$ $5 < e_{\min} < 5.4.$

By design of the example, for $e_{\min} > 5.4$ U^- is negative; also by (40B) for $e_{\min} > 5.4$, $e_n + \epsilon < e_{\min}$, so work rules are binding on good workers. U^+ is positive for $e_{\min} < 5.8$. Consequently, in the range $5.4 < e_{\min} < 5.8$ only good workers are at work, and since their effort is constrained by work rules,

(44) $\bar{e} = e_{\min}$ $5.4 < e_{\min} < 5.8.$

For $e_{\min} > 5.8$ $\bar{e}$ is indeterminate, since U^+ and U^- are both negative. The number of workers willing to work is, however, 0. Hence $\bar{e}$ is maximized according to (41), (43), and (44) at $\bar{e} = 6$ with $e_{\min}^+ = e_{\min}^-$ $\leqq 5$.

To obtain an example with unemployment rate u_0, it is only necessary to choose $\bar{l} = l_0$ consistent with u_0 and the marginal productivity condition for labor demand so that

(45) $\bar{l} = l_0 = (1 - u_0)^{-1}(\alpha^{-1}6^{-\alpha}\overline{w})^{1/(\alpha-1)}.$

Remark. This example corresponds exactly to cash poster behavior. The firm paid the same wage to all workers. One group of workers (a minority) worked at the work standard, or very close to it. Other workers worked above that standard. For reasons unspecified by Homans, but which are consistent with our model, the firm did not raise standards on either good workers or poor workers. At the equilibrium unemployment is involuntary.

VIII. CONCLUSION

This paper has explored the idea that labor contracts are partial gift exchanges. According to this idea, at least in part, wages are determined by, and in turn also influence, the norms of workers' effort; similarly, workers' effort is determined, at least in part, by these norms. A relation between the terms of exchange and norms is in our view what differentiates gift exchange from pure market exchange.

Indeed, while the norms may be greatly influenced by the same things as market prices, there is still a major difference between pure market exchange and gift exchange. In pure market exchange the maximum price at which a buyer is willing to purchase a commodity or factor service is the minimum at which the respective commodity or factor service is obtainable. Obversely, the minimum price at which a seller is willing to sell a commodity or factor service is the maximum at which the respective commodity or factor service can be sold. In gift exchange buyers may be willing to pay more than the minimum at which they can purchase a commodity or factor service because of the effect of the terms of exchange on the norms. Similarly, sellers may be willing to accept less than the maximum at which they can sell a commodity or factor service because of the effects of the terms of exchange on the norms. It has been shown that due to this behavior with gift exchange markets need not clear. Thus, the gift-exchange economy and the neoclassical economy differ in at least one fundamental respect. Future papers will explore further differences between the two models of exchange.

UNIVERSITY OF CALIFORNIA, BERKELEY

REFERENCES

Azariadis, C., "Implicit Contracts and Unemployment Equilibria," *Journal of Political Economy*, LXXXIII (Dec. 1975), 1183–1202.

Baily, M. N., "Wages and Employment Under Uncertain Demand," *Review of Economic Studies*, XLI (Jan. 1974), 37–50.

Belshaw, C. S., *Traditional Exchange and Modern Markets* (Englewood Cliffs, NJ: Prentice-Hall, 1965).

Coser, L. A., *Masters of Sociological Thought: Ideas in Historical and Social Context* (New York: Harcourt Brace Jovanovich, 1971).

Doeringer, P. B., and M. J. Piore, *Internal Labor Markets and Manpower Analysis* (Lexington, MA: D. C. Heath & Co., 1971).

Edwards, R., *Contested Terrain: The Transformation of the Workplace in the Twentieth Century* (New York: Basic Books, 1979).

Etzioni, A. W., *Modern Organizations* (Englewood Cliffs, NJ: Prentice-Hall, 1971).

Festinger, L., "A Theory of Social Comparison Processes," *Human Relations*, VII (1954), 117–40; reprinted in *Readings in Reference Group Therapy*, Herbert H. Hyman and Eleanor Singer, eds. (New York: The Free Press, 1968).

Freeman, R. L., and J. L. Medoff, "The Two Faces of Unionism," *The Public Interest*, No. 57 (Fall 1979), 69–93.

Hall, R. E., "The Rigidity of Wages and the Persistence of Unemployment." *Brookings Papers on Economic Activity*, III (1975), 301–49.

Hirschman, A. O., *Exit, Voice and Loyalty* (Cambridge: Harvard University Press, 1970).

Homans, G. C., "Status Among Clerical Workers," *Human Organization*, XII (Spring 1953), 5–10; reprinted in G. C. Homans, *Sentiments and Activities* (New York: Free Press of Glencoe, 1962).

——, "The Cash Posters," *American Sociological Review*, XIX (Dec. 1954), 724–33; reprinted in G. C. Homans, *Sentiments and Activities* (New York: Free Press of Glencoe, 1962).

Hyman, H. H., "The Psychology of Status," *Archives of Psychology*, No. 269 (1942); reprinted in part in *Readings in Reference Group Theory*, Herbert H. Hyman and Eleanor Singer, eds. (New York: The Free Press, 1968).

Leibenstein, H., *Beyond Economic Man: A New Foundation for Microeconomics* (Cambridge, MA: Harvard University Press, 1976).

Mauss, M., *The Gift: Forms and Functions of Exchange in Archaic Societies*, translated by Ian Cunnison (London: Cohen and West, 1954).

Mayo, E., *The Social Problems of an Industrial Civilization* (London: Routledge and Kegan Paul, 1949).

Merton, R. K., *Social Theory and Social Structure*, revised and enlarged edition (Glencoe, IL: The Free Press, 1957).

Okun, A., "Inflation: Its Mechanics and Welfare Costs," *Brookings Papers on Economic Activity*, II (1975), 366–73.

———, *Prices and Quantities: A Macroeconomic Analysis* (Washington, D.C.: The Brookings Institution, 1981).

Pearlstine, N., "Auto Pact Tension Eases; Strike Chances Viewed as Tied to Chrysler, GM Parleys," *Wall Street Journal*, CLXXVI, No. 48 (Sept. 4, 1970), 5, column 2.

Phelps, E. S. *et al.*, *The Microeconomic Foundations of Employment and Inflation Theory* (New York: Norton, 1970).

Roethlisberger, F. J., and W. J. Dickson, *Management and the Worker: An Account of a Research Program Conducted by the Western Electric Company, Hawthorne Works, Chicago* (Cambridge, MA: Harvard University Press, 1947).

Solow, R. H., "Another Possible Source of Wage Stickiness," *Journal of Macroeconomics*, I (Winter 1979), 79–82.

———, "On Theories of Unemployment," *American Economic Review*, LXX (March 1980), 1–10.

Stoft, S., "Cheat-Threat Theory," University of California Thesis Prospectus, August 1980.

Stouffer, S. A., E. A. Suchman, L. C. de Vinney, S. A. Star, and R. M. Williams, Jr., *The American Soldier: Adjustment During Army Life*, Vol. 1 (Princeton, NJ: Princeton University Press, 1949).

Stouffer, S. A., A. A. Lumsdaine, M. H. Lumsdaine, R. M. Williams, Jr., M. B. Smith, I. L. Jarvis, S. A. Star, and L. S. Cottrell, Jr., *The American Soldier: Combat and its Aftermath*, Vol. 2 (Princeton NJ: Princeton University Press, 1949).

Titmuss, R. M., *The Gift Relationship: From Human Blood to Social Policy* (New York: Random House, 1971).

A Model of the Natural Rate of Unemployment

By Steven C. Salop*

Since the publication of Edmund Phelps' volume, the "new" macroeconomics has treated the labor market as a dynamic process of rational search by unemployed workers for available vacancies. Wages are viewed as at least potentially flexible, though free contracting between workers and firms may lead to fixed wages in the short run. Imperfect information is a crucial element of the theory, for it implies both a need for contracting and a need for rational search rather than simple market clearing in each period.

A positive rate of frictional unemployment may exist in equilibrium, denoted as the "natural" rate. This unemployment is due to the frictions in the search process and imperfections in information rather than to any deficiency in aggregate demand. Milton Friedman defined the natural rate as

> the level that would be ground out by the Walrasian system of general equilibrium equations, provided there is embedded in them the actual structural characteristics of the labor and commodity markets, including market imperfections, stochastic variability in demands and supplies, the cost of gathering information about job vacancies and labor availabilities, the costs of mobility, and so on. [p.8]

This paper reexamines the micro founda-

tions of the natural rate in a model of labor market equilibrium in which turnover flows and imperfect information are explicitly considered. Workers may quit their current jobs to enter the unemployment pool in order to search among available vacancies for a more preferred position. Firms economize on turnover by an appropriate wage policy. The model to be presented is essentially a stationary analogue to models formulated by Dale Mortensen and Phelps (1970b), with one major difference. In this model, the internal labor market for experienced trained workers is conceptually separated from the external labor market for new employees. Moreover, the firm is constrained by morale, moral hazard, and capital market imperfections to pay an identical wage rate to all its employees, regardless of seniority. As a result, both labor markets are unable to clear simultaneously, and in general, quantity adjustments are required in one of the markets. I focus on the case in which the quantity adjustments take place in the external new applicant market.

As a result of this friction in the labor market, equilibrium entails not only the usual voluntary frictional component of unemployment, but possibly also a component of involuntary unemployment. This involuntary unemployment is permanent; it may not be eliminated through aggregate monetary or fiscal policy. Instead it is structural in the sense that it derives from the inability of all markets to clear simultaneously, a friction that is imbedded in the structure of the economy. The equilibrium also contains components of disguised unemployment and search unemployment.

*Federal Trade Commission. The remarks in this statement represent only my personal views. They are not intended to be, and should not be construed as, representative of the views of any other member of the Federal Trade Commission staff or individual Commissioners. This paper is dedicated to Al Klevorick, who convinced me to fully complete my dissertation with this paper and Edmund Phelps, who originally stimulated these ideas. David Soskice rekindled my interest in the problem and Dale Mortensen has provided continuing encouragement. I am grateful to George Akerlof, Steve Salant, Joseph Stiglitz, and the referee for helpful comments and insights, and Mary Ann Henry for superb typing and editing.

I. The Model[1]

The formal model has the following basic structure. The labor market contains no uncertainty in the aggregate, though every

[1]This section follows the author (1973b).

worker and firm does face some private uncertainty. When a new employee joins a firm, he is uncertain of the particular set of nonpecuniary characteristics offered by the firm, but learns them through experience on the job. Once these characteristics become known, if the employee is dissatisfied and believes he can do better elsewhere, he quits and joins the unemployment pool to search for alternative employment. (In order to keep the model simple, on-the-job search is ignored.) Quits depend on the tightness of the labor market, rising when unemployment is low and falling when opportunities are scarcer. Unemployment and wage rates adjust until the costs of turnover to firms and the benefits of quitting to workers are equilibrated.

Turnover is costly to firms through its direct costs such as formal orientation programs, expenditures to foremen for "breaking in" new employees as well as indirect costs such as lowered productivity during the adjustment process. As a result, firms utilize wage policy to economize on turnover. This concern for turnover occurs regardless of conditions in the external labor market. Even if a lost worker can be immediately replaced with an identical new applicant, the new applicant is less valuable than an experienced worker, since the turnover costs must be borne again.

Since experienced workers are more valuable to the firm, we would expect to observe wage rates increasing with experience and training. However, even with self-selection there is a limit to the effectiveness of these wage differentials for eliminating turnover. If the time period in which a worker is "inexperienced" is relatively short, then it may be difficult to design a wage schedule that completely compensates for the cost differences. At the limit, if training is instantaneous upon the beginning of employment, then it is impossible for the firm to pay a wage differential to "experienced" workers, for a worker becomes experienced at the very moment he is employed. In this case the only device a firm could employ is an application fee. However, its effectiveness is also quite limited. There is a moral hazard prob-

lem in that workers may foresee the firm entering the "application business" of simply collecting fees. Furthermore, workers may not have access to the capital market to borrow a possibly very large application fee.

It is surely unreasonable to explain unemployment solely on the basis of lack of knowledge of firms' characteristics. Product demand uncertainty and its role in layoffs seem to have more empirical significance. The appeal of this model rests not on its empirical validity, but on the logical structure of the analysis, and its focus on the interaction of the unemployment pool with the markets for experienced and inexperienced workers, through the costs of turnover to individual firms. While the exact formal basis for the quit decision is artificial, it does allow for a concentration on these complicated interactions without the additional complexity of an explicit model of demand uncertainty, complete with the necessity of modelling layoffs, implicit employment contracts, inventories, and other variables that would be required by a rigorous general equilibrium model.[2]

The same comment is required for the assumption that firms are unable to regulate the flow of excess applicants through a set of application fees or seniority wages. If moral hazard problems are ignored or eliminated through explicit contracts, the necessary set of markets will be complete and no involuntary unemployment will obtain in the model. On the other hand, as a practical matter, it is impossible for firms to contract away all the randomness and heterogeneity it faces in the labor market. Workers differ with respect to productivity, probability of absenteeism and quitting, and other variables that are crucial to determining a worker's value, yet are difficult to observe and write contracts on. Each of these variables could lead to incompleteness in the set of market-clearing prices required for full-employment equilibrium.

Any incompleteness in the number of prices and any uncertainty that affects the

[2]See Costas Azariadis and Martin Baily.

quit rate will enter the unemployment flows and equilibrium configuration in a manner similar to the example explored here. Thus it is useful to treat the assumptions as loose characterizations of important labor market phenomena, and build more realistic models once the logic is fully understood in a simple context.

A. *The Firm's Problem*

Assumption 1: *Firms produce output with employed labor E according to a nonincreasing returns production function*

$$Q = f(E), f' > 0, f'' \leq 0$$

Assumption 2: *The capital market is ignored. However, there is a fixed cost $F \geq 0$ for setting up a firm.*

Assumption 3: *New workers (N) must be trained at the outset of employment.* Training costs (T) take place at increasing marginal costs in output terms according to

$$T = T(N) T' > 0, T'' > 0$$

Assumption 4: *Every firm is characterized by a given set of nonpecuniary job attributes.* Workers differ in preferences for these attributes. The attributes are not known to the workers upon becoming employed, but instead, they are learned by working at a firm. Once a worker learns a firm's attributes, he trades off his current wage plus nonpecuniary benefits against the expected benefit of quitting to look for another job and makes a quit decision.[3] If we let z denote a measure of labor market tightness, say the average wage rate adjusted for the probability of getting a job (and including the average nonpecuniary utility), then a firm's quit rate (q) depends on its wage w relative to z:

$$q = q(w/z), q' < 0 \; q'' > 0$$

Thus, dissatisfied workers are more likely to quit the tighter are conditions in the labor

---

[3]Alternatively, we could generate this quit-rate function if workers have a preference for job variety. For simplicity, on-the-job search is not permitted.

---

market. In a stationary state, new hires equal quits.

$$N = q(w/z)E$$

Assumption 5: *The firm may hire new workers N only as long as it has enough willing applicants at its going wage rate.* The applicant function also depends on the firm's relative wage rate w/z, or

$$N \leq A(w/z), A' > 0$$

Assumption 6: *Firms are unable to charge an application fee.* This is a crucial assumption; the lack of competitive application fees is responsible for the incompleteness of markets and for the equilibrium unemployment.

Assumption 7: *The firm faces a perfectly competitive output market at a price equal to one (the numeraire) and chooses a wage of w.* Its optimization problem may be written as follows.

$$\max_{w,E,N} R = f(E) - wE - T(N) - F$$

subject to: $N = q(w/z)E : \lambda$

$$N \leq A(w/z) : \mu$$

Letting λ and μ denote the multipliers we have the Lagrangian

$$L = f(E) - wE - T(N) - F$$
$$+ \lambda[N - q(w/z)E] + \mu[A(w/z) - N]$$

The first-order conditions expressing the firm's wage, employment, and new-hire tradeoffs at an interior solution $(E, w, N) > 0$ are written as follows:

(1) $E > 0, \quad f'(E) - w - \lambda q(w/z) = 0$

(2) $w > 0, \quad -E[1 + \frac{\lambda}{z} q'(w/z)]$

$$+ \frac{\mu}{z} A'(w/z) = 0$$

(3) $N > 0, \quad -T'(N) + \lambda = 0$

In addition, we have the first-order conditions on the constraints,

(4) $\lambda[N - q(w/z)E] = 0$

(5) $\mu[A(w/z) - N] = 0$

In order to focus on the possibility of involuntary unemployment, it is *assumed* the firm has excess applicants. From (5), we have

(6) $$A(w/z) > N \rightarrow \mu = 0$$

The remaining first-order conditions exhibit the tradeoffs facing the firm. Substituting λ from (3) into (2), we have

(7) $$E + \frac{T'(N)}{z} q'(w/z)E = 0$$

This is the wage-turnover cost tradeoff. If the firm raises its wage by a unit, direct wage costs per employee rise by E units; turnover falls by $(1/z)q'E$ units and these workers must be replaced, each at cost T'. Rewriting (7) and (3), we have

(8) $$T'(N) = - \frac{z}{q'(w/z)} = \lambda$$

Substituting (3) into (1), we have

(9) $$f'(E) = w + q(w/z)T'(N)$$

The marginal revenue product of an additional worker equals the marginal cost of an additional worker— the wage plus the portion of the worker's turnover costs amortized for a single period.[4]

Substituting (8) into (9), we have

(10) $$f'(E) = w[1 - \frac{q(w/z)}{(w/z)q'(w/z)}]$$

Denoting the quit-rate elasticity by $\epsilon > 0$, we have a variant of the conventional monopsony formula,

(11) $$f'(E) = w[1 + 1/\epsilon]$$

Noting that hires equal quits, we rewrite the constraint,

(12) $$N = q(w/z)E$$

Equations (9), (10), and (12) may be solved for (E, w, N) as functions of the single exogenous parameters z. It is easy to show that[5]

[4]If the quit rate is q per period, then a worker's expected tenure is $1/q$ periods. The $T'(N)$ is spread over the entire period equally. The discount rate has been set equal to zero for simplicity.

[5]See the author (1973b) for the details of these derivations.

(13) $$E = E(z), \qquad E' < 0$$

(14) $$w/z = W(z), \qquad W' < 0$$

(15) $$N = N(z), \qquad N' \gtrless 0$$

If $f'(E) = 0$ (constant returns to scale), then $N'(z) < 0$. In order to demonstrate the involuntary unemployment result with as little complexity as possible, we make this assumption. As the labor market tightens (z rises), the firm finds its quit rate rising. It economizes on turnover costs by lowering employment (and new hires). However, it allows its relative wage w/z to fall, implying a higher quit rate at the new optimum. Thus, the firm adjusts its wage rate to the state of the labor market, but, as we shall show in Section II, this wage flexibility is not sufficient to completely eliminate unemployment in equilibrium.

B. *Incomplete Markets, Application Fees, and Market Clearing*

The insufficiency of wage flexibility in clearing the market is a consequence of the manner in which the applicant function enters the firm's optimization. The firm faces two interrelated labor markets, an *internal* labor market for experienced (trained) employees and an *external* market for new applicants. Since the firm has only a single wage rate with which to economize on labor simultaneously in both markets, this single wage is generally unable to clear both markets simultaneously.

Because of turnover costs, the internal labor market dominates the firm's decision making in a loose (low z) market; that is, the applicant function enters merely as a nonbinding constraint (equation (6)). The possibility of a binding constraint is discussed in Section IV.

On the other hand, as David Soskice points out, the firm could economize on applicants separately by charging an application fee in order to equate applicants to new hires. Letting the fee be denoted by $\hat{a}$, we have

(16) $$A(w - r\hat{a}/z) = N(z)$$

where $r\hat{a}$ is the (implicit) interest on the fee.

Clearly, there exists a fee $\hat{a}$ that would eliminate the excess applicants. Furthermore, if all firms charged excess applicant fees, these fees would lower the expected returns from quitting (z) and imply a labor market equilibrium with zero structural unemployment.

Unfortunately, the use of such application fees is generally limited. Union regulations, antidiscrimination laws, and morale problems generally require firms to maintain equal pay for equal work. In addition, there is a serious moral hazard problem. If the equilibrium fee is very large, workers might (correctly) fear that a firm has entered the "application" industry; that is, it would be in the firm's interest to falsely advertise vacancies to collect application fees.

Another possibility to ensure market clearing is a rising wage structure. This policy is not considered in the optimization written previously because training takes place instantaneously.[6] If training takes time, however, then the application fee may be interpreted as the wage differential between trained and untrained workers. As before, however, this policy has only limited scope. The entire training costs must be captured during the apprenticeship program. This is impossible if training costs are so large to require a negative apprenticeship wage.[7] Furthermore, since training here is firm specific, workers may be averse to bearing such costs in the absence of explicit contractual obligations on the part of the firm.

II. Market Equilibrium

In the absence of application fees or other contractual arrangements, we may solve for the free entry equilibrium in the labor market. Formally, an equilibrium is a number of firms n and wage rates, employments, new hires, and applicants $[w_i, E_i, N_i, A_i]$ for the n firms, such that the n

internal labor markets for experienced workers (quits) and n external labor markets for new applicants are cleared. Since there are only n prices attempting to clear $2n$ markets, it is not surprising that quantity rationing must serve as the clearing device in some markets, leading to the possibility of unemployment at the equilibrium.

Equations (13)–(15) summarize the demands of a single firm in this economy as a function of the aggregate variable z. For simplicity, assume that every firm has identical technology and that workers' preferences over nonpecuniary characteristics of firms are symmetric across the attributes offered.[8] Hence, no equalizing wage differentials are necessary; every firm has an identical quit-rate function and all choose identical $[w, E, N, A]$. Under these assumptions, we may easily solve for the equilibrium z^* for n, the number of firms in the market.

Let z, the summary measure of labor market tightness, equal the expected wage in the market.[9] Letting π denote the probability that an unemployed (searching) worker obtains an offer, since every firm pays an identical wage, we have

$$(17) \qquad z = \pi w$$

If the equilibrium $\pi < 1$, then involuntary unemployment is positive, whereas full employment entails $\pi = 1$. The supply of workers to the market (each supplying one unit of labor) depends on the probability of employment as well as the wage. Let supply S be given by

$$(18) \qquad S = S(z), S' > 0$$

Since $nE(z)$ workers are employed and $S(z)$ workers each supply a unit of labor, the stock of involuntarily unemployed $U(z)$ is given by

$$(19) \qquad U(z) = S(z) - nE(z)$$

---

[6]Since all trained workers are perfect substitutes, they ought to be paid identical wages at the optimum. See Joseph Stiglitz.

[7]Joanne Salop and the author and A. Weiss explore models of self-selection and apprenticeship.

[8]That is, firms are equidistantly spaced in attribute space relative to preferences. For the details, see the author (1978).

[9]To be fully rigorous, z ought to denote the expected wealth stream accruing to the worker if he quits. This approximation is used for expositional convenience and does not alter the logic of the result. See the author (1973a) for the rigorous formulation.

Note that $U(z)$ does not include those workers who are frictionally unemployed. This can be illustrated by examining the functioning of the market. The state of the market before the period begins can be described as follows: Of the $S(z)$ workers in the market, $nE(z)$ are employed and $U(z)$ are unemployed. At the beginning of a period, some workers quit (a total of $Q(z) = n\,q(W(z))E(z)$) and enter the unemployment pool. (On-the-job search has been ignored for simplicity; it could be added without changing the basic results of the model, if it is more efficient to search while unemployed.) Thus the total number of workers searching for a job are those that were previously unemployed ($U(z)$) plus those that have just quit ($Q(z)$) or a total of $U(z) + Q(z)$. Of these workers, $nN(z)$ are hired; this is the measure of frictional unemployment in the market. If hiring is done randomly among all the applicants, the probability π that any particular searcher is hired is given by

$$(20) \qquad \pi \equiv \pi^u(z) = \frac{nN(z)}{U(z) + Q(z)}$$

Since the market is in equilibrium, hires equal quits, or

$$(21) \qquad Q(z) = nN(z)$$

Thus, $U(z)$ measures involuntary unemployment and $Q(z)$ measures frictional unemployment.

Substituting (21) and (19) into (20), we have $\pi^u(z)$ as pictured in Figure 1.

$$(22) \qquad \pi^u(z) = \frac{nN(z)}{S(z) - nE(z) + nN(z)}$$

Differentiating, we have[10] $d\pi^u/dz < 0$. Substituting $W(z)$ from (14) into the definition of z in (17), we have a second expression for π.

$$(23) \qquad \pi = \pi^w(z) \equiv \frac{1}{W(z)}$$

Differentiating, we have

$$\frac{\partial \pi^w}{\partial z} > 0, \qquad \text{since } W' < 0$$

[10]Assuming $N'(z) < 0$. Recall that constant returns production is sufficient for $N' < 0$.

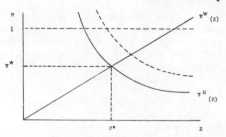

FIGURE 1. EQUILIBRIUM

We set $\pi^u(z) = \pi^w(z)$ to solve for the equilibrium value z^*, as a function of the parameter n.

$$(24) \qquad \frac{1}{W(z^*)} = \frac{nN(z^*)}{S(z^*) - nE(z^*) + nN(z^*)}$$

which defines

$$(25) \qquad z^* = z(n)$$

If $N'(z) < 0$, a unique underemployment equilibrium obtains as pictured below. $\pi^*\epsilon(0,1)$ is also necessary.

$$(26) \quad 0 < \pi^* < 1 \leftrightarrow U(z^*) > 0$$
$$\leftrightarrow S(z^*) > nE(z^*)$$

This depends quite crucially on the number of firms, n, as well as the supply of labor function.

As the number of firms increases, the $\pi^u(z)$ function shifts up[11] and π^* and z^* rise. Thus, we must ask the question of whether entry by new firms will continue to tighten the labor market until $\pi^* = 1$. In general, this need not be the case. Suppose free entry continues until profits per firm equal zero; then rewriting profits $R(z)$ as a function of z, we have

$$(27) \quad R(z) = f(E(z)) - zW(z)E(z)$$
$$- T(N(z)) - F$$

The number of firms depends crucially on the level of fixed costs F. By setting F we can essentially set the number of firms n at any level desired. Formally, we have

$$(28) \qquad R(z) = 0$$

From (25) we have $z^* = z(n)$, $z' > 0$. Equa-

[11]Since $n = qE < E$.

tions (25) and (28) may be solved for the unique equilibrium values (z, n). Uniqueness may be demonstrated using the envelope theorem.[12]

$$\frac{dR}{dn} = [-wE + \frac{\partial R}{\partial w}\frac{\partial w}{\partial z}$$

$$+ \frac{\partial R}{\partial N}\frac{\partial N}{\partial z} + \frac{\partial R}{\partial E}\frac{\partial E}{\partial z}]\frac{dz}{dn}$$

Since $\partial R/\partial w = \partial R/\partial N = \partial R/\partial E = 0$ at the optimum for each firm, we have

$$\frac{dR}{dn} = -wE(\frac{dz}{dn}) < 0$$

At a zero profit level, a new entrant will incur negative profits. Thus, *an equilibrium in the labor market may exist in which the equilibrium probability of employment (z) is less than one*. Referring back to (26), this implies that unemployment $U(z)$ is positive.

Suppose the supply of labor function shifts, due to governmental manpower programs or migration by new workers into the economy. This rise in the $S(z)$ function lowers π in the short run as more applicants compete for the available vacancies in the market. Quits fall as employed workers perceive the worsened opportunities from search which in turn allows firms to lower wage rates. Profits rise and induce entry by new firms. Surprisingly, the new equilibrium entails an identical z as originally. We may prove this as follows.

Letting the supply shift parameter be denoted by α and rewriting the equilibrium condition (24) and free entry condition (27), we have

(29) $\pi(z) \equiv \frac{1}{W(z)} =$

$$\frac{nN(z)}{S(z, \alpha) - nE(z) + nN(z)}$$

(30) $R(z) = f[E(z)] - zw(z)E(z)$
$$- T(N(z)) - F = 0$$

Equation (30) may be solved for a unique level $\hat{z}$ for all α and n; as α changes, the equilibrium number of firms n simply ad-

justs to maintain equality in (30). Thus policies that increase the supply of labor to the market have no effect on the *expected* real wage in equilibrium. The proportion of these new workers who become employed is identical to the proportion previously employed.

This unemployment $U(\hat{z})$ is a permanent state of the market. Macro-economic stabilization policies cannot eliminate it. Instead, it arises from the structure of the economy—the lack of market clearing in external labor markets in conjunction with firms' monopsony power in internal labor markets. It is involuntary in the sense that the unemployed workers would be willing to accept a job at the going wage rate; however, at the going wage, offers are not forthcoming to all the unemployed. I call this unemployment *involuntary structural unemployment*. This involuntary structural unemployment is in addition to *frictional unemployment* resulting from workers quitting one job to look for another. Frictional unemployment is measured simply by new hires (or quits) of $\hat{n}N(\hat{z})$.

III. Wage Differentials, Search Unemployment, and Disguised Unemployment

The equilibrium constructed has no wage differentials. However, if firms differ in turnover costs, they will make different optimal wage-turnover tradeoffs. This is expressed in equation (8), which may be rewritten as

$$T'(N) = -\frac{z}{q'(w/z)}$$

If there are turnover-cost induced wage differentials,[13] the optimal behavior by applicants will lead to the existence of equilibrium *search unemployment*. We may model this formally as follows.

Applicants choose a firm (a queue) in order to maximize expected return. If firm j pays a wage w_j, has vacancies N_j and applicants $A_j > N_j$, the expected wage to an applicant from waiting in firm j's queue is

---

[12]The condition that n must equal an integer is ignored. This is not an unreasonable approximation if n is fairly large.

[13]Permanent noncompensating wage differentials may also be due to differences in production functions, discount rates, etc. See the author (1973a).

given by z_j, where[14]

(31) $\quad z_j = w_j N_j / A_j \qquad j = 1, 2, \ldots, n$

Suppose there are $\bar{A}$ total applicants in the market. If each applicant observes $[w_j, N_j, A_j]$ and chooses a queue to max z_j, the number of applicants will adjust until an equilibrium queue distribution is achieved in which returns are identical in each, or

(32) $\qquad z_j = \bar{z}$ for all j

Solving (31) and (32) we have

(33) $\qquad A_j = N_j (w_j / \bar{z})$

(34) $\qquad \bar{A} = \sum A_j$

Clearly $\bar{z}$ will depend on $\bar{A}$ and $[w_j, N_j]$.

For example, suppose firms' wages were distributed uniformly in (w_a, w_b) and due to both production function and training function differentials, every firm had an identical number of vacancies N. Then solving explicitly, we have

(35) $\qquad A(w) = (w/\bar{z}) \cdot N$

This is a linear function of w. Since

(36) $\qquad \bar{A} = \int_{w_a}^{w_b} A(w) dw$

we have

(37) $\qquad \bar{z} = \left(\dfrac{w_b^2 - w_a^2}{2} \right) \dfrac{N}{A}$

In Figure 2, the area between $A(w)$ and N consists of search unemployment[15] plus structural involuntary unemployment. On the diagram, this is shown as follows. The area between $S(w)$ and N measures search unemployment and the area between $A(w)$ and $S(w)$ measures structural involuntary unemployment. Frictional unemployment is measured as the area under N, the total flow of vacancies in the market.

It may be noted that equilibrium may entail zero involuntary unemployment. (For example, $S(w)$ could measure the *total* applicants per firm.) However, equilibrium does imply that only the minimum wage firm may have a binding queue. In equilib-

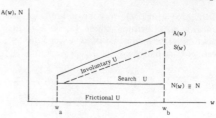

FIGURE 2. EQUILIBRIUM WITH WAGE DIFFERENTIALS

rium any firm choosing $w > w_a$ will have excess applicants.[16]

Finally, we may also measure the *disguised unemployment* that arises as a result of the existence of *structural unemployment*. If there were no structural unemployment, there would be a supply $S(w)$. However, because of the limited opportunities in the market, only $S(z)$ enter the labor force. Thus a stock of potential workers $D(z)$ never enter, where $D(z) = S(w) - S(z) \geq 0$. These workers comprise *disguised unemployment*.

IV. Full-Employment Equilibrium

The solution of the formal model demonstrates only the possibility of an equilibrium with structural unemployment, not its necessity. In the analysis it is *assumed* that the necessary condition $\pi < 1$ is fulfilled. Fortunately, some supply function $S(z)$ or fixed cost F can always be found that ensures that z equilibrates at $\pi < 1$. On the other hand, for small $S(z)$, an equilibrium with $\pi = 1$ obtains, a full-employment equilibrium.

Moreover, the analysis of Section I assumes that the applicant constraint is not binding. In my 1973b paper, the possibility of a binding applicant constraint is considered, the regions where it is binding are derived, and the expanded $W(z)$, $E(z)$, and $Q(z)$ functions are calculated. Employing that expanded analysis in the present equilibrium model, involuntary structural unemployment obtains for certain values of the technological and supply parameters of

[14]As before, the expected *wealth* in each queue should be calculated.
[15]See Robert Hall for an application of this analysis.

[16]This flows directly from (38) and (39). If for the $w > w_a$ firm, $z(w) = z_a$ and $w > w_a$, then $\pi(w) = N(w)/A(w) < 1$.

the model. Moreover, cases may exist in which there are multiple equilibria, some with full employment and some with unemployment. This is no surprise, for multiple equilibria and nonexistence often occur in models of price-setting agents and incomplete markets.[17]

When the possibility of wage differentials is included as in Section III, a similar expansion of the analysis is necessary; the involuntary unemployment area between $A(w)$ and $S(w)$ may disappear. However, as long as there are wage differentials, equilibrium must entail a positive level of search unemployment, as more applicants queue at high wage than low wage firms.

V. Conclusions

An incomplete set of market-clearing wages will prevent the labor market from attaining the classical zero involuntary unemployment equilibrium. Instead a permanent level of involuntary structural unemployment and disguised unemployment may result as quantities adjust to the nonmarket-clearing wages. This unemployment is in addition to the frictional and search unemployment of the "new" macroeconomics.

The job shortage interacts with firms' monopsony power in the labor market to ensure that the aggregate unemployment rate is not optimal. Even if the level of frictional unemployment were efficient, the three other types of unemployment are not. Search unemployment requires an equalization of *average* rather than marginal rates of substitution; disguised and structural unemployment entail quantity rather than price adjustments.

Finally, the analysis of the paper has focused on the existence of a structural unemployment equilibrium. It should be noted that an equilibrium may also exist with zero structural unemployment. Such multiple equilibria generally exist in economies with incomplete markets or market power. However, a detailed analysis of the exact conditions under which multiple equilibria obtain is left to a sequel.

[17]See John Roberts and Hugo Sonnenschein, and the author (1978) for examples.

REFERENCES

C. Azariadis, "Implicit Contracts and Underemployment Equilibria," *J. Polit. Econ.*, Dec. 1975, *83*, 1183–202.

M. Baily, "Wages and Employment under Uncertain Demand," *Rev. Econ. Stud.*, Jan. 1974, *41*, 37–50.

M. Friedman, "The Role of Monetary Policy," *Amer. Econ. Rev.*, Mar. 1968, *58*, 1–17.

R. E. Hall, "Why is the Unemployment Rate So High at Full Employment?," *Brookings Papers*, Washington 1970, *3*, 369–402.

D. Mortensen, "A Theory of Wage and Employment Dynamics," in Edmund Phelps et al., eds., *The Microeconomic Foundations of Employment and Inflation Theory*, New York 1970.

Edmund Phelps et al., (1970a) *The Microeconomic Foundations of Employment and Inflation Theory*, New York 1970.

_____, (1970b) "Money Wage Dynamics and Labor Market Equilibrium," in his *The Microeconomic Foundations of Employment and Inflation Theory*, New York 1970.

J. Roberts and H. Sonnenschein (1977), "On the Foundations of the Theory of Monopolistic Competition," *Econometrica*, Jan. 1977, *45*, 101–14.

S. C. Salop, (1973a) "Systematic Job Search and Unemployment," *Rev. Econ. Stud.*, Apr. 1973, *40*, 191–201.

_____, (1973b) "Wage Differentials in a Dynamic Theory of the Firm," *J. Econ. Theory*, Aug. 1973, *6*, 321–44.

_____, "Monopolistic Competition with Outside Goods," unpublished paper, Univ. Pennsylvania 1978.

J. K. Salop and S. C. Salop, "Self-Selection and Turnover in the Labor Market," *Quart. J. Econ.*, Nov. 1976, *90*, 619–27.

D. Soskice, "Salop and Stiglitz on Involuntary Unemployment," unpublished paper, Univ. California-Berkeley 1974.

J. E. Stiglitz, "Equilibrium Wage Distributions," unpublished paper, Stanford Univ. 1974.

A. Weiss, "Education as a Test," unpublished paper, Bell Laboratories 1977.

Job Queues and Layoffs in Labor Markets with Flexible Wages

Andrew Weiss

Bell Laboratories, Murray Hill, New Jersey, and Columbia University

Models of a heterogeneous labor market are presented in which a worker's acceptance wage is an increasing function of his ability, and in which firms have imprecise information concerning the labor endowment of particular workers. Because the expected labor endowment of a hiree is an increasing function of the firm's wage offer, industrial firms may choose not to lower wages when confronted with a queue of job applicants. Rejected job applicants will not be able to increase their probability of employment by lowering their acceptance wages. Firms may choose to simultaneously hire and fire workers.

In 1975, the administration of the Stanford Linear Accelerator Center (SLAC) declared its intention to lay off 10 percent of its work force. The workers then voted to take a 10 percent wage cut voluntarily to stop the layoffs. This offer was refused by the management of SLAC. The reason offered by SLAC was: if wages were cut, "the best workers would quit."

I. Introduction

In traditional labor-market models, wages are determined solely by their role in equating supply and demand. These models have, there-

The basic research for this paper was done in 1975 under a grant from the Sloan Foundation. I am grateful to Peter Fishburn, Bruce Greenwald, Luis Guasch, Herschel Grossman, Steven Shavell, Michael Spence, David Starrett, Joseph Stiglitz, Robert Willig, Edward Zajac, an anonymous referee, and participants in the Microeconomic workshops at the University of Minnesota and Columbia University and the Economic Theory seminar at the University of Chicago for helpful comments and suggestions.

fore, been of little use in explaining the widely observed phenomenon of job queues and the related reality of layoffs accompanied by rigid wages. However, both phenomena can be explained if we make two critical assumptions: (1) the wages received by workers are not proportionate to their productivity, but (2) the acceptance wages of workers are an increasing function of their productivity.

These assumptions generate a model of labor markets in which the wage offered by a firm affects not only the number of job applicants to the firm but also the expected labor endowment of workers hired by the firm. Suppose a wage elicits enough applicants to satisfy the firm's demand for workers. By offering a higher wage, the firm is able to attract more able workers and hence increase the expected labor endowment of a worker drawn randomly from its pool of applicants. The firm is not interested in choosing the minimum wage at which its demand for labor is satisfied but, rather, in choosing the wage which minimizes its cost per efficiency unit of labor; it is not the cost of "workers" which concerns the firm but the cost of labor inputs. Because wages affect quality, the wage which minimizes each firm's cost per efficiency unit of labor may result in an excess supply of workers to all firms. A worker on a job queue would not be able to obtain a job by offering to work at a lower wage since that offer would signal to the firm an upper bound for the worker's acceptance wage and consequently (by assumption 2) an upper bound on his labor endowment. Hence, these job queues will persist.

Now consider a firm (similar to SLAC) facing a fall in demand. There are quality differences among its workers which are unperceived by the firm but which are correlated with the alternative income those workers would receive elsewhere in the economy. If the firm cut its wages, its best workers would quit. To avoid the adverse selection ramifications of a wage cut, firms may instead arbitrarily lay off workers.

In addition to explaining job queues and layoffs, the model presented below can account for the different unemployment rates and layoff probabilities of observationally distinct groups in the population. Cost-minimizing wages are determined for each group in the population. At a given level of aggregate demand, some groups may, at their cost-minimizing wage, face an excess demand for their labor services. They would then receive a wage above their cost-minimizing one. At the same time, other workers either encounter job queues or a complete lack of hiring at their own cost-minimizing wages.

Since the quality-determining role of wages depends on the plausibility of the assumptions mentioned above, we will devote the remainder of the Introduction to a discussion of these assumptions.

Firms have several reasons for not paying wages which are pro-

portionate to productivity. The most obvious of these is that the cost
of precise information may exceed its benefit. The difficulty and cost
of precisely measuring productivity have received extensive anecdotal
treatments (Brown 1962).

Even if productivity were known with certainty, firms may choose to
pay wages which are not proportional to either output or expected
output. The risk-aversion reasons for not linking wages directly to
output have been discussed at length by Stiglitz (1975) and Pencavel
(1975) and need not concern us here except to remark that the
progressivity of the income tax further induces workers to prefer
wage policies with lower variance in earnings.

Of more concern is why firms do not pay a wage proportionate to
expected productivity, that is, a time rate for each worker proportionate to his expected output during that time period.

To the extent that work is a cooperative enterprise, wage differentials between workers in the same firm with the same readily observable characteristics could cause resentments that would lower the
productivity of each worker. For example, friction between workers
might increase the quit rate and cause some employees to hinder the
efforts of their co-workers.

These morale effects are accentuated by changes in abilities after
workers are hired. If two workers perform the same task but the more
productive worker (A) receives a lower wage than the less productive
worker (B), solely because when they were hired worker B was believed to be of higher ability than worker A, then the morale problems
and the negative impact on the effort of worker A could be dramatic.

Union pressure may also militate for a uniform wage policy. When
the median worker's output level is below the output of the mean
worker, then a democratically run union (disregarding incentive effects) will vote for a uniform wage.

There is also strong empirical evidence that firms pay workers a
more or less uniform wage rate despite ability differences. Lewis
(1960) found that only 27 percent of U.S. production workers had
their pay linked either to their own output or the output of a group of
workers. Even among workers classified as having their pay linked to
performance the connection is often extremely weak. I have studied
proprietary data on the physical output of workers in a company
which pays group incentives. Since all the workers studied belonged to
the same pay group, there were only very minor pay differences
among them (those differences were due to seniority). On the other
hand, the output of the most productive worker was often more than
three times as great as the output of the least productive worker
among fewer than 20 workers doing the same job with the same

supervisor. In addition, for the workers in question promotions and fringe benefits were not affected by performance.

Although in some companies more productive workers are more likely to be promoted, get a better choice of vacation dates, or have less stringent supervision, the assumption of a uniform wage within a job classification seems more realistic than the usual assumptions of wages strictly proportionate to either ability or performance.

The positive correlation between acceptance wages and productivity is easily justified in the context of a less developed country where acceptance wages are determined by output in agriculture or handicrafts. However, developed economies also have a large nonindustrial sector of self-employed craftsmen, professionals, individuals improving their homes, and casual laborers who are paid on a piecerate basis. This sector exists alongside an industrial sector marked by uniform wages and tests to observe productivity. In both less and more developed countries, potential earnings in the nonindustrial sector play a crucial role in determining the lowest wage at which an individual would accept a job in the industrial sector.[1] In general, we would expect productivity in the nonindustrial sector to affect acceptance wages and to be correlated with productivity in the industrial sector, resulting in a positive correlation between acceptance wages and productivity in the industrial sector.

Productivity differences between workers stem from two types of characteristics: those which are costlessly observed (such as years of education) and those which can only be measured at some cost (such as manual dexterity). We will assume that the cost of measuring the latter characteristics, and a reluctance to link pay to characteristics which are not immediately discernible to the workers, lead firms to offer the same wage to all workers having the same costlessly observed characteristics. We will first analyze the case in which workers differ only according to unobserved characteristics, so that firms only offer a single wage. Part III then considers the case where workers differ according to both observed and unobserved characteristics. In the latter case, wages will be linked to the observed characteristics and firms will offer different wages and different probabilities of being hired according to the observed characteristics of the workers.

---

[1] An alternative explanation for the positive correlation between acceptance wage and ability is given by Greenwald (1979). In Greenwald's work, firms know the ability of their workers. If a new firm makes a wage offer, that offer will be matched for some workers but not for others. As the new firm raises its wage offer, the level of "minimum ability" at which that wage offer is matched will also rise. Thus, we would derive the positive correlation between the wage a firm offers and the expected ability of the workers it attracts.

II. Observationally Indistinguishable Workers

Each worker has a labor endowment (θ) which is invariant across all jobs and an acceptance wage (w) which is an increasing function of his marginal product in the nonindustrial sector and is strictly greater than that marginal product. Therefore, the acceptance wage of a worker is a strictly increasing function of his labor endowment θ, so that $\theta = q_j(w)$ and $q'_j(w) > 0$, where j indicates the observable characteristics of the worker. This functional relationship between labor endowment and acceptance wages, as well as the normalized distribution of workers $F_j(w)$ of type j by acceptance wages, are assumed to be known by all firms. We will ignore the subscript j in Part II, where we are assuming that all workers are observationally indistinguishable. We also assume that the nonindustrial sector has a constant-returns-to-scale production technology and the price of output in the nonindustrial sector is the numeraire.

Each firm (i) is characterized by an increasing, concave, and continuously differentiable production function $g(L)$, whose only argument is efficiency units of labor, and by a fixed cost T_i which differs across firms and may represent different entrepreneurial skills. Firms are assumed to maximize expected profits π_i, and the price p of output in the industrial sector is assumed to be determined exogenously. The only unusual noninformational assumptions are exogenous price determinations and the restriction that labor is the only variable input. Both of these assumptions are made purely for expositional convenience.

Firms have two choice variables: the wage w to offer and the number of workers x to hire. We shall assume that labor is a continuous variable. Let

$$\overline{q}(w^*) = \frac{\int_0^{w^*} q(w) dF(w)}{\int_0^{w^*} dF(w)};$$

that is, $\overline{q}(w)$ denotes the expected labor endowment of a worker hired when wage w is offered. The profit function of firm i offering wage w^* and hiring x^* workers is

$$\pi_i \cong pg[x^*\overline{q}(w^*)] - w^*x^* - T_i. \tag{1}$$

The approximation in (1) is due to the concavity of the production function and the fact that the firm is sampling from a distribution $F(w)$. Therefore, we know from Jensen's inequality that the right-hand side of (1) will overstate the expected profits of the firm. However, since this approximation rapidly approaches equality as the firm's labor force increases, it will be assumed to be exact for the remainder of the analysis.

We shall now determine the equilibrium wage when labor supply exceeds labor demand and then show that this inequality is consistent with competitive equilibrium.

To ease the notation, we assume that $w/\overline{q}(w)$ has a unique global minimum, and we let $\tilde{w}$ denote the wage which minimizes $w/\overline{q}(w)$. Let $N^S(\tilde{w})$ and $N^D(\tilde{w})$ denote the economy-wide labor supply and demand, respectively, at wage $\tilde{w}$.[2]

If $N^S(\tilde{w}) > N^D(\tilde{w})$, then each firm in the industrial sector will offer a wage of $\tilde{w}$.

Suppose to the contrary that $\tilde{w}/\overline{q}(\tilde{w}) < w/\overline{q}(w)$ for all $w \neq \tilde{w}$, but some wage $\hat{w} \neq \tilde{w}$ and labor force $\hat{x}$ maximize profits. Let $x^0 = \hat{w}\hat{x}/\tilde{w}$. Then,

$$g[x^0\overline{q}(\tilde{w})] - \tilde{w}x^0 - T_i = g\left[\frac{\hat{w}\hat{x}}{\tilde{w}}\overline{q}(\tilde{w})\right] - \hat{w}\hat{x} - T_i > g[\hat{x}\overline{q}(\hat{w})] - \hat{w}\hat{x} - T_i.$$

Thus, hiring x^0 workers at wage $\tilde{w}$ is more profitable than hiring any number of workers at wage $\hat{w}$.

We can now show that job queues are consistent with competitive equilibrium. We first derive $N^D(\tilde{w})$ and then show that $N^S(\tilde{w})$ can exceed $N^D(\tilde{w})$.

Differentiating equation (1), we see that if the equilibrium wage is $\tilde{w}$, each firm chooses a size of its labor force $\tilde{x}$ such that

$$pg'[\tilde{x}\,\overline{q}\,(\tilde{w})]\,\overline{q}\,(\tilde{w}) = \tilde{w}. \tag{2}$$

Equation (2) is the usual profit-maximizing condition that the marginal revenue product of a worker is equal to his wage. In a job-queuing equilibrium, firms will enter until the marginal firm earns zero profits. Let m be the number of firms which have fixed costs less than or equal to $pg[\tilde{x}\overline{q}(\tilde{w})] - \tilde{w}\tilde{x}$. Then, $N^D(\tilde{w}) = m\tilde{x}$.[3]

Since the labor-supply function has not been specified, it is certainly possible for $N^S(\tilde{w})$ to exceed $m\tilde{x}$, in which case labor supply exceeds labor demand at the equilibrium wage $\tilde{w}$.

The intuition behind this result is that each firm wishes to pay a wage which minimizes its labor costs per efficiency unit of labor hired. If $N^S(\tilde{w}) < N^D(\tilde{w})$, then competition for workers will drive the market wage above $\tilde{w}$. On the other hand, if at wage $\tilde{w}$ labor supply exceeds

[2] We are implicitly assuming that there are no costs to switching jobs, so that $N^S(\tilde{w})$ is independent of the number of firms which have previously hired workers in this market, and that firms cannot identify unemployed workers. In Guasch and Weiss (forthcoming) this assumption is dropped. The behavior of firms is analyzed when workers incur significant costs from switching jobs.

[3] The assumption of fixed costs differing across firms is not vital to our analysis. It is merely a device to show that the job queues persist even with entry. We could have shown this persistence equally well by assuming either that prices decrease with output or that fixed costs increase with the number of firms.

labor demand, firms would not reduce their wage offers, even if they each had long queues of applicants at wage $\bar{w}$.

Although there are job queues, no individual can increase his probability of being hired by announcing a willingness to work at a wage below $\bar{w}$. By announcing a willingness to work at $\bar{w} - \Delta$, the individual reveals that his true acceptance wage is less than or equal to $\bar{w} - \Delta$ and that his expected ability is $\bar{q}(\bar{w} - \Delta)$. However, by definition, $(\bar{w} - \Delta)/\bar{q}(\bar{w} - \Delta) > \bar{w}/\bar{q}(\bar{w})$. Therefore, this individual becomes *less* likely to be hired when he announces an acceptance wage below $\bar{w}$.

Thus far, we have analyzed the persistence of a job queue in a competitive labor market but have not discussed changes in the length of that queue. By choosing the price of nonindustrial output as our numeraire and by assuming a constant-returns-to-scale technology in the nonindustrial sector, we have fixed the acceptance wage of workers. Consequently, the wage which minimizes the cost per efficiency unit of labor is not affected by fluctuations in demand. If $N^S(\bar{w}) \geqslant N^D(\bar{w})$ before a fall in the price of industrial output, then $N^S(\bar{w}) > N^D(\bar{w})$ after that fall, and $\bar{w}$ will continue to be the industrial wage. From equation (2) and the concavity of $g(L)$, we see that firms respond to falls in demand by reducing employment.

If we were to allow decreasing returns to scale in the nonindustrial sector but continue to assume that acceptance wages were proportionate to earnings in the nonindustrial sector, then the fall in the price of industrial output would still result in falls in industrial employment. In this case, however, the wage in the industrial sector would fall by a proportion equal to the percentage change in the marginal product of an efficiency unit of labor in the nonindustrial sector. This result follows directly by observing that

$$\bar{q}(w^*)\Big|_{p = p_1} = \bar{q}(\alpha w^*)\Big|_{p = p_2},$$

where $\alpha - 1$ is the fractional change in the marginal product of labor in the nonindustrial sector when p changes from p_1 to p_2. Therefore, $\alpha \bar{w}$ is the cost-minimizing wage at $p = p_2$ and firms hire the same expected quality of labor at wage $\alpha \bar{w}$ that they previously hired at $\bar{w}$. Since α is less than one only if nonindustrial output has increased, the presence of decreasing returns to scale in the nonindustrial sector cannot reverse or prevent falls in demand from causing a reduction in industrial employment.

On the other hand, if we do not put any structure other than monotonicity upon the function relating acceptance wages and earnings in the nonindustrial sector, then falls in industrial demand could increase, decrease, or leave unchanged industrial employment. Industrial employment would be increased if the acceptance wages of the less able workers were very responsive to falls in their wage in the nonindustrial sector and the nonindustrial sector were characterized by decreasing returns to scale. In that case, layoffs in the industrial sector would decrease the marginal product of labor in the nonindustrial sector by a fraction β, causing a fall in the cost-minimizing wage by a fraction greater than β. Firms would then hire workers of lower expected labor endowments and might hire more of them, despite the fall in demand. A formal proof of these results appears in Weiss (1976).

III. Heterogeneous Labor

In Part II we assumed that all workers had identical observed characteristics. We shall now treat a more general case in which differences in observed attributes among workers enable firms to partition the labor force into n "types."[4] Workers of the same type have the same observed attributes but different acceptance wages and labor endowments. These are determined by both observed and unobserved attributes.

In a competitive labor market, workers of different types will in general receive different wages. If they were receiving the same wage, the firm would almost always be making positive profits on one type of workers and those workers would be bid away by competing firms.[5] Although the arguments for a uniform wage continue to hold for workers with the same observed characteristics, wages will differ among workers with different observed characteristics.

Each group i is characterized by a firm-optimal wage $\tilde{w}_i$ which minimizes labor inputs per dollar for that group. We can rank the groups in order of increasing cost per efficiency unit of labor at each group's firm-optimal wage $\tilde{w}_i$ such that

$$\frac{\tilde{w}_1}{\overline{q}_1(\tilde{w}_1)} < \frac{\tilde{w}_2}{\overline{q}_2(\tilde{w}_2)} < \ldots < \frac{\tilde{w}_n}{\overline{q}_n(\tilde{w}_n)},$$

where $\overline{q}_i(w_i)$ denotes the expected labor input per employee of type i when wage w_i is offered.

We can now show why some groups are excluded from the industrial sector.

Groups will be hired in order of increasing cost per efficiency unit of labor at their firm-optimal wage. For $j > i$, workers of type j will be hired only if the labor-supply constraint is binding on workers of type

[4] The discussion below was motivated by a conversation with Robert Lucas, who is, of course, not responsible for its subsequent direction.
[5] The only time two groups could receive the same wage is if the same expected quality of labor was forthcoming from both groups at that wage.

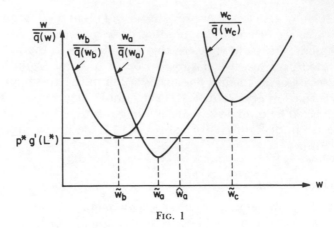

FIG. 1

i; that is, when workers of type j are being hired, there are no queues of type-i workers applying for jobs.

This result follows directly from the firm's desire to minimize cost per efficiency unit of labor. If group i is either not being hired or is experiencing job rationing, then some firm can hire members of that group at wage $\tilde{w}_i$, which, by definition, yields a lower cost per efficiency unit of labor than *any* wage offered to ability type j. Therefore, no firm would ever hire workers of type j unless the labor-supply constraint upon group i is binding.

Let us now turn to the equilibrium-wage distribution. In a competitive labor market, the wages of low-index groups will be bid up so that the cost per efficiency unit of labor is equalized among all groups being hired.

Suppose the contrary that types i and j are hired at wages w_i^* and w_j^* and that $w_i^*/\overline{q}(w_i^*) > w_j^*/\overline{q}(w_j^*)$. A firm hiring type-$i$ workers would prefer to bid type-j workers away from other firms by offering a wage above w_j^* rather than hiring type-i workers.

In equilibrium, each employed group will receive a wage $\hat{w}_k$ such that $\hat{w}_k = pg'(\cdot)\overline{q}(\hat{w}_k)$. All groups for which jobs are not rationed will receive wages $\hat{w}_k > \tilde{w}_k$.

This result is illustrated in figure 1, which graphs the expected cost per efficiency unit for three types of workers as a function of the wage offered each type. If the marginal revenue product of an efficiency unit of labor is denoted by $p^*g'(L^*)$, where $g(L^*)$ is the profit-maximizing output when the price is p^*, then no workers of group c will be employed in the industrial sector. Workers of group b receive their firm-optimal wage and may face job queues. Firms compete only for members of group a, bidding their wage above $\tilde{w}_a$.

As in the single-wage case, members of groups b and c would find that announcing "low" acceptance wages does not improve their employment prospects. The argument here is identical with that on the top of page 532.

If the output price in the industrial sector were to increase, each firm would increase its employment of group b, lowering $g'(L^*)$, and new firms would enter, further increasing the demand for type-b labor. For a large enough increase in the output price, the demand for type-b workers would exceed their supply at wage $\tilde{w}_b$, and the wage for both group b and group a would rise as each firm tried to increase the size of its labor force. Only after job queues for type-b workers have vanished and the wage of type-b workers has risen above $\tilde{w}_b$ will any type-c workers be hired.

Conversely, the only effect of small falls in the output price will be a reduction in the employment of type-b workers. In the absence of turnover costs, type-a workers will continue to be hired at wage $\hat{w}_a$ while type-b workers are being laid off. The wage offered to type-a workers will only fall below $\hat{w}_a$ when no type-b workers are employed. This is because at any wage w_a^*, where $\hat{w}_a > w_a^* > \tilde{w}_a$, the cost per efficiency unit of labor for type-a workers is less than the minimum cost of type-b labor. Therefore, the full impact of small changes in demand is borne by type-b workers.

IV. Empirical Evidence

The model presented in Part III is consistent with two recent empirical studies. Wolpin (1975) has used data from the Thorndike sample to show that the mean earnings of self-employed workers are roughly 40 percent higher than the earnings for employees of firms. The Thorndike sample is comprised of prime-age white males with at least 12 years of education who passed a sequence of preliminary Air Force qualification examinations (AFQT). Typically, individuals with these observable characteristics would not face job queues and could be termed a low-index group. Our model predicts that self-employed members of low-index groups are choosing not to work for firms and consequently have higher wages than do the employees of firms. Thus, our model is consistent both with Wolpin's data on mean earnings and with his finding that, when earnings are regressed on such observable variables as schooling, experience, and the individual's score on the AFQT, the intercept for self-employed workers is significantly higher than for employees of firms. These results hold whether professionals are included and/or the sample is limited to managers. Of course, these high earnings of the self-employed may be a return to the higher risk or variance in earnings from self-employment, or a return on capital which is perceived by the self-employed as earnings. On the other hand, self-employed individuals may substantially understate their income to avoid taxes and may receive substantial parts of their income as fringe benefits. Thus, Wolpin's data provide partial, though not conclusive, support for the model developed above.

Feldstein and Wright (1976) have remarked on (a) the very high unemployment rates for certain subgroups in the population and (b) the lack of responsiveness of these unemployment rates to changes in aggregate demand. The model presented above offers an explanation for these empirical findings based upon different distributions of ability between groups, not necessarily differences in mean productivity. Firms draw first from "favorable" distributions. Only after the labor-supply constraint is binding upon those types and their wages are driven up will the firms begin hiring from the less advantaged (high-index) groups.

V. Conclusion

The main thrust of the analysis presented above is to provide a new explanation for the failure of wages to fall when there is an excess supply of workers wishing to work in industrial firms. Salop (1973) and Stiglitz (1974) attribute the downward rigidity of wages to a desire on the part of firms to reduce labor turnover. If a firm cut its wages, its workers would be more likely to quit, increasing the labor costs of the firm. Leibenstein (1957) explained the downward rigidity of wages in underdeveloped countries as due to the direct effect of income on the nutrition, and hence the productivity, of workers. Firms would not cut wages because the fall in output per worker would outweigh the saving in the wage per worker. In each of these models, the labor force is homogeneous, and the wage offered affects the productivity of workers by affecting behavior.

This paper, in contrast, focused on the sorting effect of wages. In the model presented above, asymmetric information and the positive correlation between acceptance wages and labor endowments enable a firm offering a wage above the market-clearing wage to hire from a "better" pool of applicants.[6]

The paper also presented a new explanation of why firms lay off workers in response to a fall in demand. Azariadis (1975) and Baily

---

[6] These sorting effects of wages are similar to the sorting effect of prices in the used car market as analyzed by Akerlof (1970). Although Akerlof only analyzed market-clearing equilibria his model could easily be extended to show that potential buyers would receive higher quality cars by offering higher prices.

(1977), among others, have presented models in which firms make an implicit contract with workers not to vary wages. Instead, workers are laid off in response to a fall in demand. However, throughout the "implicit-contract" literature, workers are only laid off if their marginal utility of leisure (less turnover costs but including unemployment compensation) when laid off exceeds the value of their marginal product (less their disutility from work) when employed. Consequently, in the implicit-contract literature all layoffs are Pareto efficient (aside from their macroeconomic consequences).

In the model presented above, workers who are laid off are more productive in industrial employment than in nonindustrial employment at the time they are being laid off. In fact, all workers employed by firms have a marginal product in industrial employment above their marginal product in nonindustrial production. Consequently, government policies which increase industrial employment by payroll subsidies increase total output.

A payroll subsidy does not affect the firm's choice of a cost-minimizing wage $\bar{w}$. The industrial sector will continue to employ workers at a wage at least as great as $\bar{w}$. Wages only rise above $\bar{w}$ if the labor-supply constraint becomes binding. However, the cost per worker will fall. Therefore, equation (1) shows that the number of firms will increase, and equation (2) shows that the size of existing firms will also rise. Since no previously hired workers are being excluded, these shifts of workers from the nonindustrial sector into the industrial sector raise total output.[7]

Finally, this model allows new insights into why firms would simultaneously hire and fire workers. During a boom, high-index workers (in the sense defined in Part III) are hired. During a slump, firms may find it profitable to replace those workers with new workers whose observable attributes mark them as members of a lower-index group.

References

Akerlof, George A. "The Market for 'Lemons': Quality Uncertainty and the Market Mechanism." *Q.J.E.* 84 (August 1970): 488–500.

Azariadis, Costas. "Implicit Contracts and Underemployment Equilibria." *J.P.E.* 83, no. 6 (December 1975): 1183–1202.

Baily, Martin N. "On the Theory of Layoffs and Unemployment." *Econometrica* 45 (July 1977): 1043–63.

[7] On the other hand, subsidies which are linked to the number of employees in a firm have ambiguous effects on total output. The intuition here is that subsidies per employee, in a world where $N^S(\bar{w}) > N^b(\bar{w})$, may cause a fall in the cost-minimizing wage as each firm seeks to increase the number of workers it employs. If low-ability workers have a comparative advantage in nonindustrial employment, this shift in the composition of the industrial sector's labor force may cause a fall in total output. These policy implications are derived rigorously in Weiss (1976).

Brown, Wilfred B. *Piecework Abandoned*. London: Heinemann, 1962.
Feldstein, M., and Wright, B. "High Unemployment Groups in Tight Labor Markets." Discussion Paper no. 488, Harvard Univ., June 1976.
Greenwald, Bruce C. N. *The Labor Market as a Market for Lemons*. New York: Garland, 1979.
Guasch, L., and Weiss, A. "Adverse Selection and Increasing Returns to Late Entry." *Q.J.E.*, forthcoming.
Leibenstein, Harvey. *Economic Backwardness and Economic Growth*. New York: Wiley, 1957.
Lewis, L. Earl. "Extent of Incentive Pay in Manufacturing." *Monthly Labor Rev.* 83 (May 1960): 460–63.
Pencavel, John H. "Work Effort and Alternative Methods of Remuneration." Industrial Relations Working Paper no. 63, Princeton Univ., 1975.
Salop, Steven C. "Wage Differentials in a Dynamic Theory of the Firm." *J. Econ. Theory* 6 (August 1973): 321–44.
Stiglitz, Joseph E. "Alternative Theories of Wage Determination and Unemployment in LDC's: The Labor Turnover Model." *Q.J.E.* 88 (May 1974): 194–227.
———. "Incentives, Risk and Information: Notes toward a Theory of Hierarchy." *Bell J. Econ.* 6 (Autumn 1975): 552–79.
Weiss, Andrew M. "A Theory of Limited Labor Markets." Ph.D. dissertation, Stanford Univ., 1976.
Wolpin, Kenneth I. "Education and Screening." Ph.D. dissertation, City Univ. New York, 1975.

Hierarchy, Ability, and Income Distribution

Guillermo A. Calvo and Stanislaw Wellisz

Columbia University

Labor allocation and wage-scale formation are studied in the context of competitive hierarchic firms. We show that (1) the wage per effective laborer and his quality increase with the hierarchical position of the employee, and (2) up to a point, the imposition of a minimum wage for production labor increases the quality and quantity of production workers and reduces the wage, quality, and number of supervisors. These results help to explain the skewness of income distribution, and the wage differentials across layers which are inexplicable in terms of differences in labor quality and difficulty of tasks.

This paper presents a theory of labor allocation and of wage-scale formation within hierarchic firms facing a competitive labor market. Our aim is to give an endogenous explanation of the hierarchic differentials in worker quality, wages, and degree of supervision. We also explore the effect of minimum-wage imposition upon such firms and the related problem of interlevel conflicts of interests.

The problem of "internal wage scales" and of internal labor use looks trivial under the neoclassical assumptions that firms are able to make (and costlessly enforce) contracts with their employees in terms of labor services. The solution becomes much less obvious if, instead, we take the more realistic view that the management of human resources within firms involves a "game" between employees who seek to maximize utility and residual owners whose aim is to maximize profits and who resort to incentives and punishments to achieve their goal.

We are indebted to George J. Stigler, Oliver E. Williamson, and an anonymous referee for very helpful comments. This work was performed while the authors were visiting at the Institute for International Economic Studies, Stockholm University.

115

The study of hierarchic organizations was pioneered by Simon (1957) and Lydall (1968), who sought to explain the observed skewness of the upper tail of income distribution in terms of internal arrangements within firms. Both authors assumed that (1) the employees of a firm supervise employees on the level below and that the lowest-level employees are the only production workers, (2) the supervisor/supervisee ratio is constant across layers, and (3) the wage at any layer is a constant multiple of the wage at the layer below. Simon (1957) and Lydall (1968) show that these assumptions generate a Pareto wage distribution, but neither author gives an economic explanation of the internal wage and labor utilization structure.[1]

An endogenous explanation of the internal wage supervision structure was first proposed by Calvo (1977) and Calvo and Wellisz (1978). To elicit work from their employees, employers pay wages and supervise employees' performance. If, as is reasonable to assume, supervision is not costless, the optimal arrangement for the lowest-paid workers involves wages which exceed the workers' opportunity cost. Moreover, even if all labor is uniform, the higher the position in the hierarchy, the lower the optimal degree of supervision and the higher the wage. An intuitive explanation of this finding is that the higher the employee's position, the greater the number of production workers which may be adversely affected by his nonperformance, hence, the greater the potential loss to the enterprise. The high wage is, in a sense, a "bribe" offered to the high-level employee to keep him from shirking. In the present paper, we shall extend our analysis to the more complex and more interesting case of heterogeneous labor, and we shall show that the wage per efficiency unit rises with the hierarchic level.

Insofar as job difficulty does not always increase with the hierarchic level, it is not obvious why the higher posts should be occupied by the more able personnel. Mayer (1960) demonstrated that if one assumes that workers supervised by a more able individual are more productive than if they worked on their own, then in an optimal arrangement the more productive individuals should be placed higher on the hierarchic ladder. Without questioning the plausibility of such assumptions, we shall prove a more fundamental proposition, namely, that the same mechanism which generates the wage ladder also creates the ability ladder even if all jobs are equally difficult and even if there are no Mayer-type externalities. The compounding of the hierarchic ability assignments by the hierarchic wage per efficiency

[1] Neither Simon nor Lydall suggests any link between the hierarchic theory of wages and a more general theory embracing the self-employed and those employed in nonhierarchic organizations, whereas our approach provides for such a linkage (see Calvo 1977).

unit differentials gives an endogenous explanation why the wage distribution is more skewed than the inherent ability distribution.

We begin the descriptive part of our paper (Part I) by formulating a model of a hierarchic firm. We assume with Simon (1957) and Lydall (1968) that all production activities are carried out by level one workers who are supervised by level two employees, who in turn are supervised by level three employees, and so on. For the sake of simplicity, we assume that a worker either works at full efficiency or that he shirks, but some of our main qualitative conclusions hold under the more realistic, but less tractable, assumption that effort is a continuous function of work incentives (see Appendix A).

Our first task is to prove that an optimal arrangement at any hierarchic level is independent of the number of supervisory levels above it. This result, which is instrumental for further proofs, is interesting in itself: it shows that, ceteris paribus, the same conditions will be offered to same-level employees (always counting from the bottom up) by relatively "tall" and relatively "flat" firms.

The second, and more important, purpose of the descriptive section is to present a solution to the problem of assignment of heterogeneous workers to the different hierarchic levels. We assume that all tasks are equally attractive, that is, that if the wage were equal at all levels, all workers would be indifferent as to the levels to which they are assigned. We also rule out comparative advantage (which would render the problem quite trivial) and assume, instead, that the relative efficiency of workers remains constant across layers, that is, that for any i and any j the ratio β_{ik}/β_{jk} representing the relative efficiency of the ith and of the jth workers, when both are assigned to a kth-level task, remains constant for all k. Finally, as noted above, we rule out Mayer-type externalities. We prove that even under such stringent assumptions it is rational to assign the more efficient workers to higher tasks. We also show that the optimal interlayer wage differentials are greater than the differentials in the inherent productivity of optimally assigned workers. Our results are thus consistent with those of Simon and of Lydall, but, in contrast with the earlier analysis, we explicitly deal with firms imbedded in the competitive labor market, and we dispense with the Simon-Lydall exogenous wage scale and fixed span of control assumptions.

In Part II of this paper, we explore the effect of the imposition of a minimum wage applying to the production workers. We show that, as the wage is raised, the owner will hire better quality production workers, a result which is consistent with standard analysis. It is more surprising to find that, up to a point, the higher the minimum wage, the larger the number of production workers that will be employed. On the other hand, an increase in the minimum wage of production workers is disadvantageous to the supervisors. As the wage is raised, the optimal number, quality, and wage of supervisors decline. Up to a point, however, total employment of workers plus supervisors increases.

The explanation of these findings is that, as will be demonstrated, the hierarchic firm acts as if it were a monopsonist, even though it operates within a competitive labor market. Thus, the inclusion of the supervision element in the analysis provides a link between a behavioral theory of firms, based on monopsonistic premises, and the theory of competitive market behavior.

I. Wages and Labor Quality in a Hierarchic Firm

To bring our findings into stark relief, we present them within the context of a highly stylized model. Greater realism could only be purchased at the cost of clarity of argument; moreover, as we show in Appendix A, the relaxation of our strongest assumptions does not necessarily alter the central qualitative results.

Assumptions and Definitions

A. The firm's employees are organized into n hierarchic layers; the first-layer employees are the only production workers. All others (including the owners) perform supervisory duties, with the ith layer being supervised by the i + first layer. The symbol M_i $(i=1, \ldots, n)$ stands for the number of ith-layer employees. We assume without loss of generality that there is a single owner and that he supervises the highest layer (i.e., the members of the nth layer).

B. All tasks within the firm, including production and supervision, are, for the same wage, equally attractive to all employees and equally difficult. This means that for the same wage a worker of a given quality can perform equally well and equally willingly any level task.

C. Workers differ in quality, be it because of native ability, education, diligence, or other factors. The symbol β_i stands for an employee of quality β assigned to an ith-level task. An effective labor unit is defined as the equivalent of one employee of quality $\beta = 1$; hence, $\beta_i M_i$ stands for the ith-level effective labor force. We define the owner's effectiveness as being equal to one.

D. Workers are hired from a pool of self-employed.[2] The utility derived from self-employment is h; for the sake of verbal simplicity,

---

[2] "Self-employment" might stand for genuine self-employment, for a period on relief, etc., or, for that matter, for the participation in the Marxian "reserve army."

we shall refer to h as an employee's opportunity cost. We assume that

$$h = H(\beta) \quad H' > 0, H'' > 0, H'' \text{ continuous domain of } H = (0, \infty). \quad (1)$$

Unless the first-order condition assumption is made for the relevant part of the domain of H, it is clear that only the most productive workers will be hired. Strict convexity of H and continuity of H'' are assumed to simplify the mathematics. As will be made clear below, however, some sort of convexity of H will be necessary if firms are to employ laborers with different qualities. Some notes toward a justification of this assumption on the basis of general equilibrium considerations are presented in Appendix B.

E. Workers have identical preferences, a Von Neumann–Morgenstern representation of which is the wage w plus the amount of leisure. This implies risk neutrality.

F. Workers are hired for a single period, and they decide at the beginning of the period whether they will work or shirk. Each worker makes the (irrevocable) decision to work or to shirk the entire period.

G. A worker's product cannot be measured, but his efforts can be checked. An inspection is carried out at the beginning of the period, and any worker caught shirking is discharged and becomes self-employed. The variable P_i stands for the probability that a worker who shirks will be caught (or, the "degree of supervision"). We assume that

$$P_i = \text{Min} \left(\frac{\beta_{i+1} M_{i+1}}{M_i}, 1 \right).^3 \quad (2)$$

In what follows, we concentrate on the case in which one in equation (2) is not binding,[4] that is,

$$P_i = \beta_{i+1} M_{i+1} / M_i, \quad (2')$$

meaning that the probability that a worker who shirks will be caught is equal to the number of effective supervisors per supervisee.[5]

---

[3] We follow here the assumption made by Calvo (1977). However, all our qualitative results hold if P_i is made a nondecreasing function of the effective supervisor-supervisee ratio, i.e., of $\beta_{i+1} M_{i+1} / M_i$. The latter seems to be a reasonable assumption in the present framework where labor services are the only factor determining the level of supervision. The analysis could be extended, however, to the case where capital besides labor affects the degree of supervision if P_i is also made a function of the capital/supervisee ratio applied to layer i.

[4] When $P_i = 1$, supervision is perfect and the model specializes to the standard one in the theory of the firm.

[5] Situations where this would apply are those where difficulty of detecting when a supervisee shirks does not depend on the supervisee's ability. A polar assumption is that $P_i = \text{Min} (p_{i+1} M_{i+1} / \beta_i M_i, 1)$ or, in other words, that the difficulty of supervising rises in

H. Labor is the only factor of production; the marginal product of effective labor is constant and equal to one.

I. The firm is a profit maximizer; π_n stands for the profit, and π_n^* for the maximum profit of an n-layer firm.

J. The firm is not allowed to charge entrance fees.[6]

We can now easily derive an expression for the wage which the firm will pay to the ith-level employees. Given the supervision level P_i (> 0) and assuming that k units of leisure are derived from shirking, the firm must offer a wage w_i such that the expected utility of shirking will be smaller than the expected utility of working, if it wants to make sure that workers have a definite preference for work; that is,

$$w_i > P_i h_i + (1 - P_i)(w_i + k); \tag{3}$$

hence,

$$w_i = (1/P_i - 1)k + h_i.^{[7]} \tag{4}$$

Since the firm seeks to maximize profits, it will offer the lowest wage at which employees will refrain from shirking. Assuming that in case of indifference the employees will opt to work, the wage will be

$$w_i = (1/P_i - 1)k + h_i.^{[7]} \tag{4'}$$

Independence of Optimal Arrangements from the Number of Hierarchic Levels

We shall now prove that the optimal wage and labor quality for a hierarchic layer is independent of the number of layers superior to the one for which a choice is being made. To be more precise, if n is the number of layers in a firm, then the choice of an optimal arrangement at the ith layer (where $i \leqq n$) is independent of n. Without loss of generality, we will show this proposition by comparing a one-layer arrangement, in which the owner supervises the production workers, and a two-layer arrangement, in which the owner supervises supervisors who, in turn, supervise the production workers.

Consider first a single-layer arrangement, for which we have by assumptions A and C and by (2'):

$$P_1 = 1/M_1, \tag{5}$$

---

proportion to the ability of the supervisees. The algebra is a bit more complicated in this case, but the central results on the allocation of quality and wages across the hierarchical ladder stay the same.

[6] Results will not change if we assume, instead, that there is a positive upper bound on the entrance fee charged by the firm.

[7] The standard analysis assumes that $P_i = 1$, in which case $w_i = h_i$. A formula like (4') was also derived by Becker and Stigler (1974) in connection with a law enforcement problem.

which, with equations (1) and (4′), yields

$$w_1 = (M_1 - 1)k + H(\beta_1).$$ (6)

The profit for the one-layer firm can be written as (recall assumption H):

$$\pi_1 = \beta_1 M_1 - w_1 M_1,$$ (7)

which, when combined with equation (6), yields

$$\pi_1 = \beta_1 M_1 - [(M_1 - 1)k + H(\beta_1)]M_1.$$ (8)

By definition,

$$\underset{\beta_1, M_1}{\text{Max}}\ \pi_1 = \pi_1^*.$$ (9)

Assuming the existence of an interior solution (i.e., one where $M_1 > 0$, $\beta_1 > 0$), we get, at optimum,

$$H'(\beta_1) = 1.$$ (10)

Consider now a two-layer organization in which M_1 production workers are supervised by M_2 employees whose efficiency is β_2. Instead of equation (5), we now have

$$P_1 = \frac{\beta_2 M_2}{M_1}$$ (11a)

and

$$P_2 = \frac{1}{M_2},$$ (11b)

and instead of equation (6),

$$w_1 = (M_1/\beta_2 M_2 - 1)k + H(\beta_1)$$ (12a)

and

$$w_2 = (M_2 - 1)k + H(\beta_2).$$ (12b)

The total profit of a two-layered organization, π_2, is equal to the total product of the first-layer workers minus wage payments to first- and second-layer employees:

$$\pi_2 = \beta_1 M_1 - w_1 M_1 - w_2 M_2,$$ (13)

which, by equations (12a) and (12b), becomes

$$\begin{aligned}\pi_2 = \beta_1 M_1 &- [(M_1/\beta_2 M_2 - 1)k + H(\beta_1)]M_1 \\ &- [(M_2 - 1)k + H(\beta_2)]\,M_2.\end{aligned}$$ (14)

We shall now derive the condition for π_2^*, the maximum profit in a two-layered organization. By definition,

$$\pi_2^* = \max_{\beta_i,\, M_i | i=1,\, 2} \pi_2. \tag{15}$$

Hence,

$$\operatorname*{Max}_{\beta_2, M_2} \left(\operatorname*{Max}_{\beta_1, M_1} \left\{ \beta_1 M_1 - [(M_1/\beta_2 M_2 - 1)k + H(\beta_1)]M_1 \right\} \right.$$
$$\left. - [(M_2 - 1)k + H(\beta_2)]M_2 \right). \tag{16}$$

For the ease of notation, let $\tilde{M}_i$ stand for the inverse of the effective supervision ratio, so that

$$\tilde{M}_1 = M/\beta_2 M_2; \tag{17}$$

we obtain from equation (16):

$$\pi_2^* = \operatorname*{Max}_{\beta_2, M_2} \left(\beta_2 M_2 \operatorname*{Max}_{\tilde{M}_1, \beta_1} \left\{ \beta_1 \tilde{M}_1 - [(\tilde{M}_1 - 1)k + H(\beta)]\tilde{M}_1 \right\} \right.$$
$$\left. - [(M_2 - 1)k + H(\beta_2)]M_2 \right), \tag{18}$$

and from equations (8) and (9) it now follows that

$$\pi_2^* = \operatorname*{Max}_{\beta_2, M_2} \left\{ \beta_2 M_2 \pi_1^* - [(M_2 - 1)k + H(\beta_2)]M_2 \right\}, \tag{19}$$

which shows that the first-layer arrangement which is optimal in the single-layer case is also optimal in the two-layer case. This finding has an important methodological consequence: we can now treat the problem of optimal arrangement of layers independently of each other (the two-layer proof can be extended readily to n layers by adding a third, fourth, . . . , nth layer to the hierarchy). The finding also has a substantive interest: we have just shown that the production workers will be offered the same conditions of work regardless of the number of hierarchic layers in the enterprise, and the same will hold for the second- and higher-layer employees. The result is realistic, and, unlike some results that follow, it is reassuringly neoclassical.

Relation between Hierarchic Level, Wage, and Worker Quality

We shall now show that even if work at all hierarchic levels is equally difficult and equally onerous, a profit-maximizing enterprise will assign the better quality workers to the higher ranks and will pay them higher wages than those paid at the lower ranks to the lower-quality workers.

Comparing equation (19), the expression for maximum profit in the two-layer cases, with that for the one-layer case (eqq. [8] and [9]), we notice that the two differ from each other only in that the first term of the maximand is multiplied by one in the one-layer case and by π_1^* in the two-layer case. If a two-layer arrangement is to be utilized alongside with, or in preference to, the one-layer arrangement, it must be true that $\pi_2^* \geq \pi_1^*$, the equality holding only if both arrangements are equally profitable. Comparing equation (19) with (9), we immediately see that this condition implies that

$$\pi_1^* \geq 1, \tag{20}$$

and, if the two-layer arrangement is the more profitable,

$$\pi_1^* > 1. \tag{21}$$

A necessary condition for equation (19) is (assuming, again, interior optima)

$$\pi_1^* = H'(\beta_2). \tag{22}$$

Thus, by equations (1), (10), (21), and (22), we obtain

$$\beta_1 < \beta_2, \tag{23}$$

which implies that if labor is heterogeneous it is rational for the multilayer firm to assign the less productive workers to the lower-ranking tasks (and the more productive workers to the higher rungs of the hierarchy).

It will now be shown that the higher the rank, the lower the optimal degree of supervision. We shall utilize the finding that the addition of a hierarchic level does not alter the optimal arrangements on the lower level. We can thus consider the form

$$\underset{\beta, M}{\text{Max}} \left\{ \alpha\beta M - [(M - 1)k + H(\beta)]M \right\} \tag{24}$$

and let α take any nonnegative value. Notice that if $\alpha = 1$, (24) expresses profit maximization in the single-layer case, and if $\alpha = \pi_1^*$, it corresponds to profit maximization with respect to quality and quantity of supervisors when the quantity and quality of supervisees per effective supervisor are already optimally chosen.

Let $\hat{M}(\alpha)$, $\hat{\beta}(\alpha)$ be the values of M and β that solve (24), and assume that there is a unique maximum and that it is obtained at a regular point (i.e., an interior point at which the second-order conditions are satisfied with strict inequality). The first-order condition of (24) with respect to M is

$$\alpha\hat{\beta}(\alpha) - \{(M - 1)k + H[\hat{\beta}(\alpha)]\} - Mk = 0, \tag{25}$$

and with respect to β it is

$$\alpha = H'(\beta), \tag{26}$$

from which follows

$$\partial \hat{\beta} / \partial \alpha > 0. \qquad \text{(This implies eq. [23].)} \tag{26'}$$

The partial derivative of (25) with respect to α (utilizing eq. [26]) is

$$\hat{\beta}(\alpha). \tag{27}$$

Therefore, by (27), the standard comparative-statics calculation on the basis of (25) yields

$$\hat{M}'(\alpha) > 0, \tag{28}$$

from which it follows immediately that $\hat{M}(\pi_1^*) > \hat{M}(1)$. Remember that $\hat{M}(\pi_1^*)$ stands for the optimal number of supervisors in the two-layer arrangement; $\hat{M}(1)$ is the optimal number of workers in the one-layer arrangement and also (by the previous result) the optimal number of workers per effective supervisor in the two-layer arrangement. Thus, equation (28) proves that in a two-layer arrangement the number of supervisors is greater than the number of workers per effective supervisor. This result can be made clearer through the introduction of some additional notation. Let M_i^j stand for the optimal number of layer i workers in a j-layer case. Now, in a two-layer case at optimum,

$$M_2^2 = \hat{M}(\pi_1^*), \tag{29}$$

whereas

$$M_1^2 = \hat{M}(1)\hat{M}(\pi_1^*)\hat{\beta}(\pi_1^*) \qquad \text{or} \qquad \frac{M_1^2}{\hat{M}(\pi_1^*)\,\hat{\beta}(\pi_1^*)} = \hat{M}(1), \tag{30}$$

where $\hat{M}(\pi_1^*)\hat{\beta}(\pi_1^*)$ stands for the optimal effective number of supervisors in the two-layer organization (notice that, by previous results, the number of layer one workers per supervisor is the same in the one-layer as in the two-layer case). Now equations (28), (29), and (30) show that the number of supervisors is greater than the number of workers per effective supervisor. Recalling that, by definition, the owner's effectiveness qua supervisor is one, and remembering the inverse relation between the effective supervisor/supervisee ratio and the probability that a supervisee will be caught shirking (e.g., eq. [21]), it follows that, at optimum,

$$P_2 < P_1, \tag{31}$$

which means that in an optimal arrangement the higher the hierarchic level, the lower the optimal level of supervision.

The last point in our basic argument is that the optimal interlayer wage differentials are greater than the differentials in the effectiveness of the workers assigned to the various layers. Define

$$\omega = w/\beta = \text{wage/unit of effective labor.} \qquad (32)$$

By an argument similar to that used in the derivation of equation (6), we get

$$\omega = \frac{(M - 1)k + H(\beta)}{\beta}. \qquad (33)$$

Let $\hat{\omega}(\alpha)$ stand for the value of ω when $M = \hat{M}(\alpha)$ and $\beta = \hat{\beta}(\alpha)$. By (33) we can express the maximum in (24) as

$$[\alpha - \omega(\alpha)] \, \hat{M}(\alpha) \, \hat{\beta}(\alpha). \qquad (34)$$

It must be true that in a one-layer organization the optimal choice of M, ω, and β must result in greater or equal profits than would be the case if these variables were set at levels optimal for the supervision layer in a two-layer organization. Assuming uniqueness, the above statement holds with strict inequality, that is,

$$[1 - \hat{\omega}(1)] \, \hat{M}(1) \, \hat{\beta}(1) > [1 - \hat{\omega}(\pi_1^*)] \, \hat{M}(\pi_1^*)\hat{\beta}(\pi_1^*). \qquad (35)$$

But, from (26') and (28), we know that

$$\hat{M}(1) \, \hat{\beta}(1) < \hat{M}(\pi_1^*) \, \hat{\beta}(\pi_1^*). \qquad (36)$$

Hence, (35) and (36) imply that

$$\hat{\omega}(1) < \hat{\omega}(\pi_1^*), \qquad (37)$$

which shows that the interlayer wage differentials are greater than the differentials in effective labor per physical worker.[8]

Let us pause to give an intuitive explanation of our findings and to show what light they shed on actual labor practices. In a hierarchic organization there is, as it were, a multiplicative productivity effect. If a worker shirks, the firm loses the worker's product. If a supervisor shirks and, as a consequence, the workers under him shirk, too, the firm loses the produce of the entire productive workers' team. This is the basic reason for assigning the more productive workers to the higher-level jobs and offering them a wage higher than would be accounted for by their higher efficiency.

Our analysis, which deliberately focuses on a single aspect of man-

---

[8] As indicated above, the analysis could be extended to an n-layer form. However, the number of layers has to be assumed exogenous because in a similar way, as in Calvo and Wellisz (1978), it can be shown that if $\pi_1^* > 1$ (eq. [21]) then there would be no limit to the size of the firm. At the cost of complicating the algebra, one could, however, prove our central results and, at the same time, ensure a limit to firm size by modeling "loss of control" as in Williamson (1967) or Calvo and Wellisz (1978).

agement of a firm, namely on supervision, thus gives an endogenous explanation of a number of seemingly unrelated phenomena: the pervasiveness of the practice of offering hierarchic wage differentials, inexplicable in terms of differentials in difficulty of the various tasks; the assignment of the more able individuals to the higher rungs of the ladder; and the greater responsibility given to the higher-ranking individuals.[9]

Our findings also throw a new light on the issue of the skewness of income distribution. Since the more able individuals are assigned to higher supervisory levels, and since the optimal interlevel wage differentials are greater than the inherent ability differentials, the income distribution in a hierarchic organization will be more skewed than the distribution of ability. Moreover, the high executives in the large, multilayered firms will enjoy higher salaries than the executives of "flatter" (which, in general, means smaller) organizations. The executive of a very large company is paid a very high salary not because the wage should reflect the prestige or because the large company can afford to offer large pay, but because it is optimal for a large company to hire a very able executive and to compensate him more than his sheer ability would seem to warrant.[10]

Our analysis is consistent with the fact that some individuals may have such a high preference for self-employment as to price themselves out of the hierarchic market, while others might simply be too highly qualified to be hired by an organization. There is, therefore, no inconsistency between the finding that wage hierarchies are endogenously generated and the empirical observation that many high-income individuals are not organization men.

II. Effect of Minimum Wages

Our analysis has shown that in a profit-making hierarchic organization the production and lower administrative level workers are

[9] Management science literature takes it for granted that more able individuals should be given higher posts. Wage ladders are commonly explained in terms of differentials in "responsibility," "degree of accountability," or possibility of inflicting "discretionary damage" on the firm, but no explanation is given why such differentials should be reflected in the pay (see, for instance, Benge, Burk, and Hay 1941, pp. 102 and 106; Hoge 1955, pp. 167–68; Jaques 1956; and Lydall 1968, p. 126). Williamson (1975, p. 78) also suggests that hierarchic differentials, coupled with the possibility of internal promotion, are instituted to provide a work incentive.

[10] Our results also shed some light on the question of why, in situations where there are distinct groups of labor (e.g., "native" and "expatriate" labor in developing countries or "guest workers" and "nationals" in western Europe), and where one group is considered inherently more productive than the other, the more productive group is given supervisory and administrative posts and the less productive group is assigned to production jobs.

"exploited" in the sense that they are paid less per effective labor unit than the higher-level workers. The question arises, what would happen to the pattern of employment and of quality of workers in a hierarchic organization if the lowest-rung workers' wages were raised, say, by government fiat or by union action?

The problem facing the hierarchic firm is to maximize profits subject to a given wage. In the single-layer case (recalling eqq. [4], [5], and [7]), the problem can be stated as

$$\text{Max}_{\beta_1, M_1} \pi_1 = (\beta_1 - w_1)M_1 \qquad \text{s.t.} \qquad w_1 \geq k(M_1 - 1) + H(\beta_1) \qquad (38)$$

where w_1 is given.

In contrast with the previous analysis, now the firm is a wage taker. The constraint in equation (38) has to be added to ensure that workers will not shirk all the time (recall eqq. [4] and [5]). We will first study the impact of w_1 on optimal β_1.

Since optimal β_1 will be set larger than w_1, the constraint will always be binding for, if it were not, one could increase profits by increasing M_1. We can therefore restate the problem in the form

$$\text{Max}_{\beta_1}(\beta_1 - w_1)\left[\frac{w_1 - H(\beta_1)}{k} + 1\right] \equiv \tilde{\pi}_1(w_1). \qquad (39)$$

The first-order condition for β_1 is

$$\left[\frac{w_1 - H(\beta_1)}{k} + 1\right] - \frac{H'(\beta_1)}{k}(\beta_1 - w_1) = 0, \qquad (40)$$

where the expression in brackets equals M. Hence, at optimum,

$$M_1 = (\beta_1 - w_1)\frac{H'(\beta_1)}{k} \qquad (41)$$

and

$$\tilde{\pi}_1(w_1) = \frac{(\beta_1 - w_1)^2}{k}H'(\beta_1). \qquad (42)$$

Differentiating equation (40) with respect to w_1, we get

$$\frac{1 + H'(\beta_1)}{k} > 0, \qquad (43)$$

implying the following comparative-statics result:

$$\frac{d\beta_1}{dw_1} > 0, \qquad (44)$$

which means that as the wage is raised, a profit-maximizing firm will hire better quality workers. This finding is in line with standard results, and it is confirmed by casual empiricism: the imposition of minimum wages may price low-quality workers out of the "organized" labor market and cause them to become "self-employed."

By formula (39) and the Envelope theorem,

$$\tilde{\pi}_1' = - \left[\frac{w_1 - H(\beta_1)}{k} + 1\right] + (\beta_1 - w_1)/k. \qquad (45)$$

Thus, by equations (40) and (45),

$$\tilde{\pi}_1' \gtreqless 0 \text{ as } \qquad H'(\beta_1) \lesseqgtr 1.$$

It is clear from (46) that, if the wage were such that the associated $H'(\beta_1) < 1$, the firm could increase profits by paying a higher wage and getting a better quality work force. The (unconstrained) optimum would be reached at the wage at which $H'(\beta_1) = 1$. This case was discussed in Part I of this paper. What interests us here is the case in which $H'(\beta_1) > 1$, that is, in which a minimum wage constraint would be binding. As we can readily see from (42), (44), and (46), recalling that $H'' > 0$,

$$0 < \frac{d\beta_1}{dw_1} < 1 \qquad \text{if } H'(\beta_1) \geq 1, \qquad (47)$$

from which it follows that as the minimum wage is raised, the profit per worker declines. In addition, since the constraint in (38) is binding, we get

$$\frac{dM_1}{dw_1} = \frac{1}{k}\left[1 - H'(\beta_1)\frac{d\beta_1}{dw_1}\right], \qquad (48)$$

and, by (47) and (48),

$$\frac{dM_1}{dw_1} > 0 \qquad \text{when } H'(\beta_1) = 1.^{11} \qquad (49)$$

This finding means that if, in the initial situation, the wage is optimally set by the firm, then the imposition of a minimum wage (provided that it is not too high) will actually increase employment.[12] The statement can be made in a more assertive fashion if labor is homogeneous, for in this case, as can be readily seen by making β_1 a constant in (38), as the wage increases the owner will hire more and more workers until the point at which the wage is so high that it becomes more profitable for the owner to liquidate the firm altogether and to work alone. (Recalling owner's $\beta = 1$, the latter occurs

---

[11] We are extremely thankful to an anonymous "mathematical checker" for showing us how to simplify the proof of eq. (49) and for several other editorial suggestions.
[12] This result does not necessarily hold if P_i is defined as in n. 5 or in the variable-effort case discussed in Appendix A.

when maximum profit is less than $1 =$ profit if owner were to work by himself.) In the heterogeneous labor case, higher-quality labor is substituted for lower-quality labor and maximum employment may be reached before the shutdown point. Even in this weaker form, the finding is sufficiently novel, however, as to warrant an intuitive explanation.

The key to our result is that the payment of higher wages reduces the workers' propensity to shirk and therefore reduces the optimal degree of supervision. With a given supervisory capacity, it becomes profitable to hire additional workers. However, in a heterogeneous labor market it also becomes profitable to hire workers of a higher quality. As is implied in Part I, a given wage level provides less of an incentive for workers with a higher-quality and thus a higher-opportunity cost. The employment-augmenting effect of minimum wages is less pronounced, therefore, in the case of labor market heterogeneity. Hence, it would seem that low-level workers seeking to have their wages raised through legislative or through collective action would be well advised to oppose increased efficiency. If they are successful, they might achieve (at least in the short run) a result which standard competitive analysis considers to be impossible, namely, an increase in wages and an increase in employment.[13]

The above results hinge on the assumption that there is a constant capacity to supervise. If there is one or more supervisory layers between the owner and the production workers, the owner may react to the minimum wage increase not by hiring more workers but by cutting down on the number or on the quality of the supervisory staff. To see what are the minimum wage effects in the more general situation, we now turn to the two-layer case.

The problem of profit maximization of a two-layer firm subject to a given w_1, that is, the wage of the lowest-layer workers, can be stated as

$$\underset{\beta_i, M_i, w_i|_{i=1,2}}{\text{Max }} \pi_2 = (\beta_1 - w_1)M_1 - w_2 M_2, \tag{50}$$

subject to $w_2 = (M_2 - 1)k + H(\beta_2)$ and $w_1 \geq (M_1/\beta_2 M_2 - 1)k + H(\beta_1)$, where w_1 is given. The constraint involving w_2 is the same we discussed in Part 1, whereas that in w_1 is similar to the one in (38) and, as argued above, it will always be binding.

---

[13] This is essentially a partial equilibrium result that could, however, be extended to a general equilibrium proposition in a surplus-labor economy of the type discussed in Appendix B and in Calvo (1977). The result will look more familiar to the reader once he notices that due to the nature of the supervision process, increasing employment, M, requires also increasing wage, w_1. Thus, although the firm is a perfect competitor, it behaves *as if* it faced an upward-sloping labor supply, i.e., *as if* it were a monopsonist in the labor market. In situations like that, it is well known that the imposition of a minimum wage (thus creating a "flat" section on the labor supply function) may be conducive to higher levels of employment and wages.

Also, by the sort of argument that ought to be familiar to us by now, equation (50) is equivalent to

$$\underset{\beta_2, M_2, w_2}{\text{Max}} \ \tilde{\pi}_1(w_1)\beta_2 M_2 - w_2 M_2, \tag{51}$$

subject to $w_2 = (M_2 - 1)k + H(\beta_2)$, which, in turn, is equivalent to

$$\underset{\beta_2, M_2}{\text{Max}} \ \{\tilde{\pi}_1(w_1)\beta_2 - [(M_2 - 1)k + H(\beta_2)]\}M_2. \tag{52}$$

Thus, at optimum,

$$\tilde{\pi}_1(w_1) = H'(\beta_2), \tag{53}$$

and, therefore, recalling equation (46) and that $H'' > 0$,

$$\frac{d\beta_2}{dw_1} \leq 0 \qquad \text{if } H'(\beta_1) \geq 1, \tag{54}$$

which means that the optimal quality of supervisors falls as the (binding) minimum wage of the supervisees is increased. Since, by our previous results, the quality of the workers affected by the minimum wage improves, this means that the quality differential between supervisors and supervisees is narrowed.

We shall now show that an increase in the minimum wage of the production workers leads to a reduction in the number of supervisory personnel. As can easily be shown, optimal M_2 satisfies

$$M_2 = [\tilde{\pi}_1(w_1) \beta_2 + k - H(\beta_2)]/2k, \tag{55}$$

and by (46), (54), and (55),

$$\frac{dM_2}{dw_1} \leq 0 \qquad \text{when } H'(\beta_1) \geq 1, \tag{56}$$

where β_1 is the optimal value of that variable, given w_1. Thus, in the relevant range the number (as well as the quality) of the supervisors falls as the minimum wage of workers is raised. Notice also that since the optimal number of workers per effective supervisor is equal to M_1 as determined in the one-layer situation and, by (54) and (56), that

$$\frac{d\beta_2 M_2}{dw_1} = 0 \qquad \text{when } H'(\beta_1) = 1, \tag{57}$$

it follows, recalling (49), that in the two-layer case,

$$\frac{dM_1}{dw_1} > 0 \qquad \text{when } H'(\beta_1) = 1. \tag{58}$$

So, as in the one-layer case, if the minimum wage for workers is not set "too high," its imposition will increase lowest-level employment. Furthermore, by (56) and (58), it follows that there exists a neighborhood of the unconstrained w, such that the imposition of a binding minimum wage increases total employment (supervisors plus supervisees). The conclusion holds a fortiori if β_1 is not allowed to vary.

The analysis of the two-layer hierarchic organization thus clearly reveals the nature of the conflict between the lower-level and the higher-level employees. An increase in the minimum wage of the lower-level employees leads to a reduction in the qualifications required from the higher-level employees, to a reduction of their wage, and to a reduction in their number. Nor is union action in defense of the quality requirements likely to be of much help to the higher-level employees. For suppose that β_1 and β_2 are held constant. Optimal w_2 (recall [4'] and also that $1/P_2 = M_2$) satisfies

$$w_2 = (M_2 - 1)k + h. \tag{59}$$

Hence, it easily follows from equations (55) and (59) that

$$\frac{dM_2}{dw_1} < 0 \quad \text{and} \quad \frac{dw_2}{dw_1} < 0. \tag{60}$$

Thus, even an action to maintain the supervisors' quality will not protect their wages or their numbers.

As a final point, notice that the situation would be quite different if supervisors, instead of workers, were covered by a (binding) minimum wage. For it is easy to see that optimal w_1, $M_1/M_2\beta_2$, and β_1 would remain the same, which means that profit per effective supervisor, π_1^*, will be unchanged; on the other hand, raising w_2 over the unrestricted solution will have the same qualitative impact on M_2 and β_2 as w_1 had on M_1 and β_1 in the one-layer case analyzed at the outset of this section. So β_2 will rise and, if the increase in w_2 is small enough, the number of supervisors, M_2, will also rise. Since, as argued above, $M_1/\beta_2 M_2$ remains constant, this implies that employment of workers, M_1, will increase. The same results hold even when β_2 is not allowed to change.

Appendix A
The Variable Effort Case

We shall now abandon the assumption that workers either shirk all the time or work with full efficiency, and we shall assume instead that work can be carried out at varying intensities.

We assume that

$$e_i = f\left(\frac{1}{P_i}, w_i, \beta_i\right), \tag{A1}$$

where e_i stands for effort of ith-level workers ($e_i \leq 1$) and the other variables have the same interpretation as in the text. We assume the degree of supervision depends upon (1) the supervisor/supervisee ratio, (2) the quality of supervisors, and (3) their effort. More specifically,

$$P_i = \text{Min } (e_{i+1}\beta_{i+1}M_{i+1}/M_i, 1). \tag{A2}$$

In what follows we just look at situations where one is not binding in (A2).

Let the profit function in a one-layer firm be represented by

$$\pi_1 = e_1\beta_1 M_1 - w_1 M_1. \tag{A3}$$

This corresponds to the case where workers get the full wage during the period and punishment takes the form of dismissal at the end of the period. Assuming that e and β of the owner are equal to unity, equations (A1–A3) imply that

$$\pi_1 = [f(M_1, w_1, \beta_1)\beta_1 - w_1]M_1; \tag{A4}$$

thus,

$$\pi_1^* \equiv \underset{M_1,w_1,\beta_1}{\text{Max}} \ \pi_1. \tag{A5}$$

Let us define

$$x(M, w) \equiv \underset{\beta}{\text{Max}} f(M, w, \beta)\beta; \tag{A6}$$

in view of (A4), $x(M, w)$ is the optimal labor service per worker, given M and w. Thus,

$$\omega(M, w) \equiv w/x(M, w), \tag{A7}$$

which is the optimal wage per effective work, given M and w. Consequently, (A5) can be restated as follows:

$$\pi_1^* \equiv \underset{M_1,w_1}{\text{Max}} \ [1 - \omega(M_1,w_1)]x(M_1,w_1)M_1. \tag{A5'}$$

For the two-layer case, we get

$$\pi_2 = e_1\beta_1 M_1 - w_2 M_2 - w_1 M_1 \tag{A8}$$

and

$$\pi_2^* \equiv \underset{M_i,w_i,\beta_i|i=1,2}{\text{Max}} \ \pi_2. \tag{A9}$$

Therefore, applying an argument similar to the one given in Part I, we get

$$\pi_2^* = \underset{M_2,w_2}{\text{Max}} \ [\pi_1^* x(M_2,w_2) - w_2]M_2, \tag{A10}$$

or, recalling equation (A7),

$$\pi_2^* = \underset{M_2,w_2}{\text{Max}} \ [\pi_1^* - \omega(M_2,w_2)]x(M_2,w_2)M_2. \tag{A10'}$$

Let us denote by $[\hat{M}(\alpha), \hat{w}(\alpha)]$ the optimal values of M and w for (A5') when $\alpha = 1$, and for (A10') when $\alpha = \pi_1^*$. As in the text, we assume

$$\pi_1^* > 1, \tag{A11}$$

which corresponds to the case where the firm prefers a two-layer over a one-layer arrrangement. Assuming that optimal solutions are different from each other, we must have, recalling (A5') and (A10'),

$\{\pi_1^* - \omega[\hat{M}(\pi_1^*), \hat{w}(\pi_1^*)]\}x[\hat{M}(\pi_1^*), \hat{w}(\pi_1^*)]\hat{M}(\pi_1^*)$

$$> \{\pi_1^* - \omega[\hat{M}(1), \hat{w}(1)]\}x[\hat{M}(1), \hat{w}(1)]\hat{M}(1) \quad (A12)$$

and

$\{1 - \omega[\hat{M}(\pi_1^*), \hat{w}(\pi_1^*)]\}x[\hat{M}(\pi_1^*), \hat{w}(\pi_1^*)]\hat{M}(\pi_1^*)$

$$< \{1 - \omega[\hat{M}(1), \hat{w}(1)]\}x[\hat{M}(1), \hat{w}(1)]\hat{M}(1). \quad (A13)$$

Subtracting (A13) from (A12) and recalling (A11), it follows that

$$x[\hat{M}(\pi_1^*), \hat{w}(\pi_1^*)]\hat{M}(\pi_1^*) > x[\hat{M}(1), \hat{w}(1)]\hat{M}(1), \quad (A14)$$

which corresponds to equation (36). In addition, by (A13) and (A14),

$$\omega[\hat{M}(\pi_1^*), \hat{w}(\pi_1^*)] > \omega[\hat{M}(1), \hat{w}(1)], \quad (A15)$$

which corresponds to equation (37).

Therefore, by (A14) and (A15), one can extend to this case the proposition that the optimum wage per effective work and the optimum effective supervisee/effective supervisor ratio increase as one moves toward the apex of the hierarchical pyramid. However, the optimal pattern of quality, effort, and supervisee/effective supervisor ratio is ambiguous unless further restrictions are imposed on the relevant functions. A complete taxonomy of cases is beyond the scope of this paper. It is worth pointing out, however, that since the economy studied in the text is a special case of the present one, there must exist a "neighborhood" of economies where *all* the propositions of the text hold true.

Appendix B

Convexity of H(·)

We shall now briefly comment on the assumption $H'' > 0$. As noted before, if $H'' \leq 0$ firms will employ only the best-qualified workers and, in this case, for the maximum with respect to β to be well defined, we have to constrain the domain of H to be some finite interval $(0, \bar{\beta})$, $\bar{\beta} > 0$, where $\bar{\beta}$ stands for the productivity of the best workers. If $\bar{\beta}$-type workers are the only ones employed by firms, all our previous results hold true except, of course, the ones concerning quality differentials across layers. Thus, one can still show that supervisors will be paid higher wages than supervisees (even when they now would be of the same quality), and that a minimum wage may increase employment of the bottom-layer workers at the cost of reducing the wage and employment of supervisors.

The convexity of $H(\cdot)$ could be justified on the basis of general equilibrium considerations. To illustrate this fact, we will consider the case where if a worker gets fired his option is to become self-employed or remain idle. We will assume, in order not to prejudge the issue, that, as in the firms' sector, the self-employment sector requires labor alone and produces the same homogeneous output with constant returns to scale. A type-β individual working by himself produces $b\beta$ units of output, where b is some positive constant. Therefore, recalling Assumption E, the utility of a type-β individual if he is not employed by a firm, $H(\cdot)$, satisfies

$$H(\beta) = \text{Max } (k, b\beta), \quad (B1)$$

where, as before, k is the utility of remaining idle. Let us define β_c by the condition $k = b\beta_c$; therefore, if $\beta < \beta_c$, the individual will prefer to remain inactive,[14] and if $\beta \geq \beta_c$, he either will prefer to work by himself or will be indifferent between these two courses of action. But, more important for our present purpose, it follows that

$$H(\beta) = k, \qquad \text{for } 0 \leq \beta \leq \beta_c$$
$$= b\beta, \qquad \text{for } \beta_c < \beta \leq \bar{\beta}. \tag{B2}$$

Thus, function H will be flat at level k from zero to β_c and then will start rising at the rate b. Hence, H is convex over its entire domain and exhibits strict convexity when one takes a point to the left and another to the right of β_c. This, of course, stops short of justifying $H'' > 0$, or its existence everywhere, but it is enough for proving slightly weaker versions of the propositions derived in the previous sections.

So, for instance, if the firms' demand in the labor market is not constrained by supply, it is easy to show that (1) firms will choose only types β_c or $\bar{\beta}$, (2) supervisors will never be of inferior quality than supervisees, and (3) there are instances where supervisors are of type $\bar{\beta}$ and supervisees of type β_c. Given the number of firms, labor supply can be ensured to be greater than demand by setting the supply of β_c and $\bar{\beta}$ types sufficiently large.[15]

In more interesting models, $H(\beta)$ will reflect employment opportunities in other firms adjusted by the probability of employment, search costs, etc. Although we have every reason to believe that these elements will tend to impose a greater degree of convexity into the general equilibrium H function, a more definite statement will have to await further research.

References

Becker, G. S., and Stigler, G. "Law Enforcement and Compensation of Enforcers." *J. Legal Studies* 3, no. 1 (January 1974): 1–18.

Benge, E. J.; Burk, S. L. H.; and Hay, E. N. *Manual of Job Evaluation.* New York and London: Harper & Brothers, 1941.

Calvo, G. A. "Supervision, and Utility and Wage Differentials across Firms." Mimeographed. Columbia Univ., Economics Workshops, April 1977 (revised July 1977).

Calvo, G. A., and Wellisz, S. "Supervision, Loss of Control, and the Optimum Size of the Firm." *J.P.E.* 86, no. 5 (October 1978): 943–52.

Hoge, R. H. "Evaluating Executive Jobs." *Personnel J.* 34, no. 5 (October 1955): 166–71.

Jaques, E. *Measurement of Responsibility: A Study of Work, Payment and Individual Capacity.* Cambridge, Mass.: Harvard Univ. Press, 1956.

Lydall, H. F. *The Structure of Earnings.* Oxford: Clarendon, 1968.

Mayer, T. "The Distribution of Ability and Earnings." *Rev. Econ. and Statis.* 42, no. 2 (May 1960): 189–95.

Simon, H. A. "The Compensation of Executives." *Sociometry* 20, no. 1 (March 1957): 32–35.

Williamson, O. E. "Hierarchical Control and Optimum Firm Size." *J.P.E.* 75, no. 2 (April 1967): 123–38.

———. *Markets and Hierarchies: Analysis and Antitrust Implications.* New York: Free Press, 1975.

[14] The implications are essentially the same in the more plausible setup where workers get unemployment compensation if they remain idle.

[15] For a similar procedure in the case of homogeneous labor, see Calvo (1977).

INCENTIVES, PRODUCTIVITY, AND LABOR CONTRACTS*

Edward P. Lazear and Robert L. Moore

The relationship between age-earnings profiles and worker incentives is examined by contrasting wage and salary workers with the self-employed. It is argued that the steepness of wage and salary workers' age-earnings profiles reflects the desire to provide work incentives to those workers. Since self-employed workers do not face this agency problem, they are used as a benchmark to gauge productivity. Empirical support of the proposition is provided, and the effects of human capital accumulation are separated empirically from incentive effects. The most important conclusion is that under some strong assumptions, most of the slope in age-earnings profiles is accounted for by the desire to provide incentives, rather than by on-the-job training.

I. Introduction

Attention has been focused recently on the notion that worker productivity is not independent of the compensation scheme. Starting with early papers by Johnson [1950], Cheung [1969], and Ross [1973], a recurring theme of the agency literature is that a divergence of interests between principal and agent causes output to depend upon the contingent nature of compensation. A seemingly unrelated empirical phenomenon has also been observed (see Wolpin [1974] and Fuchs [1981]). That is that age-earnings profiles for self-employed are flatter than those for otherwise similar wage and salary workers. This is surprising, since investment in physical capital depresses observed wages for the young self-employed, while returns to that investment which accrue to the old, raise observed wages. Both tend to steepen age-earnings profiles for self-employed vis-à-vis wage and salary workers.

A major difference between self-employment and work for others is that agency problems are unimportant in self-employment. The fact that the owner and worker are the same individual eliminates any disharmony of interests. It is this aspect of the institutional arrangement that will be exploited to explain the apparent empirical anomaly and to make statements about the empirical relationship between the shape of the age-earnings profile and the shape of the age-productivity profile for the typical wage and salary worker.

More specifically, this paper discusses the way in which worker

*We are indebted to Barry Nalebuff for providing many insightful comments on an earlier draft. This research was supported by the National Science Foundation.

effort varies with contractual arrangements and the shape of the workers' age-earnings profile. It is argued that the use of an upward sloping age-earnings profile generates effort incentives which are absent when profiles are flat. By increasing the slopes of the age-earnings profile, employers induce their employees to work harder, raising the present value of their employees' lifetime earnings. Self-employment requires no internal incentive mechanisms and as such provides a test of this proposition. The main prediction and finding is that the present value of lifetime earnings rises more with the slope of the age-earnings profile for wage and salary workers than for their self-employed counterparts, presumably reflecting incentives effects.

The model leading to this argument was developed elsewhere [Lazear, 1979, 1981] and is summarized in Section II. It is then tested using data from the March 1978 Current Population Survey. The results in Section III show a definite consistency between the theory and the data: as predicted, steeper profiles imply a larger increment to lifetime wealth for wage and salary workers than for the self-employed. By comparing self-employed workers to their wage and salary counterparts, one can estimate the amount of wealth generated by upward sloping profiles that result from this incentive mechanism as opposed to a more traditional human capital explanation. If some strong assumptions are made, one concludes that most of the slope of the age-earnings profile reflects incentive-based wealth rather than human capital accumulation through on-the-job training.

II. The Model

The theme of this analysis is that the shape of the age-earnings profile and more generally, the structure of compensation, affects the productivity of workers. In this section the goal is to construct a model that can be used to determine that relationship empirically.

First, consider a worker employed by a firm that buys labor in a competitive factor market. As argued elsewhere [Lazear, 1979, 1981], steepening the age-earnings profile reduces the worker's incentive to shirk and thereby increases his productivity. At the same time, however, a steeper profile means that the employer is more likely to renege on the implicit contract because the gains to terminating a worker midstream are larger. The efficient contract is the one that maximizes expected utility, net of firm and worker cheating. This reduces to minimizing the sum of firm and worker cheating.

Although this is spelled out in detail in Lazear [1979, 1981], the following simple structure illustrates the tradeoff.

Suppose that a worker lives two periods, $t = 1, 2$. He can work at full effort, producing V dollars of output each period, or he can shirk, in which case output is $V - C$ each period. The value of shirking to workers (thought of as leisure) is $\theta_i \sim f(\theta_i)$ across workers. Assume that if a worker shirks in period 1, he is terminated with certainty before period 2.[1] Let the discount rate be zero and assume that the alternative use of the worker's time has value $\overline{W}$. If there were no other possibility of termination, the worker's period 1 shirking rule would be

$$\text{Shirk if } \theta_i > W_2 - \overline{W}.$$

Similarly, the firm may be dishonest by promising to employ the worker over two periods, but terminating him after one. If W_2 exceeds the worker's output, then the firm has an incentive to do this. To the extent that information about the firm's behavior this period is at least partially transmitted to the next generation or that morale problems are created by such action, a cost may be imposed on the firm. Let the cost of breaking the contract be $u_j \sim g(u_j)$ across firms. In the absence of a pension or other enforcement device, all workers will shirk with certainty in period 2 because retirement follows anyway.[2] Thus, the firm's cheating rule is to violate the implicit contract by terminating the worker after period 1 if

$$\mu_i < W_2 - (V - C).$$

Assume that firms and workers know the distributions $f(\theta)$ and $g(u)$, but that only the worker knows the exact value of his θ_i and only the firm knows the exact value of u_i. All workers receive W_1 in period 1. $F(\theta)$ and $G(u)$ are the distribution functions of θ and u. Given the possibility that the firm may fire the worker, the worker's shirking rule becomes

(1) $\qquad \text{Shirk iff } \theta > (W_2 - \overline{W})[1 - G(W_2 - (V - C))],$

since the worker is fired if $\mu < W_2 - (V - C)$. We can therefore define a critical level of θ, $\overline{\theta}$, as

---

1. Making the probability of termination less than one does not alter the basic story. Piece rates are ruled out here by assuming that it is too costly to monitor the amount of shirking.
2. This is a detail. Workers could be prevented from shirking in the last period by paying a large pension, contingent upon performance, but the basic point will not be affected.

(2) $\bar{\theta} = (W_2 - \overline{W})[1 - G(W_2 - (V - C))].$

The problem for the firm is to maximize the worker's expected wealth (assuming initially that workers are risk-neutral) subject to the zero profit constraint. The firm wishes to select W_1, W_2 to maximize

(3)   Expected Wealth $= W_1 + F(\bar{\theta})[1 - G(W_2 - (V - C))]\,W_2$

$$+ F(\bar{\theta})\,G(W_2 - (V - C))\,\overline{W}$$

$$+ (1 - F(\bar{\theta}))\,\overline{W} + \int_{\bar{\theta}}^{\infty} \theta f(\theta)\,d\theta \equiv P^*,$$

subject to the zero profit constraint that expected payout equals expected product:[3]

(4) $W_1 + F(\bar{\theta})[1 - G(W_2 - (V - C))]\,W_2$

$$= V + F(\bar{\theta})[1 - G(W_2 - (V - C))](V - C) - [1 - F(\bar{\theta})]C.$$

Substituting (2) and (4) into (3) and differentiating yields the first-order conditions for maximization:

(5a) $-(FG')(V - C - \overline{W}) + (F')$

$$\times \{(1 - G)(V - C - \overline{W}) + C - \bar{\theta}\}\,\theta' = 0.$$

(5b) $\theta' = 1 - G - (G')(W_2 - \overline{W}).$

(5c) $W_1 + F(\bar{\theta})[1 - G(W_2 - (V - C))]\,W_2$

$$= V + F(\bar{\theta})[1 - G(W_2 - (V - C))](V - C) - [1 - F(\bar{\theta})]C.$$

Maximization of (3) amounts to choosing W_2 so as to trade off optimally the reduction in worker shirking that results from a higher W_2 (and consequently lower W_1) against the increase in firm defaults on labor contracts inspired by higher W_2. This is the essence of (5a). There, increases in W_2 generally raise $\bar{\theta}$, which deters shirking by workers. This is captured by the second term of (5a). The first term of (5a) is the effect that increasing the second-period wage has on encouraging the firm to default on its workers. The first term is clearly negative, since $V - C > \overline{W}$ in order for it to be efficient to employ the worker during period 2. The sign of second term is determined by the sign of θ'. Under most circumstances, it is positive, since $\theta' > 0$. Then an increase in W_2 increases expected output via the deterrence of shirking.

3. Assume that the realization θ_i and μ_j are revealed to the worker and firm, respectively, only after period 1 has begun so that no problems of adverse selection arise.

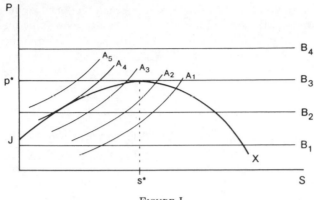

FIGURE I

When $\theta' < 0$, no interior solution exists (at least locally). The reason is that an increase in W_2 so increases the probability that the firm defaults in period 2 that it pays the worker to beat the firm to it. Under those circumstances, increases in W_2 do not deter cheating, and the only equilibrium is to pay $V - C$ in each period. If $\overline{W} > V - C$, then no work occurs. If $\overline{W} < V - C$, then work occurs at low effort levels.

The interesting case for our analysis is the one where $\overline{W} < V - C$ and $\theta' > 0$, which we conjecture is the most common situation. Here, the compensation scheme pays workers low wages in period 1 and high wages in period 2 relative to marginal product.[4]

This scheme results in an age-earnings profile that pays workers less than their VMP in period 1 and more than their expected VMP in period 2. Doing so raises lifetime VMP and therefore worker's expected utility.[5] Also, the relationship between the payment that the worker receives from the firm and the promised slope of the age-earnings profile will first rise and then, after the optimum slope is reached, decline as shown in Figure I.

---

4. Note that if $V > \overline{W} > V - C$, then work should occur at most only during the first period because it is certain that output is only $V - C$ in period 2. But if no period 2 exists, then all workers shirk in period 1. Thus, a contingent "pension" that is paid upon completion of work is required. Since V is zero, employers consider the pension size when deciding to default. As the result, it will not be optimal in general to deter all worker shirking through high pensions. Workers who shirk, work inefficiently, since $V - C < \overline{W}$. Since they do not know θ in advance, it will still pay all workers to work if expected payment (which equals expected marginal product) exceeds $\overline{W}$ or if

$$F(\overline{\theta}) V + [1 - F(\overline{\theta})](V - C) > \overline{W}.$$

In many cases, this condition will be met.

5. Profiles that pay more than VMP in period 1 and less than VMP in period 2 are not viable without slavery. I.e., another firm could always offer the worker $V - C$ in period 2.

Unfortunately, the data do not directly report the promised profile. Instead they provide us with information on some weighted average of wages paid when the firm does not default and those received if the firm does default. Specifically, if $\tilde{W}_2$ is the promised wage in period 2 and $\overline{W}$ is the wage received in period 2 if the firm defaults, then W_2, the observed wage, is defined as

(6) $W_2 \equiv [1 - G(\tilde{W}_2 - (V - C))]\, \tilde{W}_2 + [G(\tilde{W}_2 - (V - C))]\, \overline{W}.$

The inverted U-shaped relationship shown in Figure I holds for promised wages. If slope S is defined in terms of observed wage, as W_2/W_1 rather than $\tilde{W}_2/W_1$, it is necessary to examine the relationship between W_2 and $\tilde{W}_2$. Differentiating (6), one obtains

(7) $$\frac{dW_2}{d\tilde{W}_2} = 1 - G - (G')(\tilde{W}_2 - \overline{W}) < 1.$$

This is not always positive. However, it is certain that

$$\lim_{\tilde{W}_2 \to \overline{W}} \frac{dW_2}{d\tilde{W}_2} = 1,$$

since $G(0) = 0$ and $(V - C) > \overline{W}$, for there to be efficient employment.[6]

This implies at least that the relationship between slope of the observed profile and present value will start out positive. It may or may not be inverted U-shaped, depending upon (7), but it is only the positive slope that is crucial to what follows. Negatively sloped segments will be dominated as the result of worker choice.

This analysis suggests that some of the slope associated with the age-earnings profile reflects incentive generation rather than the accumulation of skills over the lifetime. In what follows, a market equilibrium is described and used to provide some initial estimates of this effect.

Market Equilibrium

Consider a worker's choice, given the available slope–present value tradeoff shown in Figure I, curve JX. If the worker were risk-neutral and if he faced the same discount rate as the firm, then the choice is the contract that offers (S^*, P^*) in Figure I. Although these conditions may hold for some workers, there is no reason to believe that they will hold for all.

6. As is always the case when second derivatives are not strictly negative, there may be discrete jumps over values of S so that similar people choose very different S's. Whether or not these possibilities are realized depends upon the actual parameters of utility, f and g functions.

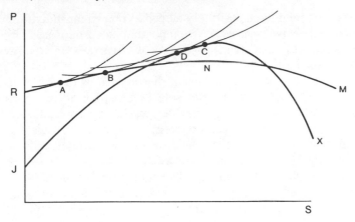

FIGURE II

First, workers with discount rates higher than the one used for computation of present value in Figure I, have positively sloped indifference curves, as shown for A in Figure II. That is, in order to induce those workers to accept steeper profiles, higher present values, as calculated using the relatively low discount rate, must be offered.[7]

Alternatively, workers may have the same discount rate as the firm, but may be risk-averse. Under these circumstances, indiffer-

---

7. Formally, if the firm has discount rate P, then constant present value to the firm implies that

(7.1) $$dPV = dW_1 + dW_2/(1 + \rho) = 0.$$

Defining slope $S \equiv W_2/W_1$ allows (7.1) to be rewritten as

(7.2) $$0 = dW_1 + \frac{dW_1}{1 + \rho}\left(S - W_1\left(\frac{W_2}{W_1^2}\right)\right) + \frac{W_1}{1 + \rho}dS \quad \text{or} \quad dW_1 = \frac{-W_1}{1 + \rho}dS$$

for present value to remain constant.

The risk-neutral worker's utility function is

(7.3) $$U = W_1 + W_2/(1 + r) = W_1[(1 + S)/(1 + r)],$$

where r is the worker's discount rate. This implies that

$$dU = dW_1 + \frac{dW_1}{1 + r}\left(S - W_1\left(\frac{W_2}{W_1^2}\right)\right) + \frac{W_1\,dS}{1 + r} = dW_1 + \frac{W_1\,dS}{1 + r}.$$

Changing slope in a way that preserves present value requires that (7.3) hold, so substituting (7.3) into (7.4), one obtains

$$dU = W_1\,dS\,(1/(1 + r) - 1/(1 + \rho)) < 0$$

if $\rho < r$. Therefore, utility falls in S for workers whose discount rate exceeds the firm's rate ρ. Since utility must be increasing in present value for a given slope, indifference curves that trade off present value against slope of the profile are positively sloped.

ence curves tend to be positively sloped as shown for individual A in Figure II because increases in slope that keep expected present value constant increase the probability of a firm default. Risk-averse workers dislike this.[8]

For reasons of either different discount rates or risk aversion, the optimal contract is one that selects a slope less than S^* and a present value less than P^*. Further, workers with relatively high discount rates or with greater aversion to risk will select $[S, P]$ combinations that lie closer to the J, while low discount, risk-neutral workers select combinations near $[S^*, P^*]$.

If all workers were employed as agents by firm owners as principals, then we would expect workers to select some point along the opportunity locus. Plotting points by occupation or industry of average slope of age-earnings profiles against average present value received in that occupation or industry would trace out (at least part of) opportunity locus JX.

The opportunity set JX may be upward sloping either because steeper slopes give workers incentives to exert effort or because

---

8. To preserve expected present value shown on the vertical axis of Figure I, we require that (with no discounting)

$$(8.1) \qquad\qquad K = W_1 + W_2$$

or

$$W_1 = K/(1 + S) \qquad \text{and} \qquad W_2 = KS/(1 + S), \qquad \text{since} \qquad S \equiv W_2/W_1,$$

where W_2 is defined as expected or observed payment in period 2. If promised wages are $\bar{W}_2$, then $1 - G(\bar{W}_2 - (V - C))$ of the workers received the promised $\bar{W}_2$, and $G(\bar{W}_2 - (V - C))$ receive the alternative wage $\overline{W}$, which results when the contract is violated. Expected utility is

$$(8.2) \qquad E(U) = U(W_1) + [1 - G(\bar{W}_2 - (V - C))] U(\bar{W}_2) + G(\bar{W}_2 - (V - C)) U(\overline{W}),$$

where $U' > 0$, $U'' < 0$.

Differentiating (8.2) with respect to S gives

$$(8.3) \qquad \frac{\partial U}{\partial S} = U'(W_1)\frac{\partial W_1}{\partial S} + (1 - G) U'(\bar{W}_2)\frac{\partial \bar{W}_2}{\partial W_2} \cdot \frac{\partial W_2}{\partial S}$$

$$+ (G')(U(\overline{W}) - U(\bar{W}_2))\frac{\partial \bar{W}_2}{\partial W_2} \cdot \frac{\partial W_2}{\partial S}.$$

From (8.1), $\partial W_1/\partial S = -K/(1 + S)^2$, and $\partial W_2/\partial S = K/(1 + S)^2$ so that (8.3) can be rewritten as

$$(8.4) \qquad \frac{\partial U}{\partial S} = \frac{K}{(1 + S)^2}\left[U'(\bar{W}_2)(1 - G)\frac{\partial \bar{W}_2}{\partial W_2} - U'(W_1)\right]$$

$$+ (G')[U(\overline{W}) - (\bar{W}_2)]\frac{K}{(1 + S)^2}\frac{\partial \bar{W}_2}{\partial W_2}.$$

If promised $\bar{W}_2$ were observed, so that $\partial \bar{W}_2/\partial W_2 = 1$, the expression in (8.4) would be steep slopes reflect investment in on-the-job training that carries with it higher wealth levels. The key to disentangling the two is the examination of self-employed workers.

Self-employment has the advantage that less monitoring is necessary. In the extreme case, where a worker employs himself in a one-man firm, all the returns to effort are captured by the worker so no shirking or default problem exists. The disadvantages may be many. The division of labor may be limited so that an individual who has a comparative disadvantage at being an entrepreneur must still undertake some of this activity. Self-employment may not be the most efficient firm type for raising capital. As such, the scale of plant may be less than optimal.

If all workers had the same entrepreneurial talent, then the situation within one occupation would be as shown in Figure II. Curve RM is the set of opportunities in self-employment, and JX is the set as a wage and salary worker. The most risk-averse or high discount rate workers select self-employment with investment return combinations shown by points A and B. The least risk averse or those with lowest time preference choose to work as wage or salaried workers with contracts shown by C and D. Present value initially increases more rapidly with S for wage and salaried workers because in addition to human capital reflected by higher S, less

---

negative because $U'(\tilde{W}_2) < U'(W_1)$, by concavity $(1 - G) < 1$, and $U(\overline{W}) < U(\tilde{W}_2)$. This implies that utility decreases in S or that indifference curves are positively sloped.

Unfortunately, $\tilde{W}_2$ is not observed, and from the definition of W_2,

(8.5)
$$\frac{\partial \tilde{W}_2}{\partial W_2} = [1 - G - (G')(\tilde{W}_2 - \overline{W})]^{-1}.$$

Substitution of (8.5) into (8.4) does not affect the second term on the right-hand side, but as long as $\partial \tilde{W}_2/\partial W_2 > 0$, it does affect the first term even for $\partial \tilde{W}_2/\partial W_2 > 0$. Since $1 - G > 1 - G - G'(\tilde{W}_2 - \overline{W})$, $(1 - G)\partial \tilde{W}_2/\partial W_2 > 1$, so $U'(\tilde{W}_2) < U'(W_1)$ is not sufficient. However, *as long as G' is small* (i.e., the distribution of firm default costs is dispersed) or if $(W_2 - \overline{W})$ is small, then $\partial U/\partial S < 0$. It is certainly true that

$$\lim_{W_2 \to \overline{W}} \frac{\partial U}{\partial S} < 0$$

or that

$$\lim_{S \to \overline{W}/\overline{w}_1} \frac{\partial U}{\partial S} = \lim_{S \to \frac{\overline{W}(1+S)}{K}} \frac{\partial U}{\partial S} < 0.$$

Therefore, at least initially, it is certain that indifference curves for observed present value and observed slope are positively sloped. In those regions where G' is large, a local interior solution may not exist. This is related to the earlier situation where $\theta' < 0$ so that no nonshirking equilibrium exists.

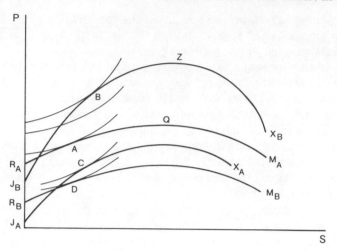

FIGURE III

shirking occurs as the result of higher S. If RM were above JX, then all workers would opt for self-employment. Further, no self-employed workers, except by mistake, should select strategies corresponding to segment NM.[9]

It seems counterintuitive that the most risk-averse go into self-employment, while the least risk-averse become wage and salary workers. This, in part, is the result of the assumption that all workers have equal entrepreneurial ability. Instead, consider two types of workers. Type A has a comparative advantage in entrepreneurship, while B is relatively more productive in a large organization as an employee. Figure III represents the situation.

Types A and B have the same preferences toward risk and same discount rates. However, type A chooses self-employment at point A, which dominates C, the best *he* could do if he were to work as a wage and salary worker. Type B chooses wage and salary at point B, which dominates D, the best he could do if he were to work in self-employment.

If we allow preferences to vary, but maintain two basic firm structures, then we shall tend to fill in $R_A M_A$ and $J_B X_B$. This relationship is estimated in the next section. Under some assumptions, discussed below, the differences in the slope of $J_B X_B$ and $R_A M_A$ is a measure of the use of profile steepness to provide incentives. Since self-employed workers need not provide incentives for themselves,

---

9. The inverted U-shape reflects that an optimal level of investment in human capital (measured by slope) exists.

the slopes of their profiles reflect investment only. Wage and salaried workers have a positive relationship between slope and present value for investment and incentive reasons.

III. EMPIRICAL ANALYSIS

The Current Population Survey (CPS) for 1978 was used to provide evidence on the issues outlined in the model section. The data contain information on 155,546 individuals. From this sample a subsample of 11,987 individuals was drawn to meet the following criteria: individuals are male nongovernment workers with some income reported during the year 1977. They also worked at least thirty weeks that year, for at least thirty-five hours per week, and were between the ages of twenty and sixty-five.

The sample was then split into workers who reported themselves as self-employed (1,795) and those who reported themselves as wage and salary workers (10,192).[10] Appendix A contains means and standard errors for the relevant variables for these groups.

To estimate the relationships discussed in the earlier part of the analysis, it was first necessary to obtain slope–present value combinations. The sample was split into categories by occupation and self-employed status and wage-experience relationships were estimated for each of these groups. The general form of the relationship estimated for each occupation by self-employment–wage and salary status was

$$(8) \quad \ln WAGE = \alpha_0 + \alpha_1(SCHOOL) + \alpha_2(EXPERIENCE) + \epsilon,$$

where $WAGE$ is the hourly wage rate, $SCHOOL$ is the highest grade of schooling completed, and $EXPERIENCE$ is defined as $AGE - SCHOOL - 6$. The results are presented in Appendix B.[11]

Lifetime wealth in an occupation i is calculated as

$$(9) \quad P_i = 2000 \sum_{t=0}^{45} \left\{ \frac{\exp\left[\alpha_0 + \alpha_1 \overline{SCHOOL}_i + \alpha_2 t\right]}{(1 + r)^t} \right\},$$

10. Self-employed were those who earned zero income through wages and salaries and reported their current status as "self-employed." For wage and salary workers, only either those who had one employer or those whose current employer was in the same occupation as his employer in the previously longest held job were included.

11. This form follows Mincer. There are other variables that other researchers sometimes use in estimating this relationship: for example, race, region, and urban-rural dummy variables, as well as experience squared. All the regressions in Appendix B were also estimated using these variables. The results reported later in Table I were not sensitive to the particular form of wage regression (equation (11)), and the conclusions reported later held whether or not these additional variables were included. The coefficient on experience was not significantly different, regardless of the form of the wage regression.

where $\overline{SCHOOL_i}$ is the mean level of schooling in occupation i and r is the discount factor. Two thousand hours are used as a typical work year. (This is irrelevant if individuals can choose the number of hours worked. It merely scales up the numbers to more familiar proportions but the wage rate is the relevant variable.) P_i is the wealth value for a typical individual who enters occupation i at age 20 and works in that occupation until age 65.

From (8),

(10) $$W_t/W_{t-1} = e^{\alpha_2(t-(t-1))}$$
$$= e^{\alpha_2} \equiv S,$$

so the measure of slope used is $e^{\alpha_{2_i}}$, where α_{2_i} is the coefficient on experience in the wage regression for occupation i.

Recall that the relationship between slope and present value should be as shown by $J_B Z$ (for wage and salary workers) and $R_A Q$ (for the self-employed) in Figure III. The present value and slope defined by (9) and (10) for thirteen different occupations is presented in Figure IV, where r equals 0.1. Wage and salary points are shown by ●, while those for self-employed are shown by Δ. The figures using the raw data resemble the shapes of Figure III. (Using alternative discount rates of 0 and 0.25 yielded figures virtually identical to Figure IV.)

This can also be illustrated by fitting a regression line through the points in Figure IV, for the self-employed, and another line for the wage and salaried workers.[12]

The results are shown in Table I and Figure V. Figure V is a close reproduction of Figure III, so at least at this level, there seems to be consistency between the theory and data. (Again, the results are the same with alternative discount rates of 0 and 0.25.) Table I reports the actual weighted regressions (on which Figure V is based) where present value (P) is regressed on the slope (S) for the thirteen occupations. Note that there is a separate regression for the wage and salaried workers and the self-employed workers and three alternative discount rates are used. The coefficient of the slope is larger for the wage and salary workers than for the self-employed. The former is significantly different from zero, while the latter is not.

---

12. Actually, the present value-slope calculations should be weighted by the reciprocal of the standard error of the estimate obtained when estimating equation (7), upon which these calculations are based. I.e., those values from equation (7) where the standard error is smaller should receive more weight. Actual estimation revealed that weighted and unweighted regressions yielded similar results. For this reason, only the weighted regressions are reported.

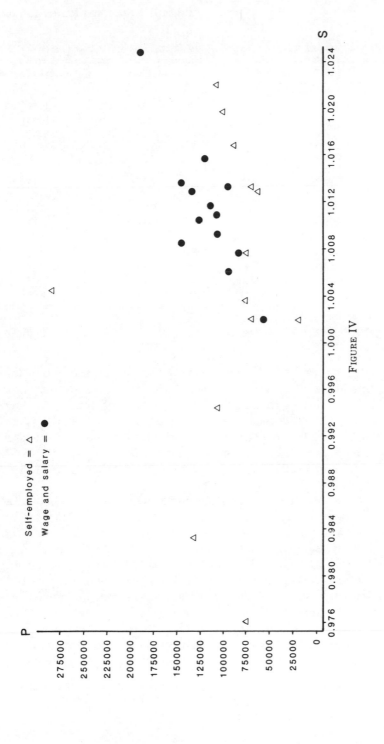

FIGURE IV

TABLE I
REGRESSIONS OF PRESENT VALUE (P) IN THOUSANDS OF DOLLARS ON SLOPE (S)*

$N = 13$	R^2	Intercept	Coefficient of slope
$r = 0$			
Self-employed	0.02	$-7,994$	8,396
		(17,309)	(17,234)
Wage & salary	0.76	$-34,482$	34,672
		(5,902)	(5,836)
$r = 0.1$			
Self-employed	0.002	-490	584
		(3,884)	(3,867)
Wage & salary	0.627	$-4,964$	5,024
		(1,180)	(1,167)
$r = 0.25$			
Self-employed	0.000	27	16
		(1,750)	(1,743)
Wage & salary	0.534	$-1,778$	1,807
		(514)	(508)

*Using Appendix B regressions, weighted by $1/SEE$.
Standard errors are in parentheses.

These results are consistent with the interpretation that there is an effect of profile slope on incentives for wage and salary workers. By increasing the slopes of the age-earnings profile, employers induce their employees to work harder, which raises the present value of their lifetime earnings. This is also a consistent interpretation of the finding that present value rises more with the slope of the age-earnings profile for wage and salary workers than for the self-employed.[13]

Note also that there is nothing mechanical or obvious about these relationships. Table I reports the relationships between present value and average rates of wage growth across occupations. This need not even be positive, much less have the shapes predicted and shown in Figure IV. That the relationship is steeper for wage and salary workers than for the self-employed lends support to the notion that wage and salary workers have steeper age-earnings profiles for incentive reasons.

It has been suggested that there are other reasons to bind workers to firms. For example, under the insurance view, there is an attempt to smooth workers' earnings out over business cycle

13. The outlier in Figure IV is the medical profession. The entire analysis was repeated omitting that group, but results did not change qualitatively.

fluctuations. In order to keep the worker during the upturn while paying him less than his marginal product, a wage greater than marginal product must be promised for some period in the future. This need not result in an upward slope over the *life cycle*, however, since the positive probability of recession next period is sufficient to keep the worker at the firm. Further, risk aversion in the presence of imperfect capital markets actually works to flatten the profile when productivity rises with experience, since workers prefer to smooth consumption over the lifecycle.

Harris and Holmstrom [1981], Nalebuff and Zeckhauser [1981], and Weiss [1982] offer consistent insurance stories that are based on worker heterogeneity that is unobserved at the time of hire. This generates profiles that on average rise faster than productivity, as firms insure workers against the contingency that they will turn out to be low productivity. Modified versions of those models carry the implication that the effect of slope on present value of earnings is larger in the wage and salary sector. It might be possible to distinguish between these two hypotheses by examining the relationship between slope and present value as it is affected by variance in wealth within the occupation. Abowd and Ashenfelter [1981] have taken a step in that direction, but we do not pursue that here.

IV. HUMAN CAPITAL VERSUS INCENTIVE EFFECTS

By making some rather strong assumptions, one can obtain estimates of the amount of variation in workers' wealth that is accounted for by on-the-job training versus that amount accounted for by incentive effects. Let us make those assumptions clear at this point.

First, in order to interpret the estimated relationship shown in Figure V, as the curves $J_B Z$ and $R_A Q$ from Figure III, one must accept that what varies across occupations is workers' risk or time preferences. Opportunities to use steeper age-earnings profiles as an incentive-generating device must be the same across occupations. As a proposition about long-run equilibrium, this is perhaps less offensive, since incentive and worker monitoring methods are likely to spread across occupations over time. Then only the most efficient methods are used, and only the most reliable firms survive.

Second, one must assume that the slope of the estimated function $R_A Q$ is the relationship that would have prevailed for wage and salary workers had they not used the age-earnings profile for incentive reasons. More specifically, we require that in the absence of any

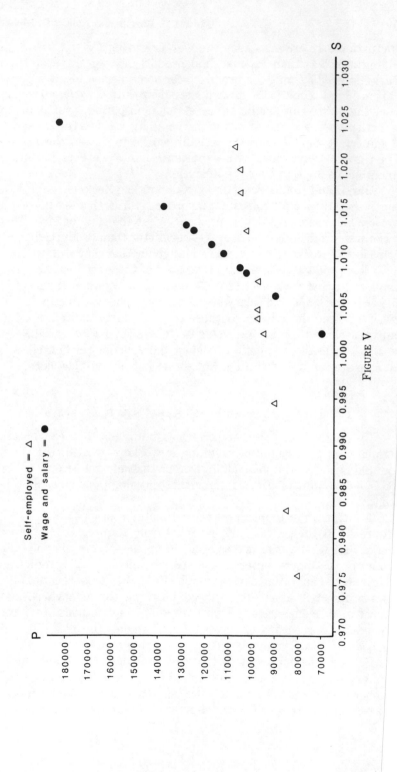

FIGURE V

incentive effects, the relationship between present value and slope for wage and salary workers would have been the same as that observed for the self-employed (ignoring intercepts).

Given these assumptions, the incentive effect on wealth distribution can be calculated. For these purposes, we use the estimates generated by assuming that $r = 0.1$.

Consider an economy where S is distributed uniformly from 1 to 1.025 (approximately the actual limits) for the wage and salary workers. Given the relationship estimated in Table I, this implies that present values of wealth levels across occupations are distributed uniformly between \$59,554 and \$186,739. This is an economy where the expected wealth from the mean occupation is \$123,146 and the standard deviation in expected wealth across occupations is \$36,715.

Now consider a wage and salary worker in a firm with $\alpha_2 = 0$; i.e., $S = 1$. Recall that the expected wealth level is \$59,554. The increase in present value associated with steeper slope that yielded the figure of \$186,739 for an $S = 1.025$ reflected human capital and incentive effects. If we assume that the growth in present value with profile slope as the result of human capital in the absence of incentive effects is the same as dP/dS for self-employed workers who enjoy no incentive effects of slope, then we can define

$$(11) \qquad \frac{d\hat{P}}{dS} = 584,000.$$

This is the estimated increase in present value for wage and salary workers associated with increases in slope that are caused by human capital or other non-incentive related effects. (It is the coefficient on S for self-employed workers in Table I.) Given (11),

$$(12a) \qquad \hat{P}(S) = \text{Constant} + 584,000(S),$$

and

$$(12b) \qquad \hat{P}(1) = 59,554$$

because neither incentive nor human capital effects are present when $S = 1$ (i.e., $\alpha_2 = 0$ implies flat age-earnings profiles). Substituting (12b) into (12a) gives the constant ($= 59,554 - 584,000$), so that the solution to the differential equation is

$$(13) \qquad \hat{P}(S) = 59,554 + 584,000(S - 1).$$

If S were distributed uniformly between 1 and 1.025 as before, then $\hat{P}$ would be distributed uniformly between \$59,554 and \$74,154.

The mean expected wealth across occupations would be \$66,854 with a standard deviation of \$4,214.

Although the standard errors are quite large, it appears that the mean level of P is much higher than that of $\hat{P}$ and the variance is much larger as well. Relative dispersion of $\hat{P}$ is much smaller than that of P: $\hat{\mu}/\hat{\sigma} = 0.063$; whereas $\mu/\sigma = 0.298$.

This can be put more forcefully. Given the assumptions, which we reiterate are quite strong, and taking the point estimates as valid, the calculation implies that in the absence of any human capital or incentive effects, the mean wealth of occupations would be 59,554 with zero predicted variance of zero. If only human capital were a factor, then the mean wealth would increase to 66,858. If both incentive effects and human capital were a factor, then the mean would be \$123,146, assuming that the distribution of S were the same under the last two circumstances. Therefore, under these assumptions, only 11 percent of the increase in present value as the result of steeper age-earnings profiles is attributable to on-the-job training. The remaining 89 percent seems to reflect incentive effects that are not present for the self-employed. In reality, this may even overstate the relative importance of human capital because the distribution of S will not be the same when we allow for both incentive and human capital effects as when only the latter are allowed. As can be seen in Figure III, as the opportunity locus $J_B Z$ gets steeper when incentive effects are introduced, this lowers the relative "price" of buying slope. As such, the distribution of S when incentive effects are introduced is likely to lie above that when only human capital effects are allowed. This implies even larger than estimated incentive effects.[14]

Still, we are reluctant to declare the results conclusive. In addition to the required assumptions, it is also necessary to ignore the fact that standard errors are quite large. In particular, intervals of the slope of the P, S relationship for the self-employed overlaps the point estimate for wage and salary workers. Additionally, there appears to be a pattern of switching to self-employment late in life. Although it is not clear what the effect of this will be on the relation between S and P (since old self-employed workers have low values of S and P), it presents another reason to use caution. Similarly, there may be other reasons why the slopes of self-employeds differ from those of wage and salary workers. However, recall that it is not the differences in slopes of profiles per se, but differences in how

14. Medoff and Abraham [1980] report a similar finding by looking at wages and experience within job categories.

slopes map into differences in present values across sector that matters for this analysis.

Perhaps the most important measurement problem is that fringe benefits may differ systematically by sector, and this may result in large differences between the observed wage and total wage. For example, the present value of pension benefits, which are becoming more important over time, tend to decline with age of retirement for wage and salary workers. (See Lazear [1982, 1983].) The same pattern is impossible for self-employed whose pension is merely a savings account. Ignoring pensions may well distort the results, making wage and salary workers' age-earnings profiles appear steeper than they are. Again, however, the effect of this on the relationship between slope of the profile and present value of (true) earnings is unclear so that even the direction of bias cannot be stated, a priori.

This also suggests a caveat. These calculations are done for a hypothetical economy rather than for the actual one. The reason is that the actual distribution of S in the human-capital-only world cannot be known without some assumptions about the distribution of tastes. However, in the spirit of the discussion above, it is possible to provide an upper bound to the human capital-induced wealth increase in the actual economy by assuming that the distribution of S in the world without incentive effects is the same as that in the actual economy which contains both human capital and incentive effects.

Table II provides information on the actual distribution of workers across occupations in the sample and on the actual values of S for that occupation. $P(S)$ and $\hat{P}(S)$ are calculated for each occupation and then using the appropriate weights, the distribution of $P(S)$ and $\hat{P}(S)$ are generated. The mean of $P(S)$ is \$115,027 with a standard deviation of \$111,740. The mean of $P(S)$ is \$65,427 with a standard deviation of \$57,007. The amount by which wealth is increased via human capital is therefore, at most $(65,427 - 59,554)/(115,027 - 59,554)$ or 10 percent of the total increase that results from incentive and on-the-job training effects. This estimate is similar to the one generated by the hypothetical economy.

These calculations are relevant only for an individual who enters an occupation and remains in that occupation over his entire worklife. Also implicit in this calculation is the assumption that individuals do not change their employment status from wage and salary worker to self-employment. Recall also that we refer here to wealth and not income. In order to talk about the way in which the

TABLE II
OCCUPATIONS OF WORKERS IN SAMPLE AND VALUES OF S

OCCUP	Number of wage and salary (W & S) workers	W & S (%)	$S_{W \& S}$	Number of self-employed (SE) workers	SE (%)	S_{SE}
1	117	0.011	1.024	76	0.042	1.004
2	1,134	0.111	1.008	124	0.069	1.021
3	2,538	0.249	1.015	258	0.144	1.016
4	328	0.032	1.005	234	0.130	1.001
5	775	0.076	1.013	98	0.055	1.019
6	398	0.039	1.010	66	0.037	0.994
7	845	0.083	1.012	98	0.055	0.983
8	1,326	0.130	1.011	94	0.052	0.975
9	817	0.080	1.010	43	0.024	1.007
10	502	0.039	1.013	32	0.108	1.013
11	998	0.098	1.009	67	0.037	1.012
12	102	0.010	1.007	39	0.022	1.003
13	312	0.031	1.002	566	0.315	1.001
	10,192			1,795		

distribution of income changes, it is necessary to be more specific about slope changes.

The conclusion under these assumptions is that most of the increase in wealth across occupations that is associated with steeper profiles reflects incentives and not on-the-job training. This conclusion is derived by comparing the way in which an individual's present value of earnings in an occupation increases with slope in the self-employed sector (where no incentive effects are possible) with that relationship for wage and salary workers. Some rather strong assumptions are made, however, and the results must be interpreted with that fact in mind.

APPENDIX A: MEANS AND (STANDARD ERRORS) OF OVERALL SAMPLE

Variable	For wage and salary workers ($N = 10,192$)	For self-employed ($N = 1,795$)
Age (in years)	39.0	44.9
	(0.117)	(0.275)
"Experience"	19.37	26.44
(age − school − 6)	(0.126)	(0.30)

(continued)

APPENDIX A (*continued*)

Variable	For wage and salary workers (N = 10,192)	For self-employed (N = 1,795)
School (highest grade completed)	12.59 (0.03)	12.45 (0.07)
White (dummy = 1 if white)	0.931 (0.002)	0.965 (0.004)
Urban (dummy = 1 if in an SMSA)	0.384 (0.005)	0.248 (0.010)
Weeks worked during the year	50.22 (0.045)	50.54 (0.091)
Hours worked per week	45.09 (0.087)	52.8 (0.325)
Annual income	16,467 (98)	14,949 (339)
(Experience)^2	537.5 (5.9)	860.6 (16.0)

APPENDIX B: WAGE REGRESSIONS (SEE EQUATION (8))

Occupation		Sample ($S_i \equiv C$)	α_0	α_1	α_2	SEE	R^2
Doctors/ dentists	W + S	117	−0.438	0.133 (0.06)	0.024 (0.005)	0.638	0.148
	SE	76	−0.161	0.152 (0.08)	0.0044 (0.0044)	0.421	0.047
Other professionals	W + S	1134	1.32	0.003 (0.008)	0.008 (0.00167)	0.592	0.027
	SE	124	−2.51	0.245 (0.044)	0.0217 (0.007)	0.973	0.21
"Other industries" (besides mnf.)	W + S	2538	0.414	0.086 (0.004)	0.0155 (0.0008)	0.518	0.186
	SE	258	0.561	0.047 (0.036)	0.016 (0.008)	1.41	0.017
Retail trade	W + S	328	1.38	0.003 (0.019)	0.0059 (0.003)	0.718	0.013
	SE	234	−0.315	0.113 (0.04)	0.0019 (0.009)	1.51	0.035
"Other"	W + S	775	0.617	0.080 (0.0009)	0.0135 (0.001)	0.479	0.123
	SE	98	0.44	0.063 (0.063)	0.019 (0.0112)	1.277	0.033
Carpenters	W + S	398	0.786	0.062 (0.011)	0.0106 (0.0021)	0.477	0.086
	SE	66	1.15	0.043 (0.042)	−0.0056 (0.008)	0.816	0.04
Other construction/craftsman	W + S	845	0.855	0.070 (0.007)	0.0127 (0.0014)	0.468	0.109
	SE	98	2.4	−0.038 (0.046)	−0.017 (0.010)	1.12	0.025
Mechanics	W + S	1,326	0.843	0.058 (0.005)	0.011 (0.001)	0.418	0.104
	SE	94	1.75	−0.028 (0.09)	−0.0244 (0.019)	2.0	0.018
All other craftsmen	W + S	817	0.899	0.065 (0.006)	0.0103 (0.0012)	0.404	0.115
	SE	43	0.64	0.041 (0.051)	0.0075 (0.010)	0.701	0.021

(*continued*)

APPENDIX B (*continued*)

Occupation		Sample $(S_i \equiv C)$	α_0	α_1	α_2	SEE	R^2
"Other than" durable/non-	$W+S$	312	0.525	0.074 (0.0110)	0.0132 (0.002)	0.547	0.105
durable	SE	32	0.036	0.089 (0.05)	0.013 (0.01)	0.597	0.097
Drivers & deliverymen	$W+S$	998	0.925	0.049 (0.007)	0.0091 (0.0014)	0.485	0.051
	SE	67	−0.066	0.085 (0.105)	0.012 (0.023)	1.84	0.010
Personal service	$W+S$	102	0.842	0.0366 (0.022)	0.0075 (0.004)	0.557	0.03
	SE	39	−0.050	0.104 (0.06)	0.003 (0.011)	0.716	0.08
Farmers & farm managers,	$W+S$	312	0.663	0.026 (0.010)	0.00215 (0.003)	0.616	0.022
paid laborers & supervisors	SE	566	−0.008	0.0026 (0.005)	0.0019 (0.0010)	0.291	0.011

UNIVERSITY OF CHICAGO and NATIONAL OPINION RESEARCH CORPORATION
OCCIDENTAL COLLEGE

REFERENCES

Abowd, J., and O. Ashenfelter, "Anticipated Unemployment, Temporary Layoffs, and Compensating Wage Differentials," in *Studies in Labor Markets*, Sherwin Rosen, ed. (NBER: 1981), pp. 141–70.

Cheung, S., *The Theory of Share Tenancy* (Chicago: University of Chicago Press, 1969).

Fuchs, Victor, "Self Employment and Labor Force Participation of Older Males," *Journal of Human Resources*, XVIII (Summer 1982), 339–57.

Harris, Milton, and Bengt Holmstrom, "A Theory of Wage Dynamics," Discussion Paper #488, Northwestern University, 1981.

Johnson, D. G., "Resource Allocation Under Share Contracts," *Journal of Political Economy*, LVIII (1950), 111–23.

Lazear, Edward, "Why Is There Mandatory Retirement?" *Journal of Political Economy*, LXXXVII (Dec. 1979), 1261–84.

——, "Agency, Earnings Profiles, Productivity, and Hours Restrictions," *American Economic Review*, LXXI (Sept. 1981), 606–20.

——, "Pensions as Severance Pay," forthcoming *NBER Conference Volume* (1983).

——, "Severance Pay, Pensions, and Efficient Mobility," NBER Working Paper #854, 1982.

Medoff, J., and K. Abraham, "Experience, Performance and Earnings," this *Journal*, XCV (Dec. 1980), 703–36.

Nalebuff, Barry, and Richard Zeckhauser, "Involuntary Unemployment Reconsidered: Second-Best Contracting with Heterogeneous Firms and Workers," Institute for Research on Poverty Discussion Paper #675-81, University of Wisconsin—Madison, 1981.

Ross, S., "The Economic Theory of Agency," *American Economic Review*, LXIII (May 1973), 134–39.

Weiss, Yoram, "Output Variability and Academic Labor Contracts," Stanford University, 1982.

Wolpin, K., "Education and Screening," Ph.D. thesis, CUNY, 1974.

Work Incentives, Hierarchy, and Internal Labor Markets

James M. Malcomson

University of York

This paper argues that contracts with payment based on a ranking of employee performance can provide performance incentives even under asymmetric information that prevents payment based on individual performance only being enforceable. Such contracts also fit with five features of labor markets that have aroused considerable interest: (1) hierarchical wage structures; (2) internal promotion; (3) wage rates that rise with seniority and experience more than productivity; (4) the variance of earnings increasing with experience; and (5) wage rates attached to jobs rather than individuals with differentials set by administrative procedures rather than by reference to external market wages.

Introduction

The literature on the principal-agent problem has been concerned with the nature of optimal contracts when there is difficulty in monitoring all aspects of an agent's performance. For the most part, this literature has considered models in which payment based directly on a measure of output provides an enforceable contract. For a recent example, see Grossman and Hart (1983). This requires that information about an agent's output be symmetric so that both parties know what payment is due under the contract and, at least in principle,

I wish to thank Arnold Arthurs, Lorne Carmichael, Oliver Hart, Keith Hartley, Ravi Kanbur, Peter Lambert, Andrew Oswald, Robert Solow, an anonymous referee, and participants in numerous seminars for valuable comments on earlier versions of this paper. They are, of course, none of them responsible for any remaining errors.

157

could get that payment enforced legally if necessary. The output measure does not have to be perfect as long as neither party is in a position to impart a systematic bias to it. However, in many employment situations, information about an agent's output is asymmetric in the sense that the agent cannot verify the principal's observation of it. As Greenwald (1979, p. 8) and Williamson, Wachter, and Harris (1975) have emphasized, performance is frequently something that can be assessed only subjectively by, for example, the judgment of a supervisor. This is particularly the case where there is a genuine team element in production of the type that Alchian and Demsetz (1972) argue is a fundamental reason for the existence of firm, as opposed to purely market, organization of production. Under such circumstances a payment scheme based directly on a measure of individual performance ("payment by standard," as it has become known in the literature) is unenforceable, and, unless some other kind of incentive scheme is available, the principal will be unable to enforce more than minimal compliance by the agent in the performance of his task.[1]

It is the contention of the present paper that in the context of a principal employing many agents, which characterizes much employment by firms, contracts with payment based on an ordering of employee performance, and hence in the spirit of the rank-order tournaments of Lazear and Rosen (1981), can still be made enforceable as a means of providing performance incentives even under asymmetric information. This provides a wider set of circumstances than those analyzed by Green and Stokey (1983), that is, situations in which stochastic elements unobservable by the principal are correlated across agents, under which such tournaments are preferable to payment schemes based on individual performance only.

The essence of the argument is that a firm can offer a contract specifying that a certain proportion of its work force will be paid a higher wage than the rest. Whether or not it abides by this is something that can be verified by employees. Since the firm is then committed to paying a higher wage to a certain proportion of employees, it has every incentive to pay that higher wage to those employees who

---

[1] Piece-rate payment is one such form of incentive scheme. If the basis for piece-rate payment can be the true marginal product of an employee, then the situation essentially reverts to a principal-agent problem in which the agent's output is verifiable by both parties. The problem with piece rates is that the unit of output used as the basis of payment must be verifiable by both parties at reasonably low cost and hence tends to be a quantitative measure that neglects all but the crudest quality dimensions. As Stiglitz (1975) has observed, "because piece rates reward speed, they tend not to provide the correct incentives for quality or proper care of equipment." Under such circumstances, even with piece-rate payment, it may be possible to improve efficiency with the use of schemes of the type that form the focus of this paper. Note also that profit-sharing bonuses are not an adequate substitute in a large enterprise because they do not directly reward individual effort.

perform best because this provides the greatest incentive for employees to perform well. But this type of contract amounts to a contract with payment based on an ordering of employees' performance, since it rewards the best no matter what the overall level is. Moreover, because a promotion scheme that ensures that a given proportion of employees is promoted exactly fits the requirements of such a contract, reward schemes of this type would seem to be important in practice.

In a repeated game of the principal-agent type, it may not be necessary to have full legal enforceability of a contract to achieve de facto enforceability, as has been shown by Radner (1981). If the principal and agent have a very long relationship with each other, then an equilibrium in which neither defaults may exist even when it pays to default in the short term. The essential reason is that a no-default equilibrium can benefit both parties in the long term, so that, with a long enough time horizon and a low enough discount rate, the cost to the principal of losing a reputation for honesty, and hence not being trusted not to default in the future, may exceed the short-term gain from defaulting. Such an equilibrium may not, however, exist and is never the only equilibrium since, when a no-default equilibrium exists, there always exists a Nash equilibrium based on the assumption that the principal will default. Hence such an equilibrium, even when it exists, may well not prove robust. The use of a contract basing reward on an ordering of employee performance is, however, always available when there are many agents and can produce efficiency gains without relying on anything more than Nash strategies.

The use of such contracts also fits with certain features of employment arrangements, particularly in large organizations, which have aroused considerable interest. These are:

1. The wage structure within an organization is hierarchical in the sense that there is a tendency for the number of employees being paid higher wages to be less than the number being paid lower wages. This is what Stiglitz (1975) terms "horizontal hierarchy."

2. A high proportion of those in higher-paid jobs have been promoted from lower-paid jobs within the same organization, and new entrants are for the most part appointed only at specific points in the hierarchy. These are characteristics of the internal labor market structure documented by Doeringer and Piore (1971).

3. Wage rates rise more with seniority and experience than productivity does. This has been documented by Medoff and Abraham (1980). For many employees it is associated with a mandatory retirement age.

4. The variance of earnings increases with experience (Mincer 1974).

5. "[W]age rates attach mainly to jobs rather than to workers" (Williamson et al. 1975). While not entirely unambiguous, the fundamental idea here seems to be that, once assigned to a particular job, there is little scope for an individual to bargain over the rate for that job. Moreover, the wage differentials between jobs are often set more by administrative procedures than by reference to external market wages (see Doeringer and Piore 1971).

One reason for the interest in these features is that they are, for the most part, inconsistent with the simplest notion of employees being paid a wage in every period equal to their marginal product in that period. Moreover, they cannot just be ascribed to collusive action on the part of trade unions since they are not present only in highly unionized markets.

The existing literature is not short of explanations for these features, but many of those explanations are directed to just one and do not fit easily with all the others. It is not the purpose of the present paper to deny the validity or importance of these earlier explanations. Indeed, many of their insights are incorporated here. As will be shown, however, the different features fit together in a natural way when contracts base rewards on an ordering of employee performance.

The literature on feature 1 stems from the work of Simon (1957) and Lydall (1968). Their explanation of hierarchical structure is somewhat mechanical since it assumes that a supervisor can supervise several employees and is always paid a wage higher than those he supervises. Calvo and Wellisz (1979) provide an explanation in terms of the optimal monitoring structure when increasing supervision improves work performance by increasing the probability of detecting shirking. The higher wage for supervisors in their model, however, follows from the somewhat special assumption that, while more able individuals cannot be distinguished by the firm from less able ones before they are hired, the firm knows that they have a higher reservation wage.

Feature 2 arises naturally in any model that involves firms' acquiring better information about an employee's ability on the job than can be acquired from characteristics apparent at the time of hiring and information available from previous employers. Then early periods of employment act as a screening process. The wage offered to new entrants to the firm therefore will reflect the mixed ability of newly hired employees, and the more highly paid will be those who have worked for the firm previously and have been revealed to have greater ability. This would also generate feature 4. Explanations of this type have been offered by Williamson et al. (1975), Greenwald (1979), and Harris and Holmstrom (1982). In Greenwald's model of adverse selection, however, wages fall relative to the expected productivity of an individual, which does not fit with feature 3, and Harris and Holmstrom's result on this fits with feature 3 only in a rather special sense. Moreover, to the extent that feature 2 involves promotion to a different job or grade, it is only necessary as a means of rewarding higher productivity if feature 5 holds. This feature is ascribed by Williamson et al. (1975) to an attempt to reduce bargaining costs in the face of what they call idiosyncratic exchange—that is, when job-specific skills give individual employees a measure of monopoly power in wage bargaining—but no formal model of this has been offered.

The existence of job-specific skills acquired by experience forms the basis of Carmichael's (1983) explanation of features 2 and 3. In his model, a fixed number of employees who have acquired the skills are offered a higher wage than their equally skilled colleagues on the basis of seniority in order to reduce quitting by the skilled. This has better efficiency properties than a separation penalty paid by the party initiating the separation to the other party. The reason is that it provides no incentive for the party wishing to separate to act in such a way as to avoid incurring the penalty by inducing the *other* party to initiate the separation. The results of the present paper, however, make it clear that the existence of job-specific skills is not a necessary condition for the type of employment arrangement characterized by features 2 and 3 to emerge.

Holmstrom (1981) generates feature 3 as a result of the use of state-contingent implicit contracts that allow risk-neutral firms to bear some of the risk that would otherwise be borne by risk-averse employees. In common with many other implicit contract models, however, this model uses the crucial assumption that firms are not allowed to pay severance payments to employees. The explanation for this feature closest in spirit to the model used here is that of Lazear (1979, 1981), which can be outlined as follows. To encourage employees not to shirk, employers pay less than marginal product in the early years of employment and more than marginal product in later years. This increases the costs to an employee of being dismissed for shirking, as a result of which less shirking occurs and a Pareto improvement is possible. Mandatory retirement occurs at the point at which an individual's reservation wage becomes greater than his marginal product, which is socially efficient. But with the wage above marginal product at this time the individual would not choose to retire so that mandatory retirement needs to be written into the employment contract.

Two features of Lazear's model are not wholly satisfactory. One is that performance is rated either as satisfactory or as unsatisfactory. There are no degrees of satisfactoriness, and this leads to an indeterminacy as to the optimal path as long as the cumulative wage paid by any date is less than the cumulative marginal product. The other is an enforceability problem. In his model a firm can dismiss an employee for shirking even though he did not shirk and so capture the difference between the cumulative wage paid and the cumulative marginal product to the date of dismissal. Then, of course, there can only be a solution with the cumulative wage to any date less than the cumulative marginal product if there is a cost to a firm of defaulting in this way. Otherwise, it would always pay firms to default at the point where the difference between these is at a maximum. Lazear assumes that there is such a cost that arises because a firm that acquires a reputation for defaulting will not be able to use such an incentive arrangement in the future and hence will incur higher labor costs per unit of output. This of course amounts to a repeated game of the type discussed briefly above and for which the existence of a no-default equilibrium is by no means guaranteed. As this paper will show, however, the essential spirit of Lazear's insight can survive the removal of both these special assumptions when contracts basing payment on an ordering of performance of employees are used.

The next section of this paper shows how such contracts can be made enforceable as a means of providing performance incentives even with asymmetric information about employees' performance and also shows that promotion schemes are a way of achieving this. Subsequent sections analyze a formal model of such a scheme, show that it can lead to efficiency improvements over other enforceable types of contract, and demonstrate how it can generate the five features of employment arrangements discussed above.

Enforceability of Contracts

To see precisely the implications of asymmetry of information about employee performance, consider the following simple model. A firm may hire employees of different generations. All individuals are identical (apart from belonging to different generations) and may work for up to 2 periods (indexed by $j = 0, 1$, respectively, for each generation) so that at any one date individuals of two generations may be employed. Each individual has a utility function $U(e_0, y_0, e_1, y_1)$, where e_j is work effort and y_j is consumption in period j. It is assumed conventionally that $U_1(\cdot)$, $U_3(\cdot)$, $U_{11}(\cdot) < 0$ and $U_2(\cdot)$, $U_4(\cdot) > 0$. Employees maximize expected utility. The firm is perfectly competitive, which, in terms of purchasing labor, means that it takes as given the minimum expected utility level, $\bar{U}$, that its employment contract must offer if it is to hire employees and it believes it can hire as many employees as it wishes at that expected utility level. Also, for expositional simplicity, constant returns to scale are assumed so that output is proportional to effort. This allows the firm to choose the optimal contract for any one generation of employees independently of any other generation. All the results do in fact continue to hold as long as the firm's revenue function is concave, but the proofs become more complicated and no additional insights arise. The firm's revenue from a unit of effort from a period 0 employee will be normalized at one. To allow for experience-related increases in skills, that for a period 1 employee will be denoted s_1. The firm is assumed to be able to borrow and lend on a perfect capital market at an interest rate $(1/r) - 1$.

The firm makes a subjective assessment of each employee's work effort, subject to measurement error. In the spirit of the preceding discussion, it is assumed that this assessment is not verifiable by employees. Let $f(x - e)$ be the probability density function for observed effort x given true effort e. This form makes the implicit assumption that the distribution depends only on the error and not on the level of e, which simplifies the proofs without losing the essential idea. Also, for simplicity, it is assumed that $f(x - e)$ is differentiable and strictly positive for all values of $(x - e)$ strictly between its upper and lower bounds. In what follows, one can either interpret e as the true output of an employee and $(x - e)$ as a measurement error or interpret x as true output related to effort by a random variable with zero mean. In the latter interpretation the expressions given below for the firm's profit are, in fact, just its expected profit. There is one further assumption about work effort. As some level of effort (e.g., whether an employee is actually present on the job) is objectively verifiable at low cost and may yield some output, it will be assumed that the firm can enforce some minimum effort level $\bar{e}$ as a condition of payment.

The variable e can be interpreted in a number of ways. If employees are hired by the day, month, or year, it can represent the hours they actually work. If hired by the hour, it can represent how hard they work during the hour. On an assembly line job, it can represent how well they perform their task, for example, how soon after leaving the factory the component they are responsible for needs attention. Whichever interpretation is appropriate, it is important to note that forms of industrial action such as a "work-to-rule" or a "go-slow" would impose a cost on the firm only if actual performance is in fact above the minimum the firm is able to enforce.

In this context, the firm cannot provide an incentive for work effort greater than $\bar{e}$ by making the wage paid depend on x. Since x cannot be verified by employees, such a payment scheme would be unenforceable. Indeed, the only payment based directly on a standard that is enforceable is a prespecified wage that is paid conditional only on effort of at least $\bar{e}$, but, with $U_1(\cdot) < 0$, this would never induce work effort greater than $\bar{e}$. However, a payment scheme based on ordinal performance can both be made enforceable and provide such an incentive. To see this, note that the firm can offer a contract in which, provided they perform at least at the level $\bar{e}$, employees receive one of two wages, w_1 and w_2, with $w_2 > w_1$, and the higher wage w_2 is paid to a specified proportion P of employees. As long as the proportion P actually paid the higher wage is verifiable by employees, such a contract is enforceable. Moreover, since x and e are positively correlated, the contract provides an incentive for increasing work effort provided the firm makes up the proportion P who are paid the higher wage from those at the top of the distribution of observed effort. The firm, of course, has every incentive to do just that. Since P, w_1, and w_2 are all specified in the contract, it cannot reduce its wage bill by dissembling in any way. Falsifying the ordering of employees' observed effort would merely reduce the incentive to increase effort without reducing its wage bill. Moreover, understating the observed effort of all employees has no effect whatever since P, w_1, and w_2, and hence the firm's costs, are independent of the absolute values of the observed effort levels.[2]

In fact, in the present model specifying P, w_1, and w_2 is precisely equivalent to being able to specify a value of x, say x^*, with all employees having observed effort greater than x^* paid the higher wage and all those having observed effort lower than x^* paid the lower wage, at least as long as the firm is sufficiently large that the sampling variation in the observed values of x is negligible. Then, making up the proportion P from those employees at the top of the observed effort distribution is equivalent to defining x^* by

$$P = 1 - F(x^* - e), \tag{1}$$

where $F(x - e)$ is the cumulative distribution function of observed effort. Note that, for the contract to provide a genuine incentive for effort, P must lie in the range $0 < P < 1$ since if either nobody or everybody is paid the higher wage no incentive effect remains. When $P = 0$ or $P = 1$, the contract simply reduces to paying a fixed wage conditional on effort at least as great as $\bar{e}$ (i.e., payment by a standard). In fact, of course, there is no need to limit the number of wages on offer to just two. One could have a whole range of possible wage rates with specified proportions of employees being paid each. Since, how-

---

[2] Strictly speaking, if employees had no way of assessing either the true or observed effort levels of other employees, they could not actually tell whether the firm was in fact rewarding effort, so the firm could save itself the trouble of measuring x by determining those to be paid the higher wage at random. Implicitly, then, it is assumed that employees observe enough of their colleagues' behavior eventually to find out if merit goes systematically unrewarded. That does not seem unreasonable.

ever, most of the interesting issues arise in the simple case, such complications will be neglected here.

As was suggested above, one particular form of reward that has the characteristics of an ordinal system is a promotion scheme. Instead of offering a 1-period contract with a higher wage going to a specified proportion of employees, the firm could offer a 2-period contract with the same wage w_0 paid to all employees for work in period 0 of their working lives and a specified proportion promoted to a higher-paid grade for period 1 of their working lives. Then P becomes the proportion promoted, w_2 the wage in period 1 for those promoted, and w_1 the wage in period 1 for those not promoted. The incentive characteristics of such a 2-period contract are similar to those for the 1-period contract.

There are, however, good reasons for the use of the 2-period form of contract in practice. The 1-period form would require payment to be made at the end of the period over which work performance is reviewed. Because ranking of employees for payment purposes is not, in general, completely costless to the firm, such reviews will take place only at discrete intervals of time. But employees will want to consume during that period and, since firms typically have cheaper access to capital markets than employees, it will be efficient for firms to finance this consumption by paying in advance of the performance review a wage w_0 that obviously cannot depend on the result of that review. Payment of the performance-related component will then be used to finance consumption in the subsequent period. Since in the present model there is no reason for an employee not to work for the same firm in the second period as in the first (indeed, if firm-specific human capital is at all an important aspect of employment, it would be inefficient for him not to do so), the payment of the performance-related component of the wage can be treated simply as part of the wage for working in the second period. Moreover, since in this model there is no reason for firms to set w_0 higher than the optimal consumption level in the first period, consumption in each period will be the same as income in each period. This is what is assumed in what follows.

On the other hand, since employees retire at the end of period 1, the 2-period contract cannot elicit work effort above $\bar{e}$ in period 1 since no further promotion is possible at that stage. To induce $e_1 > \bar{e}$ would require something like a retirement bonus paid to a specified proportion of retiring employees on retirement, and without that there would be some loss as compared with the sequence of 1-period contracts. In fact, of course, however many periods individuals work, it is only the final period to which this problem applies so that over a long working lifetime the difference becomes negligible. Since the reasons for the 2-period contract appear important in practice, that is the form of contract with payment based on an ordering of performance that will be considered formally in the rest of this paper. Moreover, since the complications of adding a third period of life in which individuals are retired (as would be required to model a retirement bonus properly) do not seem to add any essentially new insights, the possible use of such a bonus will be neglected.

In practice, employment contracts are not usually as fully specified as that suggested here. In an uncertain world there are, of course, costs to contracts that are inflexible unless they are complete in the sense of covering every eventuality. However, even with implicit or nonbinding agreements, there are clear advantages to dealing with terms verifiable by both parties. It is then immediately obvious when a firm is living up to its reputation or when customary procedures are being breached. This increases the cost to a firm of "cheating" in two ways. First, employee work effort will be adjusted straightaway, rather than with the lag that would occur if breaches were not immediately obvious. Second, employees can more quickly take other steps, such as collective action, to try to reimpose what they believe to be the implicit agreement. This latter aspect has been explored in Malcomson (1983) and hence will not be investigated further here. For the present, the terms of the 2-period contract are taken to be explicit and binding.

Work Effort of Employees

Consider an individual offered the 2-period contract of the previous section with specified values of w_0, w_1, w_2, and P in a firm with a large number of employees. He will accept the contract if his expected utility is at least $\bar{U}$. If he accepts the contract, he works for period 0 at the wage w_0. If his observed effort in period 0 is greater than the x^* defined by equation (1), he will be promoted and be offered wage w_2 in period 1; otherwise he will be offered wage w_1 in period 1. With a large number of other employees his own contribution to average work effort that, with P, determines x^* via (1) is negligible, so in determining his e_0 he will treat x^* as a parameter. (This is precisely analogous to individual agents treating price as a parameter in a perfectly competitive market.)

An employee might not, however, wish to continue to work for the firm in period 1 if the wage he is offered is less than the wage other firms would be prepared to offer him for a 1-period contract in period 1 or less than his reservation wage for not working at all. Call the higher of these W_1. With a legally binding contract, the firm might be able to force an employee to continue to work, but it seems more realistic to assume either that it could not or that the costs of enforcing the contract are so high that it would not.[3] Define $w_1^* = \max\{w_1, W_1\}$. Then the employee will always determine period 0 behavior on the assumption that w_1^* is the wage he will receive in period 1 if not promoted. For reasons discussed earlier, $e_1 = \bar{e}$ always. Hence his expected utility, which will be denoted $V(e_0, w_0, w_1^*, w_2, x^*)$, is given by

$$V(e_0, w_0, w_1^*, w_2, x^*) = F(x^* - e_0)U(e_0, w_0, \bar{e}, w_1^*) \\ + [1 - F(x^* - e_0)]U(e_0, w_0, \bar{e}, w_2). \tag{2}$$

He will choose e_0 to maximize this subject to $e_0 \geqq \bar{e}$. For an interior solution for e_0, the first-order condition for this maximization is

$$f(x^* - e_0)[U(e_0, w_0, \bar{e}, w_2) - U(e_0, w_0, \bar{e}, w_1^*)] \\ + F(x^* - e_0)U_1(e_0, w_0, \bar{e}, w_1^*) \tag{3} \\ + [1 - F(x^* - e_0)]U_1(e_0, w_0, \bar{e}, w_2) = 0.$$

It is assumed that the utility function and density function have properties that ensure that the solution to (3) is unique. Denote that solution by $e^* = g(w_0, w_1^*, w_2, x^*)$. Then

$$e_0 = \max\{e^*, \bar{e}\}. \tag{4}$$

Note that, since $U_1(\cdot) < 0$ and $U_4(\cdot) > 0$, there can be an interior solution for e_0 only if $w_2 > w_1$ and if $f(x^* - e_0)$ is strictly positive so that there is a positive probability of promotion. This is as one would expect.

Crucial to the optimal contract that the firm offers is how effort responds to the variables in the contract. The contract does not, however, determine x^* directly. It specifies P, which, via (1), determines x^*. As argued above, for an individual acting competitively x^* is taken as given. But for a firm choosing the optimal contract, a change in P affects the work effort of all employees and hence, again via (1), x^*. The same applies to changes in w_0, w_1, and w_2. Hence the firm is interested in the effort supply function with P, not x^*, as an argument. Denote this effort supply function by

$$e_0 = h(w_0, w_1^*, w_2, P). \tag{5}$$

The derivatives of $h(\cdot)$ can be found from the first-order condition (3) using standard comparative static methods provided the effects of changes in effort on x^* are incorporated. Note from (1) that, for $0 < P < 1$, $\partial x^*/\partial e = 1$ and $\partial x^*/\partial P = -1/f(x^* - e)$. For $P = 0$ and $P = 1$, $f(x^*$

---

[3] In the present model, unlike that of Carmichael (1983), there is no reason for employees to switch firms because of mismatching, so there is no efficiency loss in tying an employee to a specific firm for 2 periods. The point here is concerned with the legal problem of preventing employees' switching for their own personal gain.

$- e) = 0$ and $\partial x^*/\partial P$ is infinite. Then

$$\left(V_{11} + V_{15}\frac{de_0}{de^*}\right)de^* + V_{12}dw_0 + V_{13}dw_1^*$$

$$+ V_{14}dw_2 - \frac{V_{15}}{f(x^* - e_0)}\,dP = 0,$$

(6)

where e_0, not e^*, enters the probability density function since it is the actual effort of employees that determines x^*. From this, assuming for simplicity that the utility function is additively separable between periods, one gets the following derivatives at an interior solution for e_0 and P:

$$h_1(\cdot) = \frac{-U_{12}}{U_{11}} \gtreqless 0 \text{ according as } U_{12} \gtreqless 0;$$

(7)

$$h_2(\cdot) = f(x^* - e_0)\frac{U_4}{U_{11}} < 0;$$

(8)

$$h_3(\cdot) = -f(x^* - e_0)\frac{U_4}{U_{11}} > 0;$$

(9)

$$h_4(\cdot) = \frac{f'(x^* - e_0)[U(e_0, w_0, \bar{e}, w_2) - U(e_0, w_0, \bar{e}, w_1)]}{[f(x^* - e_0)U_{11}]}$$

$$\gtreqless 0 \text{ according as } f'(x^* - e_0) \lesseqgtr 0 \text{ for } w_2 > w_1^*,$$

$$= 0 \text{ for } w_2 = w_1^*,$$

(10)

where U_4 must be evaluated at w_1^* for (8) and at w_2 for (9). Note that, as expected, increasing w_2 raises work effort while increasing w_1^* lowers it. The effect of w_0 depends on the sign of U_{12}. The effect of changing P is more complicated. The crucial element is whether the probability density is increasing or decreasing with work effort. For $f(\cdot)$ symmetric and unimodal, $h_4(\cdot) \gtreqless 0$ according as $x^* \gtreqless e_0$ (i.e., $P \lesseqgtr \frac{1}{2}$).

The Optimal Contract for the Firm

Now consider the firm's choice of what contract to offer. It offers employees either 1-period contracts at fixed wages in both periods 0 and 1 of their working lives or a 2-period contract with a chance of promotion for period 1. In the latter case it could also hire period 1 employees on a 1-period contract at a fixed wage by offering sufficient to attract those who chose not to work, or who worked for other firms, in period 0.

Consider the 2-period contract denoted by $\{w_0, w_1, w_2, P\}$. To attract employees this must provide a minimum expected utility level $\bar{U}$, a constraint that can be expressed formally in terms of (2) with the effort supply function (5) inserted. For $w_1 \geqq W_1$, period 0 employees not promoted will return to work for the firm in period 1. For $w_1 < W_1$, they will not. Hence the firm's profit for each 2-period employee, $\pi(w_0, w_1, w_2, P)$, for any given 2-period contract is

$$\pi(w_0, w_1, w_2, P) = \begin{cases} h(w_0, w_1, w_2, P) - w_0 + r[s_1\bar{e} - Pw_2 \\ \quad - (1 - P)w_1], \quad \text{for } w_1 \geqq W_1; \\ \\ h(w_0, W_1, w_2, P) - w_0 + rP[s_1\bar{e} - w_2], \\ \quad \text{for } w_2 \geqq W_1 > w_1. \end{cases} \tag{11}$$

Clearly it could also be the case that $w_2 < W_1$, but this is equivalent to setting $P = 0$ in the lower part of (11) and hence does not need to be treated separately. The firm will choose its contract $\{w_0, w_1, w_2, P\}$ to maximize $\pi(\cdot)$ subject to the minimum expected utility constraint and the constraint $0 \leqq P \leqq 1$.

Now consider the alternative of hiring employees by 1-period, fixed-wage contracts only. In this case work effort is always $\bar{e}$ so, if the fixed wages for periods 0 and 1 are denoted w_0 and w_1, respectively, the firm's profit per employee is

$$\pi = \begin{cases} \bar{e} - w_0 + r(s_1\bar{e} - w_1), \quad \text{for } w_1 \geqq W_1; \\ \\ \bar{e} - w_0, \quad \text{for } w_1 < W_1. \end{cases} \tag{12}$$

But for any given w_0 and w_1, (12) gives the same profit as (11) with $P = 0$ since $P = 0$ implies $h(\cdot) = \bar{e}$. Hence the firm could never be worse off by offering the 2-period contract, and therefore only the solution for the optimal 2-period contract needs to be considered here. Whenever that gives a profit per employee strictly greater for $0 < P < 1$ than for $P = 0$, the 2-period contract is strictly preferable to the 1-period, fixed-wage contracts.

The formal discussion of the optimal 2-period contract is relegated to the Appendix, and detailed proofs are presented there. Here the results of economic interest are summarized.

The first result (proposition 1 of the App.) is that for risk-loving employees the firm has strictly greater profits per employee from offering a contract with the proportion promoted, P, strictly between zero and one and $w_2 > w_1^*$. The intuition for this is obvious since, with risk-loving employees, offering a gamble enables the firm to reduce the cost of offering a given expected utility level. This is also optimal (proposition 2) for risk-neutral and risk-averse employees provided that the marginal utility of income in period 1 is sufficiently large relative to the rate at which the marginal disutility of effort in period 0 increases (i.e., provided $-U_4/U_{11}$ is sufficiently large) over the relevant range. Again the intuition is straightforward. From (9), for any given P with $0 < P < 1$, $-U_4/U_{11}$ determines the rate at which e_0 increases as w_2 increases, and if the increase in effort is sufficiently large it will more than compensate for the additional wage costs.

Since a 2-period contract with $0 < P < 1$ and $w_2 > w_1^*$ is a contract with payment based on an ordering of employee performance, these results establish that, under the conditions of propositions 1 and 2, such a contract dominates contracts based on individual performance only, of which the only examples available in the current context are the 1-period, fixed-wage contracts or the 2-period contract with $P = 0$, $P = 1$, or $w_2 = w_1^*$. Moreover, with $0 < P < 1$ and $w_2 > w_1^*$, there is genuine internal promotion in the model since only employees working for the firm in period 0 will be considered for the high wage w_2 in period 1. New employees enter the firm only at w_0 (or at their marginal product $s_1 \bar{e}$ if they worked for another firm in period 0). Hence the model generates the characteristics of an internal labor market, feature 2 from the Introduction. Indeed, in this model the only promotion is internal promotion, but that obviously may not be the case in more general models.

To see how the model ties up with feature 3 from the Introduction, consider the zero-profit condition that must hold in equilibrium. This is given by setting $\pi(\cdot) = 0$ in equation (11). Note that employees are free to work for a different firm in period 1 from their employer of period 0 if they can get a higher wage. Moreover, other firms would always be prepared to offer them a wage equal to their marginal product in that period so that, as long as there are other firms around in which they are equally productive, they would be able to get $s_1 \bar{e}$, that is, $W_1 \geq s_1 \bar{e}$. With $w_2 > w_1$, it follows immediately that the terms in brackets in (11) must be negative. But in both upper and lower parts of (11) this term is the difference between marginal product and average wage in period 1 for employees on the 2-period contract. Hence 2-period employees are, on average, paid more than their marginal product in period 1. This is, as can be seen by setting $\pi(\cdot) = 0$ in (11), exactly offset in present value by their being paid less than their marginal product in period 0 so that, over their working life, the present value of expected wages equals the present value of marginal product. Hence the ratio of the average wage to marginal product rises over employees' working lives, which is precisely the relationship described under feature 1. Whether the real wage itself rises or falls between periods 0 and 1 depends on a number of factors. Individual effort falls since $e_0 \geq \bar{e}$, but this is countered by any experience-related increases in skill, that is, $s_1 > 1$. Medoff and Abraham (1980) find no significant relationship between experience and productivity within a given grade, and for the present model to be consistent with that, the experience-related increase in skill would have to just counterbalance the decline in work effort, that is, $e_0 = s_1\bar{e}$. It then follows from what was said above that $w_2 > w_1 > w_0$, and hence wages rise with length of service. Of course, since e_0 is endogenous to the model, one can express the condition $e_0 = s_1\bar{e}$ in terms of the parameters, but there seems little to be learned from that. Note also that the variance of earnings increases with experience (feature 4) since all period 0 employees earn w_0 whereas some period 1 employees earn w_2 and some w_1^*.

In view of the relationship between the wage and the marginal product it generates, the model preserves Lazear's (1979) insight into the reasons for mandatory retirement. Formally this can be included in a straightforward way by incorporating a third period into the model in which an individual's reservation wage is always greater than his productivity. Then, as in Lazear's model, at the time the employment contract is made both parties would agree to the contract specifying retirement at the end of the second period since this gives the maximum gain to be shared between the parties. But that does not mean that individuals would choose to retire at the end of the second period if they were able to continue at their second period wage since that wage is above their marginal product and hence may be above their reservation wage. This is the essence of Lazear's point.

It is also interesting to note that, since period 2 employees are paid more than their marginal product, the firm would always have a short-term interest in laying them off, although it would obviously undermine the credibility of the incentive structure if it did so. This makes it clear why the firm would be prepared to bind itself to last-in-first-out or seniority rules for determining the order of layoffs and redundancies.

Next consider the question of hierarchy. At any given date there are two generations of individuals employed by the firm. All period 0 employees are paid w_0 whereas period 1 employees are divided between those earning w_1 and those earning w_2. As long as the firm is not declining in size, it is certainly true that there are more employees earning w_0 than w_1 or w_2. With $w_2 > w_1 > w_0$ there are then certainly more employees at the bottom of the hierarchy than in either of the upper echelons. To have fewer at the top than in the middle, however, requires $P < \frac{1}{2}$, so that there are fewer earning w_2 than w_1. Conditions under which this happens are explored in the Appendix. Unfortunately, I have been unable to find a general way to characterize the economic conditions under which it occurs. Certainly for $f(\cdot)$ a normal distribution, $P < \frac{1}{2}$ for a not implausible class of utility functions. One example is when the utility function for income in period 1 displays constant relative risk aversion between 0 and $\frac{1}{2}$. See the Appendix for details.

This shows how the present model can generate the first four features of employment structures discussed in the Introduction. The fifth is slightly more tricky. The sense in which it fits easily is the following. To enhance the distinction between those promoted and those not promoted, and hence simplify the employees' monitoring of firm behavior, the firm would wish to label them as two different grades, to which the wages w_1 and w_2 are attached. Then the wage an individual receives depends only on what grade he is in since in all other respects the individuals in the two grades are identical. There is obviously no scope for individual bargaining over the rate for his grade, since wages in each period do not depend directly on productivity in that period but, at least for period 1, on the incentive effects the firm wishes to generate for the previous period. Moreover, the wage for any given grade is not directly related to external market wages, though obviously there is an indirect connection through the level of utility $\bar{U}$ that a firm's contract must offer. The relationships among w_0, w_1, and w_2 are determined by the incentive requirements of the firm. This would appear consonant with differentials being determined by administrative procedures, as discussed in Doeringer and Piore (1971), rather than by external market forces.

It is not quite the same, however, as wages being attached to jobs since, strictly speaking, within the present model everybody is doing the same job. That, of course, reflects the simplicity of the model. If, for example, one introduced supervisors of the type considered by Calvo and Wellisz (1979), who would have an obvious role to play monitoring $\bar{e}$, it may well make sense for the firm to use those promoted in a supervisory capacity as a means of reinforcing the distinction between those promoted and those not promoted. Then the wage paid would be attached not just to the grade but also to the job to which an individual is assigned.

Concluding Remarks

It has been shown that the use of contracts with payment based on a ranking of employees' performance can be made enforceable as a means of providing performance incentives even in a situation of asymmetric information in which employees cannot verify an employer's observations of their performance so that a contract specifying a wage directly dependent on individual performance is unenforceable. Under certain conditions 2-period contracts with promotion are preferable to 1-period and 2-period fixed-wage contracts, which are the only systems with payment by standard enforceable in the model. Note that this result is in no way dependent on the existence of stochastic elements in performance correlated across employees and so provides a wider set of circumstances than those discussed by Green and Stokey (1983) under which contracts based on an ordering of employees' performance are preferred to contracts based on individual performance only. Moreover, it has been shown how the internal incentive structure of such contracts can generate the five features of labor organization outlined in the Introduction.

It is also of interest to consider the properties of a competitive equilibrium in a model with 2-period contracts of the sort analyzed here. When the conditions for propositions 1 and 2 in the Appendix hold, such an equilibrium is a strict Pareto improvement over a competitive equilibrium with payment based on individual performance only. The reason is clear. In a competitive equilibrium with constant returns to scale, firms always earn zero profits per employee so that they are never worse off under 2-period contracts with promotion. But when such contracts give higher profits per employee for a given level of employees' expected utility, an equilibrium with zero profits gives higher expected utility for employees. Hence employees are better off.

One final point to note is that it is straightforward to generalize the model used here to many different types of individuals. Indeed, if one indexes the utility functions, effort levels, and contracts by i, all the arguments used above can be repeated for each i. It is, however, interesting to note that the different types of individuals would in general be offered different 2-period contracts with different profiles of lifetime earnings and probabilities of promotion so that, in practice, one would expect a variety of different job ladder structures to emerge.

Appendix

This Appendix is concerned with the nature of the optimal contract arising from the choice of w_0, w_1, w_2, and P to maximize the firm's profit per employee, $\pi(\cdot)$ defined by equation (11), subject to the minimum expected utility constraint and the constraint $0 \leqq P \leqq 1$. Note that, given additive separability between periods and $e_1 = \bar{e}$ exogenous, the utility function may be written

$$U(e_0, y_0, \bar{e}, y_1) = U^1(e_0, y_0) + U^2(y_1).$$

Then the minimum expected utility constraint is given by

$$U^1[h(w_0, w_1^*, w_2, P), w_0] + (1 - P)U^2(w_1^*) + PU^2(w_2) \geqq \bar{U}. \qquad \text{(A1)}$$

Analyzing this problem is somewhat complicated by the fact that the expression for profit given in (11) is not differentiable at $w_1 = W_1$.

The initial concern is to show under what conditions the optimal contract has $0 < P < 1$ and $w_2 > w_1^*$. It is useful to define the class of contracts in which employees bear no risk.

DEFINITION: A certainty contract is one with $P = 0$, $P = 1$, or $w_2 = w_1^*$.

Since for any certainty contract with $w_2 = w_1^*$ or $P = 1$ there is always an equivalent certainty contract with $P = 0$, only the latter case need be of concern here. As argued in the text, for a certainty contract $e_0 = \bar{e}$ always.

PROPOSITION 1: For risk-loving employees, the optimal contract has $0 < P < 1$ and $w_2 > w_1^*$.

PROOF: Any certainty contract can always be written in a form with $P = 0$ and $w_2 > w_1^*$. Hence it suffices to rule out that this is optimal. For $P = 0$, $e_0 = \bar{e}$ always. For positive P and $w_2 > w_1^*$, work effort is certainly no less than $\bar{e}$. But for risk-loving employees, the actuarial cost to the firm of providing employees with expected utility $\bar{U}$ is less if the wage for period 1 involves a gamble than if it is certain, and this can always be achieved by raising P and lowering w_0. Hence there exists a $P > 0$ that gives at least as much output and lower cost than $P = 0$.

REMARK: The obvious route to proving this result, that is, raising w_2 and lowering w_1 to leave the actuarial cost of wages to the firm unchanged, is not always available. The reason is that it may be that $w_1 = W_1 = s_1\bar{e}$ for a certainty contract so that lowering w_1 would merely ensure that employees not promoted left the firm and then the firm's profit per employee would necessarily fall.

For risk-averse employees the equivalent result is more complicated. The reason is that then the firm's profit per employee always has a local maximum at that certainty contract that, over the class of certainty contracts, maximizes the firm's profits per employee subject to the expected utility constraint. This is because under a certainty contract the constraint $e_0 \geqq \bar{e}$ is always strictly binding; that is, the solution to (3) always has $e^* < \bar{e}$, so that a local variation in the contract never increases work effort and any change in the contract that satisfies the expected utility constraint by introducing a gamble always raises the actuarial cost of wages to the firm. Hence one needs to consider the effect on profits per employee of a discrete change in the contract. In addition to the assumptions in the main text, it is assumed that $U^{2'}(w)$ ($\equiv U_4[\cdot]$) is bounded away from zero. The following lemma is used.

LEMMA 1: For some $0 < P < 1$, there exists a w_2 such that, for any w_0 and w_1^*, the solution to (3) is $e^* = \bar{e}$ for any finite $\bar{e}$.

PROOF: For $e^* < \bar{e}$, it follows from (6) that

$$\frac{\partial e^*}{\partial w_2} = -\frac{V_{14}}{V_{11}} = -\frac{f(\cdot)U^{2'}(w_2)}{U_{11} - f'(\cdot)[U^2(w_2) - U^2(w_1^*)]}.$$

For given P, $f(\cdot)$ and $f'(\cdot)$ are fixed, and there certainly exists a $0 < P < 1$ such that $f(\cdot) > 0$ and $f'(\cdot) > 0$. Then, for $w_2 > w_1^*$, $\partial e^*/\partial w_2 > 0$ and is bounded away from zero. Hence there exists a w_2 such that e^* exceeds any given number $\bar{e}$, so proving the lemma.

PROPOSITION 2: For risk-neutral and risk-averse employees, there exist utility functions such that the optimal contract has $0 < P < 1$ and $w_2 > w_1^*$ for finite $\bar{e}$.

PROOF: Suppose the optimal contract were a certainty contract. Then, since any certainty contract has an equivalent certainty contract with $w_2 = w_1^*$ and P arbitrary, without loss of generality denote the optimal contract by $\{\bar{w}_0, \bar{w}_1, \bar{w}_1, P\}$ with P arbitrary. Choose a $\bar{P}$ for which lemma 1 holds and let $w_2^*(\bar{w}_0, \bar{w}_1, \bar{P})$ be the w_2 defined in lemma 1 for which $e^* = \bar{e}$. Now consider an increase in w_2 from $\bar{w}_1$. This cannot violate the minimum expected utility constraint, since employees can always choose effort $\bar{e}$ and be certain of income $\bar{w}_1$ in period 1. For any $w_2 < w_2^*$, profit per employee π falls since there is no increase in work effort. For any $w_2 > w_2^*$,

$$\Delta\pi = \int_{w_2^*}^{w_2} \left(\frac{\partial e_0}{\partial w_2}\right) dw_2 - rP(w_2 - \bar{w}_1).$$

But it follows from (6) that, for $w_2 > w_2^*$,

$$\frac{\partial e_0}{\partial w_2} = - \frac{f(x^* - e_0)U^{2'}(w_2)}{U_{11}(\cdot)},$$

so that since, for given P, $x^* - e$ is given,

$$\Delta\pi = f(x^* - e_0) \int_{w_2^*}^{w_2} \left[\frac{U^{2'}(w_2)}{-U_{11}(\cdot)}\right] dw_2 - rP(w_2 - \bar{w}_1).$$

Since there is no restriction on the size of $U^{2'}(w_2)/-U_{11}(\cdot)$, there certainly exist utility functions with sufficiently large values of this that $\Delta\pi > 0$, contradicting that the certainty contract was optimal.

REMARK: Formally, imposing the condition that the utility function satisfies

$$\max_{w_2,P} \ f(x^* - e_0) \int_{w_2^*(\bar{w}_0,\bar{w}_1,P)}^{w_2} \left[\frac{U^{2'}(w_2)}{-U_{11}(\cdot)}\right] dw_2 - rP(w_2 - \bar{w}_1) > 0$$

is sufficient for the proof of the proposition.

The remaining proposition to be proved concerns conditions under which $P < \frac{1}{2}$. For any certainty contract this is trivial since there is always a precisely equivalent contract with $P = 0$ that certainly satisfies $P < \frac{1}{2}$. Consider therefore the other cases. The firm's profit per employee, $\pi(\cdot)$ given by (11), is a differentiable function of the contract variables except at $w_1 = W_1$. Let λ denote the Lagrange multiplier attached to the minimum expected utility constraint (A1). Then, for any contract maximizing (11) subject to (A1) with $0 < P < 1$ and $w_2 > w_1^*$, the following first-order necessary conditions must be satisfied, with inequalities bracketed together being complementary:

$$[1 + \lambda U_1^1(\cdot)]h_1(\cdot) - 1 + \lambda U_2^1(\cdot) = 0; \tag{A2}$$

$$\left.[1 + \lambda U_1^1(\cdot)]h_2(\cdot) + (1 - P)[\lambda U^{2'}(w_1) - r] \begin{matrix} \leqq 0 \\ w_1 \geqq W_1 \end{matrix}\right\} \ \text{if} \ w_1 \geqq W_1; \tag{A3}$$

$$[1 + \lambda U_1^1(\cdot)]h_3(\cdot) + P[\lambda U^{2'}(w_2) - r] = 0; \tag{A4}$$

$$[1 + \lambda U_1^1(\cdot)]h_4(\cdot) + \{\lambda[U^2(w_2) - U^2(w_1)] - r(w_2 - w_1)\} = 0; \tag{A5}$$

$$\left.\begin{matrix} U^1[h(\cdot), w_0] + (1 - P)U^2(w_1) + PU^2(w_2) \geqq \bar{U} \\ \lambda \geqq 0 \end{matrix}\right\}. \tag{A6}$$

Note from (11) that in the case $W_1 = s_1\bar{e}$ (i.e., employees would choose to work in period 1 at a wage equal to their marginal product), the firm would always have lower profits for $w_1 < W_1$ than for $w_1 = W_1$.

Before deriving the remaining proposition it is useful to establish the following lemmas:

LEMMA 2: For risk-averse employees, an optimal contract with $w_2 > w_1 \geqq W_1$ and $0 < P < 1$ implies

$$\lambda U^{2'}(w_1) - r > 0, \ \lambda U^{2'}(w_2) - r < 0, \ \text{and} \ 1 + \lambda U_1^1(\cdot) > 0. \tag{A7}$$

PROOF: From (8) and (9) of the text, $h_2(\cdot) < 0$ and $h_3(\cdot) > 0$. For a risk averter, $U^{2'}(w_1) > U^{2'}(w_2)$. Hence (A3) and (A4) can both be satisfied only if (A7) holds.

LEMMA 3: For risk-averse employees, an optimal contract with $w_2 > w_1 \geqq W_1$ implies that $\lambda > 0$ and hence that the minimum expected utility constraint is binding.

PROOF: Follows directly from lemma 2 and the fact that $U^{2'}(\cdot)$, $r > 0$.

LEMMA 4: For an optimal contract with $w_1 \geqq W_1$,

$$\lambda \leqq r \left[\frac{1 - P}{U^{2'}(w_1)} + \frac{P}{U^{2'}(w_2)} \right]$$

with equality holding when $w_1 > W_1$.

PROOF: Divide (A3) by $h_2(\cdot)$, noting that $h_2(\cdot) < 0$ so that the inequality is reversed, and (A4) by $h_3(\cdot)$. Subtract the latter expression from the former to give

$$\frac{(1 - P)[\lambda U^{2'}(w_1) - r]}{h_2(\cdot)} - \frac{P[\lambda U^{2'}(w_2) - r]}{h_3(\cdot)} \geqq 0$$

or

$$\lambda \left[\frac{(1 - P)U^{2'}(w_1)}{h_2(\cdot)} - \frac{PU^{2'}(w_2)}{h_3(\cdot)} \right] \geqq r \left[\frac{1 - P}{h_2(\cdot)} - \frac{P}{h_3(\cdot)} \right].$$

Substitution of (8) and (9) of the text for $h_2(\cdot)$ and $h_3(\cdot)$ with appropriate cancellation of terms—note that $U^{2'}(w) \equiv U_4(\cdot)$—yields the required result.

LEMMA 5: For an optimal contract with $w_1 > W_1$,

$$\frac{\partial \lambda}{\partial P} = r \left[\frac{1}{U^{2'}(w_2)} - \frac{1}{U^{2'}(w_1)} \right] \gtreqqless 0$$

according as employees are risk averse, risk neutral, or risk loving.

PROOF: Follows from lemma 4 and definitions of risk aversion, risk neutrality, and risk loving.

PROPOSITION 3: For $W_1 = s_1 \bar{e}$, $f(x - e_0)$ normal, $U_{111}(\cdot) \leqq 0$, and $U^2(w)$ displaying risk aversion and satisfying

$$\tfrac{1}{2} \left[\frac{1}{U^{2'}(w_1)} + \frac{1}{U^{2'}(w_2)} \right] [U^2(w_2) - U^2(w_1)] - (w_2 - w_1) < 0 \quad \text{all } w_2 > w_1,$$
$$(A8)$$

the optimal contract has $P < \tfrac{1}{2}$.

PROOF: For any certainty contract there is always an equivalent contract with $P = 0$, so for certainty contracts the proposition is trivially true. For $W_1 = s_1 \bar{e}$, $w_1 \geqq W_1$ always, as argued above, so that for any contract other than a certainty contract, the conditions for lemmas 2–4 are satisfied. From (10) of the text and $f(x - e_0)$ normal, it follows that $h_4(\cdot) \gtreqqless 0$ according as $P \lesseqqgtr \tfrac{1}{2}$ and also that, when $U_{111}(\cdot) \leqq 0$, $h_{44}(\cdot) < 0$. By lemma 2, therefore,

$$X_1 \equiv [1 + \lambda U_1^1(\cdot)]h_4(\cdot) \gtreqqless 0 \quad \text{according as } P \lesseqqgtr \tfrac{1}{2}, \qquad (A9)$$

where X_1 is defined implicitly. Since for any given w_1 and w_2 ($w_2 > w_1$) and, in particular, an optimal w_1 and w_2, $h_4(\cdot) \to \infty$ as $P \to 0$, it follows that $X_1 \to \infty$ as $P \to 0$. Hence, since the optimal contract has $w_2 > w_1$, X_1 can take on any positive value at the optimal w_1 and w_2 for some $0 < P < \frac{1}{2}$. But, when (A8) holds and for any given $w_2 > w_1$, it follows from lemma 4 and $r > 0$ that

$$X_2 \equiv \lambda[U^2(w_2) - U^2(w_1)] - r(w_2 - w_1) < 0 \text{ for } P = \frac{1}{2}, \qquad \text{(A10)}$$

where X_2 is implicitly defined, and from lemma 5 that, when $w_1 > W_1$, $\partial X_2/\partial P > 0$. Hence, at an optimal w_0, w_1, and w_2, $X_2 < 0$ for any $0 < P < \frac{1}{2}$. Equation (A5) requires that, at an optimum with $0 < P < 1$, $X_1 = -X_2$, which must be the case for some $0 < P < \frac{1}{2}$. But $h_{44}(\cdot) < 0$ ensures that there is only one P for which this is true at any given w_0, w_1, and w_2. Hence for $w_1 > W_1$ the proposition holds. For $w_1 = W_1$, it follows from lemma 4 that, for any given P, w_1, and w_2, X_2 is bounded above by its value for $w_1 > W_1$, so the conclusion holds for that case too.

REMARK: The conditions for proposition 3 are only sufficient conditions. In fact $f(x^* - e_0)$ normal and $U_{111}(\cdot) \leqq 0$ are much stronger than required but have the virtue of easy interpretability. Unfortunately I have found no economic interpretation of (A8). It is, however, satisfied by certain plausible classes of utility functions. One example is the class of constant relative risk aversion utility functions $U^2(w) = w^a$ for $\frac{1}{2} < a < 1$.

References

Alchian, Armen A., and Demsetz, Harold. "Production, Information Costs, and Economic Organization." *A.E.R.* 62 (December 1972): 777–95.

Calvo, Guillermo A., and Wellisz, Stanislaw. "Hierarchy, Ability, and Income Distribution." *J.P.E.* 87, no. 5, pt. 1 (October 1979): 991–1010.

Carmichael, Lorne. "Firm-specific Human Capital and Promotion Ladders." *Bell J. Econ.* 14 (Spring 1983): 251–58.

Doeringer, Peter B., and Piore, Michael J. *Internal Labor Markets and Manpower Analysis.* Lexington, Mass.: Lexington Books, 1971.

Green, Jerry R., and Stokey, Nancy L. "A Comparison of Tournaments and Contracts." *J.P.E.* 91 (June 1983): 349–64.

Greenwald, Bruce C. N. *Adverse Selection in the Labor Market.* New York: Garland, 1979.

Grossman, Sanford J., and Hart, Oliver D. "An Analysis of the Principal-Agent Problem." *Econometrica* 51 (January 1983): 7–45.

Harris, Milton, and Holmstrom, Bengt. "A Theory of Wage Dynamics." *Rev. Econ. Studies* 49 (July 1982): 315–33.

Holmstrom, Bengt. "Equilibrium Long-Term Labor Contracts." Discussion Paper no. 414. Evanston, Ill.: Northwestern Univ., Kellogg Grad. School of Management, January 1981.

Lazear, Edward P. "Why Is There Mandatory Retirement?" *J.P.E.* 87 (December 1979): 1261–84.

———. "Agency, Earnings Profiles, Productivity, and Hours Restrictions." *A.E.R.* 71 (September 1981): 606–20.

Lazear, Edward P., and Rosen, Sherwin. "Rank-Order Tournaments as Optimum Labor Contracts." *J.P.E.* 89 (October 1981): 841–64.

Lydall, Harold F. *The Structure of Earnings.* Oxford: Clarendon, 1968.

Malcomson, James M. "Trade Unions and Economic Efficiency." *Econ. J.* 93 (suppl.; March 1983): 51–65.

Medoff, James L., and Abraham, Katharine G. "Experience, Performance, and Earnings." *Q.J.E.* 95 (December 1980): 703–36.

Mincer, Jacob A. *Schooling, Experience, and Earnings.* New York: Columbia Univ. Press (for N.B.E.R.), 1974.

Radner, Roy. "Monitoring Cooperative Agreements in a Repeated Principal-Agent Relationship." *Econometrica* 49 (September 1981): 1127–48.

Simon, Herbert A. "The Compensation of Executives." *Sociometry* 20 (March 1957): 32–35.

Stiglitz, Joseph E. "Incentives, Risk and Information: Notes towards a Theory of Hierarchy." *Bell J. Econ.* 6 (Autumn 1975): 552–79.

Williamson, Oliver E.; Wachter, Michael L.; and Harris, Jeffrey E. "Understanding the Employment Relation: The Analysis of Idiosyncratic Exchange." *Bell J. Econ.* 6 (Spring 1975): 250–78.